You Cannot Predict the Future

Raccoonosaur and Puppydogosaur

Contents

1
Preface

"Those who cannot remember the past are condemned to repeat it." – George Santayana

While I cannot predict the future – I surely don't want to be condemned to repeat the past. As you hold this book in your hands, you are probably thinking "What do they mean *You Cannot Predict the Future*?" and "Who is *Raccoonosaur and Puppydogosaur*?"

Ironically, when I started writing this preface, I thought to myself, "I know I can predict the future … of what you, the reader probably will think about this book." It will stop and make you think (if you can take the time to reflect on the words and connect the dots), you will be entertained (if you allow yourself that guilty pleasure of uploading from traditional media), and you will not agree with everything (maybe passionately) that is being said, but similarly there may be some new ideas or old ideas interpreted in new ways that you will find mildly or radically provocative.

Moving on to addressing the second question "Who is Raccoonosaur and Puppydogosaur?" They are obviously avatars. I have known the Raccoonosaur for over 20 years and valued his insights that come from years of experience (and frustration) working in numerous roles in the Software Engineering industry. When I was the editor of ACM SIGSOFT (Association of Computer Machinery Special Interest Group on Software Engineering) *Software Engineering Notes*, I was impressed by his contributions and encouraged him to continue developing and refining (and sharing) his thoughts. I am please to say that they have culminated in this book.

So, what do you need to know about what's in this book? Let me offer up an annotated version of the table of contents and challenge you, as you read each chapter, to see if the expectations I am setting have been met.

Introduction: Your right shoe probably won't fit on your left foot, but you still might try.

Unknownness: You don't know what you don't know and maybe never will.

Sponsoring Organizations versus Project Teams: Who are these know/no-it-alls?

Sponsoring-Organization Obligations: Can these know/no-it-alls grow up?

The Blob of Agile versus the Bride of Waterfall: Agile and Waterfall got married, but won't stop bickering.

Determinism versus Emergence: What you think you know won't be all you end up knowing.

Five Tides: Knowing where you came from may help to show where you will end up.

A Sunrise Primer: Why I am (almost) certain that the sun will rise tomorrow and your software will have bugs.

Polish versus Rot: Software maintenance is one step forward and two steps backward – or vice versa.

A Subjective Search Primer: Statistically speaking, hedging your bets is probably the reasonable thing to do.

The Best Laid Plans of Mice and Men: Ready, Aim, Fire. But you are never ready and your aim probably will be off since you are firing at a moving target (and might not have the right ammunition).

To paraphrase the words of the Bo Diddley song, "You Can't Judge a Book by the Cover," you can't judge this book by this preface. I encourage you to be patient, take your time, and if you are curious, dig down into some of the many references this book provides. You will find that you may not be able to predict the future, but you will be better prepared not to make some of the mistakes that have been made in the past.

Will Tracz, PhD
Lockheed Martin Fellow Emeritus
Past Chairman of the ACM SIGSOFT

2
Introduction

Caution

People should not read this book. Only those who feel comfortable with doubt and uncertainty and pain should do so. Unfortunately, such people don't exist. Dan Gilbert recently said, "people never want uncertainty, they eschew it." We don't want to argue with anyone's current beliefs and we don't want to increase anyone's cognitive dissonance, so please read anything else instead. You'll have more fun.

If you are a member of the IEEE, please reread *SWEBOK*. If you admire the SEI, please reread *Managing the Software Process* by Watts Humphrey. If you are a manager, please reread *The Mythical Man-Month* by Fred Brooks. Those books will reaffirm your current beliefs and warm the cockles of your heart with nostalgia. Those books will reassure you that by using the right processes and gathering enough data and by planning, you too will feel confident. Everyone else should maybe read an escapist novel.

Everything in Requirement and Software Engineering Predicts the Future

The notion that the future can and should be predicted from the past is deeply embedded in both requirement and software engineering. We will go so far as to claim that almost everything that analysts, programmers, testers, and managers do involves predicting the future based on experiences from the past. If users told analysts that they wanted a feature yesterday, then developers will try to deliver it tomorrow. If a feature worked in test last week, then users will expect it to work in the real world next week. If a manager approved a budget or schedule last month, then the team will be expected to meet it next month.

Analyzing, architecting, programming, testing, budgeting, and scheduling may not look like predicting the future, but they are. The past is often a useful guide because the future often repeats the past. But the future may also differ significantly from the past: users may change their minds about what they want, production environments may differ from test environments, everyone makes mistakes, and so on.

People can often make good guesses about the future but nobody knows how to predict it, and without actually predicting it, nobody can avoid all mistakes and changes. Analysts cannot reliably predict who will use an app or how it will get used, so they cannot reliably write requirements. Developers cannot reliably predict how code will get changed and reused, so they cannot reliably write code. Testers cannot reliably predict where bugs will hide, so they cannot reliably write test plans. And, managers cannot reliably predict how projects will unfold, so they cannot reliably make budgets and schedules.

Accepting Doubt and Uncertainty

Everyone really should feel uncertain about a lot of things. The term that describes all of those things is "the future." In fact, that is what "the future" means. Nobody can predict the future, not us (the authors) and not you (the readers).

Requirement and software engineers cannot predict the future of their projects either. If they could, then they could also convert any other problem into a software project and solve it as well. For example, they could translate predicting weather or elections years ahead or solving poverty into software projects. The whole future of the world would become predictable. Reductio ad absurdum.

Unfortunately, the authors of books like *SWEBOK* and *Managing the Software Process* describe tools and practices that if used properly would enable people to predict the future. SWEBOKers wrote that one can resolve all uncertainties by consulting textbooks or journals or by asking colleagues or stakeholders or (as a last resort) by using some mythical risk process. (SWEBOK, page 11-10) Watts Humphrey wrote that software processes "must be predictable." (Humphrey, page 3) Even Barry Boehm and Richard Turner wrote about "change-prescient" plans and architectures. (Boehm and Turner, pages 115, 119, and 138 to 139) But since nothing can predict the future, their plans, processes, certifications, architectures, and standards cannot possibly work as well as advertised – they provide partial solutions at best. In retrospect, those authors seem both well-intended and seriously-deluded. They fooled themselves and way too many others for way too long.

It's time to get a grip. We are trying to cut through the magical thinking and the salesmanship. We are trying to be as honest and aware as we possibly can. We are trying to say what needs to be said. Of course, we have our own issues, but at least we are not limited by human delusions about predicting the future.

Anyone who demands perfect predictions about the future should not work on software projects. If you really need accurate requirements, architectures, budgets, and schedules, then you really should hire a professional fortune teller. That is the only solution we know.

Based on CRM

Many observations in this book come from Customer Relationship Management (CRM) projects. CRMs invariably need tweaking. They must invariably access remote data sources. In support departments, titles like "agent" and "customer advocate" can mean specific things and users can get upset when they are not exactly right. We believe that CRM-like relationships between sponsoring organizations and project teams will be revealed in most projects, sooner or later.

In CRM projects, non-software people (for example those in sales and customer-support) become directly involved. CRM administrators and developers interact directly with those users, who often start out knowing very little about software and therefore learn a lot and change their minds a lot over the course of each project. CRM practitioners require additional skills when dealing with those users (such as emotional intelligence) than when dealing with traditional clients (like computer engineers building embedded systems). Goal-setting becomes more collaborative and the politics of sponsoring organizations affect projects directly.

Themes

Every chapter concerns both unknowns and contexts, as shown in table 1.

Table 1: Chapters versus Themes					
	Unknowns	Users, Technologies, Organizations	History	Probability	Psychology, Sociology
Unknownness	✓				✓
Sponsoring Organizations versus Project Teams	✓	✓			✓
Sponsoring-Organization Obligations	✓	✓			✓
The Blob of Agile versus the Bride of Waterfall	✓	✓	✓		
Determinism versus Emergence	✓		✓		
Five Tides	✓		✓		
A Sunrise Primer	✓			✓	
Polish versus Rot	✓	✓			
A Subjective Search Primer	✓			✓	
The Best Laid Plans of Mice and Men	✓				✓

Unknowns

We believe that unknowns lie at the root of all problems in software engineering. Unknowns arise whenever anyone tries to predict the future. If anyone knew what users really wanted or what code would get written, then software would be easy. Unknowns underlie everything in this book.

Many contemporary tools and practices work well when everything is known, including languages like Java, IDEs like Eclipse, repositories like Git, and team processes like Scrum. Of course, we have complaints about each of them, but nothing that more-focused researchers and developers aren't already working on. However, none of those tools and practices can resolve all unknowns. None of them can point out all of the errors and omissions and changes in requirements, architectures, source codes, test plans, budgets, and schedules. None of them can predict the future.

The meanings of the words "uncertain" and "unknown" overlap in common usage in both society and software engineering, though they have distinct biases. The word "uncertain" tends to imply bounded unknowns, such as classic probability or gambling or Gaussian distributions. It allows people to believe that their "guesses" could be or even should be close to the right answer. It enables people to expect that by using statistics, they can predict the future. In contrast, the word "unknown" tends to imply unbounded unknowns or Hyperbolic distributions, which cast people adrift at sea. Unknowns can be arbitrarily wrong.

Unknowns are vexing because many people simply refuse to acknowledge that they exist. After all, requirement and software engineers are paid to confidently solve problems. Nobody wants to hear about doubts or uncertainties. "To acknowledge uncertainty [is] to admit the possibility of error." (Lewis, page 221) Most people seem to prefer over-confidence in predictions. We (the authors) distrust confidence because when people cannot predict the future, they can only be confident about outcomes through delusion and denial.

Coping is essential whenever unknowns are revealed, changes occur, and plans don't work out. Idealistic Waterfall and Bride-of-Waterfall practices, planning, and factories simply get stuck. Pragmatic Agile and Bride-of-Agile practices, technical debt, and Subjective search provide workarounds. The ability to cope is not what anyone wants, it is merely what everyone needs.

Contexts

Nothing exists in a vacuum. Everything and everyone inhabits one context or another and feels the influences of those contexts. Practitioners rarely worry much about those contexts and probably shouldn't because they can do little about them in any case. However, we believe that understanding those contexts enables everyone to set better expectations about what they can and cannot control, such as the limits of knowledge and how quality changes over time.

Users, Technologies, Organizations: Users and technologies provide the contexts for programs and standards. Sponsoring organizations provide the contexts for projects. And, projects provide the contexts for practitioners.

History: History sheds light on the ephemeral nature of today. The debate over determinism and emergence has been raging within philosophy and science for millennia and is raging within requirement and software engineering today. Given the steady stream of changes within software engineering since the 1940s, everyone should expect changes to continue for the foreseeable future, which philosophers call "pessimistic induction."

Probability: Probability theory provides a foundation for dealing with unknowns by describing "rigidly defined areas of doubt and uncertainty," as Douglas Adams wrote. Subjective probability can help people to better understand unknowns, but it can also delude people into thinking that they know more than they actually do. The Sunrise problem and Subjective probability are the mathematics of unknowns, especially when very little objective data exists.

Psychology and Sociology: Contemporary psychology and sociology show that people are not rational. They delusionally crave certainty and confidence. Half of what people believe is simply made up by their brains. Expecting flawless code is unrealistic in part because human brains systematically succumb to biases and create errors. Setting individual goals involves perception and decisions, which are psychology. Setting group goals involves politics, which is sociology.

Chapters

Unknownness: We enumerate and describe a variety of the sources of unknowns to clarify how hard they are to understand and overcome. Sources of unknowns include ignorance, size and complexity, change, the future, obliquity, arbitrariness, error, and irrationality. If we revised the chapter again, we would add politics. Lots of details in software-engineering projects are unknown and that will always remain true. Unknowns cause all problems in software because otherwise someone could easily fix them.

Sponsoring Organizations versus Project Teams: Sponsoring organizations and project teams make complementary contributions to projects. Sponsoring organizations can only acquire resources and solve political problems with politics. Project teams can only solve technical problems with technology. One side cannot substitute for the other, so each side must carry out its full job; projects cannot escape the influences of their sponsoring organizations; and projects catalyze progress.

Sponsoring-Organization Obligations: Authorities in sponsoring organizations (like managers and accountants) must learn to cope with unknowns and changes because they cannot predict the future any better than anyone else; they cannot delegate such predictions; and project team members cannot compel anyone outside of the team to do anything. The initial version of Bride-of-Agile practices includes coping with ongoing change, fostering diversity and debate, and dealing with problem stakeholders.

The Blob of Agile versus the Bride of Waterfall: The term "Agilefall" refers to the decades-long transition from the Pure-Waterfall era to the Pure-Agile era. It embodies the stubborn conflicts between Bride-of-Waterfall practices in sponsoring organizations and Agile practices in project teams. The transition occurs in two phases. The first phase has already occurred within most project teams. But, sponsoring organizations are only slowly coming to accept that they should adopt Bride-of-Agile practices. The Bride of Waterfall continues extracting her revenge by resurrecting waterfalls whenever she can.

Determinism versus Emergence: The deterministic half of software engineering emphasizes knowns and stabilities. Algorithms, languages, IDEs, repositories, and processes embody the wisdom of the past. The emergent half of software engineering emphasizes unknowns and changes. All analysts and programmers strive to change programs in new ways that will affect society. In practice, everyone needs both determinism to use contemporary tools and practices and emergence to write new programs. We place the conflicts between Waterfall and Agile into the 2500-year-long debate over causality and free will within philosophy and science.

Five Tides: Today, programming differs significantly from what it was seventy years ago when the first electronic computers were built and from what it was fifty years ago during the NATO conferences. Five tides (Machine, Language, Waterfall, Agile, and Post-Agile) embody the key points of stability during the evolution of programming. Waterfall processes arose at the culmination of the deterministic, clockwork model of reality and were spurred on by computers and statistics. Agile processes arose with the reacceptance of an emergent, human-centered reality.

A Sunrise Primer: The Sunrise problem sheds light on the accuracy of small statistical samples, on what can be deduced from minimal evidence, and on the notion of *good enough for now*. Richard Price and Pierre Simon Laplace, two of the founders of probability theory, proposed the exponential and linear equations. We propose a new hyperbolic equation. The Sunrise problem provides a foundation for the many rules of two, three, six, and twelve from analysis and design.

Polish versus Rot: Polish and rot are the two forms of emergence. Project-team members influence software through polish (analysis, programming, and testing) during development. Other people in society influence software through rot (changes in expectations, usages, and technologies) at all times but especially after development ends. Over the life of each program and standard, quality ebbs and flows in the patterns described by the Sunrise and Decay equations. Technical debt embodies the economic tradeoffs of deferring both polish and rot.

A Subjective Search Primer: We introduce Subjective search as a foundation for contemporary Agile and Bride-of-Agile practices. When a lot of coherent, objective data exists, classical statistics (called Frequentism) works well. Bayesian statistics becomes essential when objective data is hard to get, especially when predicting the future. Subjective search can use objective data when it exists and opinions and arbitrary rules otherwise. Subjective search shows how to be less wrong.

The Best Laid Plans of Mice and Men: Plans are essential for clarifying shared goals and expectations. But, people convert plans into promises for well-known psychological and sociological reasons, they just do, which leads to problems every time that errors, ambiguities, and changes are revealed. All plans are flawed and yet people routinely get blindsided by the flaws in their plans. Plans invariably lead people astray.

Arc of Relevance

Like the wave of polish and rot, this book will also rise and fall.

Born of Failure: We accidentally wrote this book while trying to write a book about something else. We only realized what this book said after it was done, after all of these chapters turned out to contradict what we wanted them to say. We had been trying to use information about the past to make predictions about the future. We had our own delusions and we also learned the hard way that we cannot predict the future. It was painful. This book is our consolation.

Current Problems: This book contains our current best thoughts and understandings but, of course, it comes up short. Reviewers caught many of the flaws in this book, but surely not all. We suspect that many errors and ambiguities remain. If we had enough knowledge or imagination to identify those flaws, we would fix them as we write this. But alas, they will only be revealed in time. We apologize for the difficulty of the material. We satisficed and called it done because otherwise we would continue to edit this forever. If we were better writers and had more time, this book would convey twice as much meaning in half as many words.

Destined for Failure: These chapters will likely remain *true* for decades because they mostly describe historical events, but they will not remain *important* or *relevant*. Due to the half-life of facts, most of this book will eventually become wrong or irrelevant. We merely hope that for now it is less wrong and less irrelevant than contemporary alternatives.

That said, we enjoyed thinking and writing about these ideas and we hope that you will find value in reading about them.

Authors

Raccoon and Puppydog are cute and fuzzy, if scruffy and annoying. They take themselves way too seriously but, if they didn't, nobody else would. Raccoon loves to delve into unknowns. He stays up all night while contemplating software engineering. He prefers to eat sushi and wants to grow up to be like Rocket. Puppydog merely wants to ponder cool ideas and to catch up on his sleep. He naps all day while daydreaming about software engineering. He prefers to eat pizza and wants to grow up to be like Hobbes. They work in Albuquerque. They can sometimes be contacted at raccoon@swcp.com.

This book is based on four years of observing CRM projects, specifically Salesforce projects, in a variety of organizations from mom-and-pop retailers to Fortune 20 corporations. Raccoon and Puppydog spent another three decades observing commercial and consulting projects for PCs, the web, and mobile devices. They usually watched from the ground level, often from a backpack dropped under a desk where they listened to the humans delude themselves about their plans, budgets, and schedules. The authors observed people do both good and bad things in many, many different situations. They attempt to distill the essence of what people actually do.

Acknowledgements

We would like to thank our friends and colleagues who contributed many ideas and refinements to this book as well as decades of friendship and encouragement: Anthony J. Giancola, Robert Schaefer, Suzanne Sluizer, and Michael Wing. We especially want to thank Will Tracz and Mina Yamashita (in memoriam), without whom this book would not be possible.

Bibliography

Douglas Adams, *Hitchhiker's Guide to the Galaxy*, Del Ray, 1995.
Barry Boehm and Richard Turner, *Balancing Agility and Discipline*, Addison Wesley, 2003.
Frederick P. Brooks, Jr., *The Mythical Man-Month, Anniversary Edition*, Addison Wesley, 1995.
Dan Gilbert, "You 2.0: Decide Already!," on NPR Hidden Brain, 22:27, August 21, 2018.
Watts S. Humphrey, *Managing the Software Process*, Addison Wesley, 1989.
Michael Lewis, *Undoing Project*, Norton, 2016.
SWEBOK V3, https://www.computer.org/web/swebok/v3/.

3
Unknownness

"We don't know a millionth of one percent about anything." – Thomas Edison

Ideally, REs and SEs would have complete and perfect information about their projects, but really, they never will. REs and SEs do know many things; but lots of things, possibly even most things, remain unknown.

Unknownness arises from a wide variety of sources, all of which frustrate the creation of effective requirements and architectures. We believe that REs and SEs routinely encounter all of the following sources of unknownness: ignorance, size, change, the future, obliquity, arbitrariness, error, and irrationality.

The boundaries between different sources of unknownness can be murky. For example, ignorance and error are related because people often make mistakes when they lack vital information, while conversely, errors show that somebody was ignorant about something. An unknown password could be considered either ignorance (because we don't know what it is) or size and complexity (because it would take a lot of work to try all possibilities).

Some sources relate to others by scale: size is an unbounded source of ignorance; the future is an unbounded source of change; obliquity is an unbounded source of arbitrariness; and irrationality is an unbounded source of error. Some sources, like the future and size, come from the outside world and affect everyone the same. Other sources, like irrationality and error, come from within and affect each person differently.

Laying out this chapter helped us to appreciate the broad scope of unknownness and the limits of knowledge. REs and SEs can neither avoid nor ignore unknownness; they will make mistakes; they cannot be certain about their plans; and they will inevitably do things differently than they want or expect.

Ignorance In RE

The first source of unknownness for REs is ignorance or simply not knowing. Requirements embody the intentions of stakeholders. Unfortunately, nobody really knows what those intentions are or should be.

Users are not technologists. They often don't know what they want or need, or they cannot articulate it. They may want their app to "pop" even though they cannot explain what that means. Users often don't know what is reasonable or possible or effective.

GUI design books urge REs to pander to user mental models, but user mental models are difficult to fathom. (Cooper, Reimann, and Cronin, pages 28+) All UIs should be understood (at least partly) from the perspective of psychology and sociology, perhaps even behavioral economics, with all of the difficulties and inconsistencies that they entail.

Individual Decisions Can Be Arbitrary: How many times has someone dithered over a simple decision, such as which restaurant for breakfast? Clients can have similar problems making simple choices about what an app should do. Given the complexities of software, users may be truly unable to evaluate tradeoffs or make decisions. When asked a question, some users and clients will make arbitrary (in other words bad) decisions to avoid looking naïve or foolish. Conversely, a client may obsess over one fact that he thinks he understands, which is actually irrelevant.

Group Decisions Can Be Political: How many times has a group of people been unable to agree on where to go for lunch? Many software decisions are essentially political, which means that somebody will lose and the group will change its decision whenever the political tides shift. The losers of a political decision may have deceptive or malicious intentions, for example to hijack the project or embarrass a rival.

Many software decisions are purely arbitrary: no better than coin tosses or die rolls. Increasingly consumers tire of answering business surveys and more and more often make up wrong answers. Users may eventually regret their software decisions, AKA buyer's remorse, but that won't help the current project.

9

User Input is Not Enough: Doing what users say they want is not enough. Company after company bit the dust after doing exactly what their users said they wanted. WordPerfect and AltaVista devoted enormous efforts to understanding what their users wanted. WordPerfect had thousands of requests for some features, which they fulfilled, but they still died. Based on numerous failed projects, we believe that doing what users say they want may be politic, but is not necessarily good for the long run. Somebody needed to have done something else for these projects to have survived.

Many UI Conventions Work Poorly

On one hand, many contemporary UI conventions work well. For example, GUIs enable users to browse and choose by pointing or tapping.

On the other hand, many UI conventions work poorly. In *About Face*, Cooper and colleagues list many problems with contemporary user interfaces, including data retrieval, data entry, undo, files, and saving work. They also recommend using fewer dialogs. Our complaints about GUIs include that preferences are hard to find and understand; options for modal dialogs tend to be hard to change; error handling and reporting remain ad hoc; search needs to include meta information; and users need to tolerate and curate incomplete or erroneous data in databases.

One of our pet peeves is the Ok button. We believe that every requirement that states "the warning dialog shall be dismissed by clicking the Ok button" is wrong. We tire of mousing to tiny buttons that appear in random locations on the screen. For most warnings, one might click almost anywhere on the dialog, or even on the whole screen, to dismiss it. Tortoise SVN uses Ok to mean both "Commit all current changes" and "Dismiss this log dialog," which mean nearly opposite things. In many apps, clicking a Cancel button brings up a confirmation dialog with new Ok and Cancel buttons, and we always have to stop and figure out what each button actually means. REs probably continue to spec Ok buttons because dialog defaults make it easy and they have gotten away with it for so long, not because it helps.

Web-based apps (from cloud computing) are ugly and arbitrary. Too many web-based apps embody RESTful or database concepts, rather than application or user concepts. Data entry is slow and clunky. It is too easy to lose entered data due to timeouts or network hiccups. Facebook's HTML5 app was a well-documented failure. As web-based apps proliferate, the average UI only seems to get worse and users tolerate them at best. There are big advantages to web-based apps, but there are also big disadvantages.

Some RE Practices are Questionable

Market Research Mostly Recreates the Status Quo: This has been stated in many ways by many people. "Mainstream market research used to emphasize asking people what they wanted." (Sims, page 135) Traditional market research asks people what they want, but it does not work for new ideas. Asking users will only recreate obvious, known solutions. There is a status quo bias. (Sims, page 110) But, no one gets ahead by copying the status quo. (Kelley, page 278)

There are many reasons why customers shouldn't design products. "Customers may lack the vocabulary or the palate to explain what's wrong, especially what's missing." (Kelley, page 27) Neither the public nor the experts know what features to cut. (Kelley, pages 258 to 259) When users and clients think that they know more than they actually do, they may insist on "suboptimal" decisions. But as Tom Kelley notes, "It's not their job to be visionaries." (Kelley, page 27)

Representative Agents Can Lead One Astray: Software requirements and architectures are full of "representative agent" rationales, which divide users into groups, for example into men and women or noobie and power users or common and unusual cases. (Watts, page 66) WordPerfect categorized their users as legal secretaries, students, writers, and so on. A set of representative agents can approximate who users are in the same way that a list of requirements can approximate what users need, but in fact both reductionisms contradict the holism or gestalt of the resulting app. Each user experiences the app as a whole. Period. The representative agent model ignores the macro-micro problem. (Watts, page 67) Cooper and colleagues repeat this mistake when they encourage designers to use personas.

Early Adopters Can Lead One Astray: In *Crossing the Chasm*, Geoffrey Moore argues that early adopters are often helpful when designing new products. But, they can have their own agendas. Windows 8 was released with minimal documentation because early adopters seemed to enjoy the Easter Egg hunt for hidden menus and features. But normal users hated searching blindly for the features they needed, simply to get their work done.

Extremes, not Typicals: In the movie *Objectified*, Dan Formosa commented, "Look at the extremes: the weakest, arthritics, athletes, the strongest, fastest. The middle will take care of itself." Cutting edge designers no longer design for average or typical users because their needs will be subsumed by the needs of the extremes. REs may eventually adopt this perspective, even so, it will require great finesse.

Users cannot accurately describe what they need. UI conventions do not tell anyone what the project should do. RE practices do not guide anyone to discover what the project should do. So, many requirements are destined to remain murky or unknown.

Ignorance In SE

Like for REs, the first source of unknownness for SEs is ignorance, or simply not knowing. The authors of *Making Software* provide tons of empirical evidence for ignorance in SE.

In "Where Do Most Software Flaws Come From?," Dewayne Perry analyzes bugs in a large embedded project. "Lack of knowledge tended to dominate the underlying causes [of modification requests]." (Oram and Wilson, page 491) Perry attributes 60% of the underlying causes of modification requests to what we would call unknowns: incomplete/omitted design 25%, lack of knowledge 18%, ambiguous design 10%, incomplete/omitted requirements 5%, and ambiguous requirements 2%. (Oram and Wilson, page 473)

One could debate whether incomplete or ambiguous requirements come from ignorance or from errors. Perry claims that the project followed process rigorously. "The system was developed and evolved using the current 'best practice' techniques and tools with well-qualified practitioners." (Oram and Wilson, page 491) All design documents were reviewed by 3 to 15 peers and all code was reviewed by 3 to 5 peers. (Oram and Wilson, page 455) Perry does not state specifically how requirements were reviewed, though we presume that they were treated comparably. So, if requirements or designs had incomplete or ambiguous details, then at least 4 and up to 16 professionals were oblivious to the need for more clarity. Clearly, many professionals were ignorant about many details. Also, these flaws were not due to lack of time, since they would have been categorized as "submitted under duress."

Perry attributes 43% of the means of prevention to what we would call the sharing of information: application walk-throughs 25%, expert person/documentation 16%, training 2%. (Oram and Wilson, page 478) He shows that, weighted by fix cost, faults prevented by training are the hardest to fix, followed by formal methods, then expertise and documentation. (Oram and Wilson, page 479) "Knowledge intensive activities tended to dominate the means of prevention." (Oram and Wilson, page 492)

Perry quotes Curtis, Krasner, and Iscoe writing that, "a thin spread of application knowledge is the most significant problem in building large systems." (Oram and Wilson, page 478) Perry argues that ignorance even shows up when everything is fine. "The fact that 16% of MRs are 'no problem' indicates that *lack of system knowledge* is a significant problem." (Oram and Wilson, page 490)

In "Code Talkers," Robert DeLine studies communication between developers, who spend about 75 minutes every day communicating informally with other developers, face-to-face, by phone, email, and so on. (Oram and Wilson, page 297) DeLine claims that 87% of this communication (more than an hour per day) is finding out things that programmers do not know, but need to know, in order to do their jobs, for example "What code caused this program state?," "What is the program supposed to do?," or "Is this a legitimate problem?" DeLine notes that a lot of communication is about understanding the rationale behind the code. (Oram and Wilson, page 300)

DeLine notes that the tasks that were the most frustrating (that wasted the most time without providing answers) were about unknowns. "What code caused this program state?" 61% unsatisfied. "Why was the code implemented this way?" 44%. "In what situations does this failure occur?" 41%. "What code could have caused this behavior?" 36%. "How have the resources I depend on changed?" 24%. And, "What is the program supposed to do?" 15%. (Oram and Wilson, page 303) Communication is not enough to create understanding.

DeLine notes that documentation could reduce the need for communication, but developers make many decisions every day. He further argues that since documentation is a speculative investment, developers should only document the decisions with the biggest scope, the most stability, and the widest audience. The remaining decisions should be shared through on-demand communication. (Oram and Wilson, pages 308 to 309)

In "Novice Professionals: Recent Graduates in a First Software Engineering Job," Andrew Begel and Beth Simon study novice programmers at Microsoft. They state, "There is so much new infrastructure to learn, it becomes the norm to have only partial knowledge of a tool or some code." (Oram and Wilson, page 507) "Novices had difficulty orienting themselves in the low-information environments presented by their project team, code base, and resources." (Oram and Wilson, page 506) In our experience, these observations apply to seasoned developers doing new tasks, as well.

Begel and Simon argue that novice programmers spend a lot of time communicating, even so, more communication would improve their productivity again. (Oram and Wilson, page 503) "Novices struggle to 'know when they don't know.'" (Oram and Wilson, page 507) They don't know to ask for help. (Oram and Wilson, page 507) "In general, novices do not ask questions soon enough, and often struggle to ask questions at an appropriate level." (Oram and Wilson, page 506)

According to their chart, novice programmers spend nearly half of their time either communicating or reading documentation, in other words, finding out things that they do not know. (Oram and Wilson, page 502)

The root causes of problems are poor communication skills and social naïveté. (Oram and Wilson, page 512) "Asking questions [is very productive, but] reveals to your coworkers and managers that you are not knowledgeable." (Oram and Wilson, page 508) "Asking for help is hindered by the power inequality and social anxiety, which are problems for all organizations." (Oram and Wilson, page 508) Managers also have a hard time asking for help.

In the essays "Conway's Corollary" and "Evidence-Based Failure Prediction," Christian Bird, Nachiappan Nagappan, and Thomas Bell write that organizational structure is the best indicator of the quality of components. (Oram and Wilson, pages 194 and 423 to 426) It predicts quality better than lines of code, code churn, code complexity, dependencies, test coverage, and pre-release bugs. (Oram and Wilson, page 199 and 430) Organizational structure measures things like "percentage of organization contributing to development [of a component]" and "number of ex-engineers [who worked on a component]."

The authors suggest that there is a direct link between knowledge and quality. Programmers and teams who know a chunk of code best will write fewer bugs and should make changes, while programmers and teams who do not know the code will write more bugs and should be kept away. When the organization of people resembles the organization of code, software works better. (Oram and Wilson, page 205)

None of the authors detail specifically how each component of the model affects quality, for example they don't state exactly how much employee turnover matters. But, when employees leave, knowledge will be lost and quality will suffer. In a different essay, Dewayne Perry advises, hire people with domain knowledge. (Oram and Wilson, page 491) We would add, "Retain knowledgeable people."

In "The Art of Collecting Bug Reports," Rahul Premraj and Thomas Zimmermann state that incomplete information is the biggest problem in getting bugs fixed. "Among the problems experienced by developers, incomplete information was, by far, most commonly encountered." One developer in the study commented, "The biggest causes of delay are not wrong information, but absent information." (Oram and Wilson, page 444) The authors note that bugs with stack traces got fixed sooner, readable bugs got fixed sooner, and bugs with code samples got fixed sooner. (Oram and Wilson, page 449) Ignorance causes delay.

Over time, SEs become expert at the code they are working on. When the task ends, they usually switch to work on code that they know less well and then begin to forget details of previous work. Every time they acquire the expertise to fix a bug or implement a feature, they are assigned to work on a different part of the code, which they either forgot or never learned. Cooper and colleagues argue that most software users are perpetual intermediates. (Cooper, Reimann, and Cronin, page 43) We would apply this same concept to SEs. Real programmers know some things about their code bases, but not everything, perpetually learning the rest of what they need to know to do their jobs.

Size and Complexity

The second source of unknownness is size, or simply too much work. All projects are constrained by limited resources, and many tasks require more work than can possibly be done, a classic example of which is combinatorial explosion. Problems that are too large, that consume more time and effort than is available, will get done poorly, if at all.

Features: At one company, which shipped millions of copies of its apps, developers removed all dialog-based and control-based contextual help from the GUIs because it was too much work to properly maintain, given their resources. Of course, their topic-based and index-based help remained. They decided it was better to not support contextual help at all than to do it poorly.

Apps: Some apps are so big and complex that entire companies are devoted to incrementally refining the many special cases, including operating system device drivers, office suites, graphics suites, and speech recognition apps.

Tools: Programming environments, tools, techniques, and processes embody tons of arcane details that developers must remember. No wonder most developers use so many software tools poorly, if at all.

Ilities: Many properties of code (such as performance, quality, maintainability, and reliability) emerge from the ways that every line of code interacts with every other line of code. Structure and encapsulation can reduce the amount of this interaction, but cannot eliminate it.

Analysis: In *About Face*, Cooper and colleagues urge designers of new apps to interview four to six users for each "role." Why not interview ten or fifty users for each role to better understand what the app should do? That would probably take more time and effort than is available, and diminishing returns make it seem not worth the effort. The term "analysis paralysis" applies to every situation where analysis takes more time than desired.

Development: Every coding bug proves that code works differently than programmers believe it does. This means that programmers have a subjective reality that only loosely tracks the objective reality of the code. The bigger the body of code, the more difficult it will be to understand. If they had time, developers would systematically memorize the code, but that is impossible.

Testing: If testers had unlimited resources, then they would do the million-year, million-monkey trying out of every possible sequence of actions. For example, many bugs and memory leaks only occur after arcane sequences of steps. Of course, professional testers do exercise the most important and most common sequences of use, but due to limited resources, end users always do the final testing.

Change

The third source of unknownness is change, which occurs routinely and without warning. Users change their minds about what they want; budgets get cut, forcing project goals to be revised; and so on. We believe that most change comes from learning or from circumstance, rather than from caprice, so we see most change as constructive and hopeful, if annoying to deal with. Coping with all forms of change requires continuing engagement.

Normal Change

Changing One's Mind: Users frequently realize that they want or need something different than what they previously thought. They may use the app and realize that different features would be more helpful. Users may see a feature in another app and realize it would help them, too. Users may rethink their own processes and come to a better understanding of what they actually do.

Evolving Resources: CPU power, graphics power, network bandwidth and connectivity continue to improve, driven by Moore's Law. While CPU clocks no longer get faster, systems are still getting smaller, cheaper, and more powerful. Battery life continues to improve. Touch screens are ubiquitous. All of these resources enable apps to do things that were never before possible or cost effective.

Evolving Expectations: Evolving resources enable programs do more for users with less effort. Users want to do more with fewer clicks. They want better speech recognition and better image processing. They want more powerful search, drill down, and better error correction. Users want their data available wherever they go, any time of day. User expectations evolve continually.

Change in the Environment: Some apps continually respond to change in the environment. Examples include search engines, virus checkers, spam filters, and tax preparation software.

Black Swans: Technologies come and go. Occasionally, a new technology sweeps the field, changing expectations dramatically: in the 1960s, text-based time-sharing; in the 1980s, GUIs; in the 1990s, the World-Wide Web; in the late 2000s, mobile (smart phones and tablets with touch input). Cloud seems to be underway, today. We expect that black swan technologies will continue to surprise us for decades to come.

Kevin Kelly (in his TED talk) argued that technology evolves just like life, becoming increasingly ubiquitous, diverse, specialized, complex, and social (symbiotic). Technologies evolve to exploit opportunities and to cope with competition.

Improving Flawed Models

George Box famously wrote, "All models are wrong; but some are useful." Requirements, architectures, and source codes are all models, just like statistical models. Norbert Weiner wrote, "The best model of a cat is another, or preferably the same, cat." But, Nate Silver notes that our models are simplifications of the world. (Silver, page 45) Models have many different kinds of flaws: some flaws are unknown; some are imprecise, such as numerical computations; some are incomplete and need more work; some are just plain wrong; all will eventually be supplanted.

Consider that GUIs (in the U.S.) usually represent people's names as first name, middle initial, and last name. But, some people have one name: Sting, Björk, Socrates. Others have four names: J.R.R. Tolkien, George H.W. Bush, L.B.S. Raccoon. Others use their middle names: J. Paul Getty and J. Paul McCartney (the guy from the Beatles). In one payroll UI, a new employee without a middle initial had to entered it as "DNA" for "does not apply." Unfortunately, the system would then print payroll checks like "Suzi DNA Smith," so a DBA had to fix the database by hand. Few GUIs capture Asian or African name order, where the family name should be printed first. These flawed models do not cause problems for most people in the U.S., who have three names and use a middle initial, but the models are wrong for millions of people. Yes, apps improve. But seemingly, for every app that improves the naming model, two new apps are created that start over poorly.

Fads

A lot of change is more style than substance. Fads do not change what is possible, so they may seem unimportant, yet fads often embody important changes in perspective. They show ongoing effort. One can sometimes look at a chunk of code or at a GUI and know the approximate date when it was last maintained, and how well. Consistency of style indicates effort, which may indicate quality. Fads help everyone to understand what is being kept up to date. They help us to identify what has been done and is widely agreed upon. There is no further need to discuss old fads, so we can focus on more contemporary issues.

Identifiers: Identifiers in C and other languages evolve through fads. K-and-R style (which was popular for decades) emerged when programs were small and disk space was expensive. K-and-R style was a big improvement over Fortran and Assembler style, less cryptic, though still overly terse. Hungarian notation and camel case emerged when apps got larger and GUI APIs evolved into monstrosities, while name spaces remained flat. Developers assumed that disk space was plentiful and cheap. Now, Linux style has evolved again: names and types are encapsulated in structs, akin to objects, type info is removed from names, and underscores separate words. Modern IDEs make this style possible because autocomplete makes typing long names easier and definitions are one click away. At every step, developers needed more clarity and fads embodied the best practices of the times. Even so, the functionality of identifiers in C has remained the same. We expect that the preferred style of identifiers will change many more times.

Programming Languages: Paul Graham argues that much of programming language design is based on popularity and fashion. (Graham, pages 180 to 182) All languages are capable of doing the same things, with varying degrees of effort. But important decisions, like syntax and typechecking, come and go.

Applications: Apps come and go. Fish tank screen savers came and went. Phone and tablet apps are trendy, as are using tabs rather than multiple document windows in GUIs or using flat buttons rather than 3D buttons with shadows.

However, fads are not always useful and can even be distracting. Users can want real improvements as well as change for its own sake. Peer pressure encourages people to catch up with the state of the practice as well as to waste effort on popular frivolities. Tradition has the opposite problem.

People can insist on tradition in order to retain the best of the past as well as to avoid change for its own sake, in other words, laziness.

Some changes lie outside of the control of REs and SEs, who are subject to the whims of fate. A client pays to add a seemingly random feature to an existing app. A competitor adds a feature that you must match. A telecom buys out the whole supply of a chip used in your device, so developers must write new device drivers to support a different chip. Everyone simply responds. Adapt or die.

Other changes lie within their control. While implementing an existing design, an RE may realize a better way to provide the same functionality with fewer dialogs. An SE may discover a way to refactor a chunk of code, to simplify and generalize it. REs and SEs can choose whether and how to respond to these changes.

The Future

"Predictions are hard, especially when they are about the future." – Yogi Berra

The fourth source of unknownness is the future. Duncan Watts notes that "The future is not like the past." (Watts, page 142) The future differs from the past by how everything changes right now. Watts also notes that simple historical models are hard to beat. (Watts, page 195) In general, not much changes from day to day. Yet, the part that does change cannot be predicted by any model that was based on the past.

Because projects take time to deliver, there will come a point in time for every project, when it will be used in the future, though it was designed and written in the past. As such, all requirements, architectures, source codes, and test plans predict the future.

The difference between gambling and knowing is time. If a roulette player could delay betting on red or black until 30 seconds after the ball is thrown, then he or she would raise the odds of winning from nearly 50% to 100%. Software is similar. If REs and SEs could rearrange time, they would know exactly what will happen.

Requirements: All change orders and all user complaints embody failures to predict the users' needs, and suggest once again that REs will never fully succeed. If REs knew what features would make the client happy (or not), then REs could always please the client. Especially in consulting, some clients with use-it-or-lose-it budgets, may have to guess today (before they are ready) about software that they will need in the future (after their budgets go away). Watts wrote, "People have reasons for what they do, but it doesn't necessarily allow us to predict in advance either what they will do or what their reasons will be for doing it." (Watts, page 52)

Code: Source code seems objective and transparent in that we can look at it after it is done, but SEs only design and edit the code before it is done. All refactorings and all bugs embody failures to predict and write the correct source code, and suggest again that developers will never accurately predict what code they should write.

Testing: Test plans predict the future. A manager once told a friend of ours, "Give me a list of the bugs that you will find during the next release so that we can make a plan to avoid them."

Most people can predict many details about what will happen tomorrow: where they will live and work, what chores they will do, and how they will spend their evening. But what about 5 or 10 or 20 years from today? A calf was born two weeks ago. John has lifted the young bull onto his shoulders every day since then. Will John be able to lift the bull every day for the next year? How do we know? Our ability to foresee consequences (whether intended or not) is limited. Peter Neumann's *Risks* Column in SEN enumerates many unintended consequences of software.

The future is our salvation because it is where we will find the time to write all the requirements and codes that we want. But by then we will also want many new things. The dilemma is that we only live today, while the future is opaque and deep beyond our comprehension.

Problems Are Oblique

The fifth source of unknownness is obliquity, which resembles the macro-micro problem and the complexity gap. Obliquity is challenging because the link between cause and effect gets lost. Individual lines of code rarely link directly to user goals. Video game players blasting away at an alien invasion don't directly experience or appreciate the "i++;" buried deep in the code. Conversely, "i++;" could mean almost anything from counting to locking to proceeding. SEs can only futz with lines of code, which map to user ideas and experiences only indirectly.

Frame Problem: The frame problem in AI concerns when two situations are alike. What features are relevant? (Watts, page 45) When skilled developers match a problem to a solution, they can match important similarities, ignore spurious similarities, and fill in missing details. Yet, many problems match existing frames poorly. And, larger contexts extend beyond frames. "For problems of economics, politics, and culture, the combination of the frame problem with the macro-micro problem means that *every* situation is [unique]." (Watts, page 110) We would add software engineering to the list and read this as "Every software project is unique: applying lessons from the past will always be problematic."

Users don't want software in their car brakes, they only want to brake safely. Users don't want spreadsheets, they only want their numbers to add up. In *About Face*, Cooper and colleagues argue that users don't want to "do work," they only want to impress their boss or client, or get a promotion, or be competent or engaged. (Cooper, Reimann, and Cronin, pages 13 to 14) Users really don't want software; they only want to solve their own non-software problems, which are always oblique to software solutions. The purposes of software from a user's or manager's point of view differ totally from the purposes of software from an RE's or SE's point of view.

Adam (an entrepreneur) wants to earn a million dollars. Chuck wants to find the love of his life. Doris wants a greener world. Edward wants world peace. None of these people necessarily want software because software does not and cannot solve any of their problems directly.

People have many non-software options to solve their problems. Adam could open a stylish restaurant. Chuck could Tango. Doris could plant trees. Edward could host an international student exchange. People must do these sorts of things, regardless of whether they also use software.

Yet often, software can help. A new game for tablets could allow Adam to sell apps. A website that matches personality profiles could help Chuck find a date. Software that remotely controls lights and HVACs could help Doris to save energy and reduce carbon emissions. A social media app or website could help Edward to foster friendships around the world. In many cases, software is an excellent tool for helping people to get what they want.

But, software alone cannot solve these problems. Other people would have to buy Adam's app. A woman who matches Chuck's profile would also have to want a date. Electrical and environmental system manufacturers would have to apply Doris's technology. Other people would have to share their personal stories on Edward's website. In every case, other people would have to actually use those apps and technologies, or the effort to create them would be wasted. Since most people are already busy with their own lives, getting cooperation can be hard.

Every piece of software creates additional work and cost, due to installation, administration, maintenance, training, security, marketing, coping with abuse, and so on. For every two steps forward that software enables, it also creates one step back. At best, software is an indirect or oblique tool for helping users to get what they want. Software doesn't solve problems, it changes them.

The only areas where software directly solves problems (where requirements and codes can be exact) is in artificial environments that are isolated from real users and the real world, where the only users are other computer and software engineers. Problems that can (almost) be solved directly with software include compilers, interpreters, operating system kernels, databases, and network interfaces. Inventory and shipping systems track boxes with bar codes. NASA defines its own interfaces for telemetry and control.

We note that these software systems are discrete components within much larger systems, the complexity gap is narrow, or they are ancillary to (i.e. removed from) the final system. For example, compilers remove source code from executables.

Details Are Arbitrary

The sixth source of unknownness is arbitrariness. If REs could reduce problems to "type 'blah blah blah' lines of code," then SE tasks would already be reduced to knowns and would essentially be done. One could hire a typist to finish it all up. In hardware and software, there are many ways to solve most goals, and many goals (at all levels) remain fuzzy and arbitrary. The complexity gap is always bigger than anyone wants it to be.

Requirements: Software goals may seem more concrete than user goals. Yet, most real software goals remain fuzzy: many different scopes of solution are possible and, within each scope, many different solutions are possible.

Game Example: Consider writing a tablet game for Adam. The possibilities are wide open. A new game could be solitary or social; physical or mental; easy or hard; strategy or luck; educational or entertaining; for kids, teens, or adults. It could be a first-person adventure, a sports simulation, a logic puzzle, a battle of wills, or a treasure hunt. Deciding to write a game app hardly adds a single constraint. Adam wants a game that sells, not a specific game, yet a real game must be a specific game. Every choice that narrows down the details of the game to make it more concrete and implementable makes the choice more speculative and takes Adam further from his stated goal to make money.

Configuration Example: Programs often store configuration data. They can store this data in flat files in "Documents and Setting" using XML or JSON or Windows Ini format or a custom format. Or, they can store this data in a database in the cloud or in the registry or wherever. There are valid if contradictory reasons for each choice. Data in the cloud can easily be shared, but not when the network is down or the user is in a rural location. Flat files are easy to copy, but are also easy for users to find, edit, and mangle.

Arbitrariness and obliquity complicate design (the mappings between high- and low-level decisions) and traceability (the mappings between requirements and code). Unless a requirements specification or architecture is shallow throughout, i.e. the complexity gap is narrow, most of the purposes of individual lines of code will be to implement arbitrary, artificial, intermediate goals, rather than the high-level project requirements.

Protocol Example: A network protocol can be written using TCP/IP level 7 (which has good support for standards), XML over HTTP (which like duck tape is very flexible and easy, even though it is big, slow, and clunky), custom packets on UDP (very fast and flexible, but you have to build your own reliability and security, and firewalls are a problem). Each choice has different advantages and disadvantages.

Once a high-level decision is made, the challenge becomes to use and implement it effectively. Suppose you choose XML over HTTP, then the next questions are "which values should be implemented as elements and which as attributes?" and "which tag and attribute names should be picked?" But these decisions are independent of the top-level protocol and choices may or may not impact overall quality. Being arbitrary, tag and attribute names should not be part of the requirements. Choosing TCP/IP level 7 would force completely different arbitrary low-level decisions.

Code and Architecture Example: Every line of code must be a specific line of code, even though many different lines are possible. The names of variables and classes and the boundaries between methods are not in the architecture and are independent of the functioning of the code.

Many decisions in an app are not part of the requirements or architectures because nobody can make all of the decisions. If nobody else chooses, then developers will choose the details themselves. Working requirements and codes are the sums of all decisions.

Error

"I now understand enough about my propensity to err that I can accept it as a fact of life." – Donald Knuth (Oram and Wilson, page 58)

The seventh source of unknownness is error. Human brains are hard-wired to make mistakes and optical illusions prove it. No matter how hard anyone studies an illusion after the truth is revealed, the brain will still succumb and perceive the shorter line as longer. (Hallinan, page 20) Human brains are hard-wired to make up information and the blind spot proves it. The blind spot in the eye is not empty, but filled in with information made up by the brain. (Schulz, page 57) Simple mistakes like typos, mousos, and thinkos will always happen. Some human thoughts and behaviors exacerbate errors.

Miscommunication

Some errors come from miscommunication. Even when users understand what they want and need, they are notoriously poor at articulating it because they rarely speak software-ese.

Misspeaking and Mishearing: Little errors always creep into conversations, resulting in exchanges like "That's what you said." "But, that's not what I meant." In the film *Spinal Tap*, the guitarist Nigel sketched a Stonehenge prop on a napkin, and wrote 18" (inches), but he meant 18' (feet). During requirements discovery, users may talk too fast or talk over each other and important details may get overlooked or written down wrong. People cover over mistakes in communication by using their experiences and imaginations, however some of their guesses will be wrong.

Interpretation: REs and SEs must never take what clients say literally because one rarely knows why they say what they say. Inputs and reactions need careful interpretation. When users dislike a demo, it may be a proxy for a fight they had with their spouse last night. When users like a demo, they might be thinking of their upcoming vacation and letting things slide. Customers say nice things, even when they struggle to use a product. (Kelley, page 27) Customers can be too polite to tell the truth. (Kelley, page 27) Half the time when you ask users, "do you want *x*?" they say "yes," simply because what else are they going to say?

Just because two people use the same words, does not mean that they understand each other. Conversely, just because two people use different words, does not mean that they misunderstand, but one suspects it. The Windows, Mac, and Linux communities each use their own words to represent the same concepts, though translating is "usually" easy.

Ambiguity: In development, many features and tasks are ambiguously scoped. For example, users may want to display and edit a list of names. The small, simple version would allow strings to be added and removed. A more complete version would allow them to be edited, reordered, imported, exported, and so on. A queue needs to hold some elements. Will it hold a thousand or a billion elements? A system will pass messages. Will it pass hundred character texts or megapixel images? The small and the complete versions of each can take very different amounts of time and resources. Users and developers may each assume different behaviors because each had always done it a different way. Ilities, like performance and fault tolerance, are often ambiguously scoped.

Omission: During discovery, the client will sketch out the features on his or her mind and then leave analysts and developers to fill in the rest. When the client forgets a detail that an RE might know, the RE acquires a new question. Did the client not need it or did he forget? For example, the client may not mention printing, which other clients have asked for in the past. Should an RE devote any effort to asking? Getting clarification about this one issue may preclude clarifying another, possibly more important issue. When everyone forgets about a detail, then REs acquire an even bigger problem, but nobody knows what it is.

In our experience, requirements are frequently omitted. The number of requirements that are present in any document is finite, while the number of requirements that might have been omitted is infinite. Details stated in the requirements can be wrong, but are usually in the ballpark. Unstated requirements can wreak havoc and sink a project. After delivery of one project of our acquaintance, developers were informed that auditors needed to be able to review data as it was being entered, forcing a significant rewrite and making everyone unhappy.

Misprioritization: One person might assess priority by tone of voice and another by order of discussion. Developers may misjudge how important a particular feature is to the client and refine the less important features, first.

Brains Use Models and Then Oversimplify Them

Joseph Hallinan notes that the brain makes mental models. Things are so complex that people use mental models, which contain flaws. (Hallinan, page 179) The problem is that human brains tend to oversimplify what they know, which is not a character flaw, but a simple biological fact.

Model making is automatic and fast. The brain fills in missing information so seamlessly that people are unaware of how many assumptions they make. They use it every time they sit in a chair or set a coffee cup on a table. They use it every time they read a class interface and project how it is implemented or read a function and project how it is used. "The machinery that allows us to perceive the world is not only deeply embedded, it's also automatic. The brain connects the dots in ways that we don't [realize]." (Hallinan, page 43) This filling in is used in art, so that people can believe that stories and movies are real. This filling in also makes people susceptible to pranks. Studies show that about half of what people believe is made up by their own brains without anyone realizing it. "The vast majority of our mental models are implicit, yet essential." (Schulz, page 93) We necessarily confuse models with reality. (Schulz, page 107)

People don't have photographic memories; instead, they use complex hierarchies of information. (Hallinan, page 121) Stories of what happens to us are also jumbled hierarchies. They are not narratives. Events do not occur in words. (Hallinan, page 129) Real requirements and codes don't either.

The Brain Simplifies Models: Brains simplify what they remember. Inconvenient details get pruned. Facts that don't fit get forgotten, de-emphasized, or reinterpreted. (Hallinan, pages 126 to 127) For example, people straighten up the maps they remember, and in doing so, distort the details. We remember cities within states and the positions of states, not the relative positions of cities. Most people believe that all cities in Nevada are east of all cities in California, even though Reno lies west of San Diego. (Hallinan, pages 120 to 122) Developers should follow coding conventions because they will not accurately remember inconsistencies in their code bases. Unconsciously, their brains tidy up what they believe.

The Brain Changes What It Remembers: The brain remembers what it likes and forgets everything else. We remember good things more than bad, for example school grades, gambling results, parenting actions. (Hallinan, page 58) "The tendency to see and remember in self-serving ways is ingrained and so subtle that we often have no idea that we're doing it." "Most people reconstruct their past opinion, they believe they always thought that." (Hallinan, page 59) Old-timers who reminiscence about the good-old days when they had perfect requirements and wrote perfect object-oriented code using assembler or C are delusional in this way.

People Think They Know More Than They Do: In *Everything is Obvious*, Watts writes "Our common sense misleads us into thinking that we know more than we do." (Watts, page 29) In *Being Wrong*, Shultz writes "We don't gather the maximum possible evidence to reach a conclusion; we reach the maximum possible conclusion based on the barest minimum of evidence." (Schulz, page 125) "Believing things based on meager evidence is what people do." (Schulz, page 114) We have all heard people interrupt each other during arguments, without even listening to what the other person says. "We are bad at saying, 'I don't know'" and "We are bad at knowing, 'I don't know.'" (Schulz, page 82) During planning and development, SEs use their memories and commonsense guesses about their code bases, but the real code bases are probably very different.

Many Thoughts and Behaviors Exacerbate Error

People See What They Expect: (Hallinan, page 21) Hallinan states this in many ways. "We see things not as they are but as (we assume) they ought to be." (Hallinan, page 113) "We think we see all there is to see." (Hallinan, page 12) We only see a fraction of what we think we see. (Hallinan, page 12) "We notice on a need to know basis." (Hallinan, page 14)

People Don't See What They Don't Expect: Conversely, people often fail to see what they don't expect to see. Inattentional blindness occurs when people look at something and cannot see it, especially when they are distracted or angry. (Hallinan, page 81) "There are many examples of novices catching errors that experts simply could not see." Children caught typos in a Brahms score and errors in NASA estimates for asteroid collisions. (Hallinan, page 112) Most radiologists failed to notice the "Gorilla in the X-ray." (Google it) Looked-but-didn't-see errors occur when we miss important details in front of our noses. (Hallinan, page 12)

People Skim: When people see stereotypes, they stop looking for details and skim. (Hallinan, page 19) Whenever REs and SEs need deep understanding (like during inspection or testing) and they see patterns, they will start skimming. When asked to cross out the letter 'e' in a text, people miss 32% of 'e's in 'the' and often missed the second 'e' in a word. People pay attention to the starts. (Hallinan, page 110) When skimming, we see things as they ought to be, we miss a lot of mistakes. The second time through we miss more. (Hallinan, page 113) Skimming gives us speed and fluidity, not accuracy. (Hallinan, page 111) "The problem is, we think we've noticed when we haven't. We don't know when we are skimming." (Hallinan, page 19)

Complications

Some behaviors increase errors. Many people are aware of these issues, but seem unable to help themselves, while living in today's frantic culture.

Avoid Distraction and Multitasking: People do not multitask well, even though everyone thinks that they themselves do. (Hallinan, pages 77+) Multitasking interrupts short-term memory, so people repeatedly forget things and it can take 15 minutes to regain focus after an interruption. (Hallinan, page 80) So, 20 phone calls or emails or Facebook updates per day means 5 hours at less-than-your-best focus. With meetings and breaks, REs and SEs won't have a single effective minute during a workday. (Hallinan, chapter 5)

Some companies now encourage distraction-free times, for example one morning a week when employees are encouraged to turn off their cell phones, emails, and browsers to get a small amount of real work done. Concentration is a key part of intelligence, so to paraphrase Miller, "The more you use your smart phone, the less intelligent you are."

Avoid Stress, Get Some Sleep, Be Happy: Gary Higabee notes that rushing, frustration, fatigue, and complacency all increase errors. "Sleepy people make mistakes." (Hallinan, page 216) "Happy people tend to be more creative and less prone to the errors induced by habit." Happy people solve problems faster. (Hallinan, page 218) Depressed people make more errors.

Avoid Habits: Habit kills the ability to see novelty. (Hallinan, page 214) But, people easily fall into ruts. Functional fixity occurs when people solve similar problems in the same way, even when better answers are at hand. (Hallinan, page 180)

Three Phases of Error

Here, we tweak Schulz's analysis from *Being Wrong* and identify three phases to an error.

Before: According to Schulz, before you know there is an error, it feels like you are right: before you know, the error resembles Coyote after going over the cliff and before he looks down. Error is a 'truth for now.' (Schulz, page 33) "A theory that hasn't been proved wrong, yet." (Schulz, page 32) Before you see the bug report, errors are blind ignorance, pure unknown. Even feeling a vague, looming unease is still feeling right for now because feelings are useless until they become actionable.

Transition: Something going demonstrably wrong for somebody reveals an error. Or, a developer inspects some code and spots an error. When developers finally see bug reports or change orders or feature requests, their realities change. The transition strips away one level of unknownness, revealing something underneath, which could be either a known or a simpler unknown. When a spacecraft slammed into Mars, SEs at NASA transitioned from "everything is alright" to "something is wrong."

Sometimes the transition lasts only an instant: on hearing the symptom, we instantly know the cause. Other times, the transition lingers: when we cannot reproduce the bug or understand the feature request because "it works for me" and "it might be user error," the status quo remains in limbo. We often delay reproducing bug reports as long as we can, to avoid shifting from the possibility (read illusion) of being right to accepting yet another of our own stupid mistakes. During the transition, REs and SEs come to terms with their own errors.

After: After we accept an error, specifically after we can reproduce it, it becomes something new, something between a known known and a known unknown. Either way, the error gets reduced to another task in the backlog. Developers may or may not fix it, depending on priorities, costs, etc. Some errors get fixed immediately. Some errors will be left intact because we are willing to live with them, for example, a button that is a few pixels too narrow, or incomplete functionality with a simple workaround. Some bugs are too hard or expensive to fix and will be left untouched. The rest will be fixed in due time.

Schulz writes that there is no experience of 'being wrong.' Saying 'I am wrong' is a paradox because by the time we say it, we already know that we are right in a new way. However, there is lots of experience with 'realizing we are wrong.' (Schulz, page 18)

Perry attributes 36% of the underlying causes of the modification requests on his large embedded project to what we would call "normal mistakes:" none given 21%, incorrect fix 7%, submitted under duress 7%, incorrect modification 1%. (Oram and Wilson, page 473) Perry interprets "none given" as mistakes that are so simple, they are not worth describing. (Oram and Wilson, page 490) Perry attributes 42% of the means of prevention to tools for avoiding normal mistakes: guideline enforcement 13%, requirements/design templates 10%, better test planning 10%, other 7%, design/code currency 2%. (Oram and Wilson, page 478)

People Are Irrational

The eighth source of unknownness is irrationality. Users, REs, and SEs are irrational and unpredictable, just like everybody else. More generally, they are subject to systemic biases. (Hallinan, page 2) People believe they are impartial, even when they are very biased. (Hallinan, pages 69 to 70) We just have to live with these facts.

Perhaps the biggest conceit in RE and SE is that people are rational and deliberate. REs and SEs may even be rational and deliberate to some limited extent within the context of writing code because everyone has technical backgrounds and works with deterministic computers. But, we believe that REs and SEs are just as crazy as everyone else because they too often fail to get the full scope of psychological and social support that they need.

Easily Influenced

Everything that users, REs, and SEs think, say, and do is influenced by everything and everyone around them. People's opinions are influenced much more than they know. (DiSalvo, page 162) David DiSalvo notes that it is unclear what all this influence means, however people are clearly not self-determined. "Self-control is at least half misnomer." (DiSalvo, page 169)

Environmental: People are influenced by their environments. Whether someone holds a warm or cold beverage affects how he or she sees others. People associate warmth with closeness. (DiSalvo, page 178). Whether a speaker holds a light or heavy clipboard affects how they are perceived. People associate weight and heavy with importance. (DiSalvo, page 177). Background music influences the choice of wine in stores, but only 14% of people were aware of it. (Hallinan, page 93)

Social: When people are praised for their efforts, they will gear up for harder tasks. When they are praised for being smart, they will prefer to attempt easier tasks. Some people respond more to a task that is described as a "challenge" and others respond more to a task that is described as "fun," even when it is the same task. (DiSalvo, page 102) The "N-Effect" states that motivation varies inversely with the size of our pond. People compete harder in smaller ponds. (DiSalvo, page 105) People are influenced by the examples set by others in prior moments, when they see others help or cheat. People are influenced by discussions with peers around watercoolers. Humans are gullible. It is easy to invent memories in others. (DiSalvo, page 193) We don't differentiate seeing something from doing it. (DiSalvo, page 168)

Individual: Every individual has biases from his or her genetics and experiences. Right-handed people see orientation better than lefties. (Hallinan, page 13) "Men tinker more, while women are more likely to follow directions." (Hallinan, page 143) People judge others by faces more than anything else, especially when voting for politicians. (Hallinan, page 45) People are influenced by their own previous actions. Writing down values is a 'blame antidote.' Writing down as many of the Ten Commandments as they can remember causes people to behave more ethically. (DiSalvo, page 168)

Desire for Control

Users: Clients often want at least some control over the software they purchase. Users may see a feature on another web site and want it, too, whether or not it is related to their project. Oatmeal complained about clients who wanted talking pet avatars to greet users on web sites. Users are aware of many conflicting ideas and standards and they often want to pick and choose. We speculate that companies pay for consulting and customization at least in part to exert control.

REs: Strong-willed REs can be so practiced at or excited about a particular technology that they fail to appreciate that they are doing something different than what the user wants. It is well known that doctors should listen more to their patients, but after decades of being encouraged to do so, doctors still don't. We are hard pressed to believe that REs actually listen any better than doctors. Being of taciturn nature, the authors excel at listening while others say what they want, yet we seem to always pick out the wrong details as most important.

Think of strong-willed, visionary architects like Le Corbusier and Frank Lloyd Wright. (Louridas, "Rereading the Classics," pages 372 to 375) REs may strive to use the latest technologies, out of personal pride or professional competitiveness. REs may take shortcuts when it suits their purposes, repeating their last project, out of familiarity or ease, simply because the user never said anything to shake that opinion.

SEs: For decades, everyone has seen SEs as undisciplined, ego-driven cowboys. SEs often want to use particular technologies or develop particular features, simply because they are cool.

21

People are Libertines

People Want What They Want: After visiting a restaurant supply store, a friend said, "They had 2-foot-long monster immersion blenders. I have no need for one, but I really want it." "Rachel's Mom: The reason that I'm calling is that I saw an ad in the paper for free health insurance for pregnant women, and I know you're not pregnant…. You're not pregnant, right? Rachel: No, I'm not pregnant. Mom: *laughs* Well, I just thought you could call them and check it out and see if they'll get you some insurance. Rachel: I don't think they'll give me insurance because I'm not pregnant. Mom: Well, if you did get pregnant then you could get it. If you got pregnant you and Brett would probably get married. And then you could just be on his insurance. But you won't be ready to get married for a while. Not until you're at least 30." (Rachel, quoted by permission)

People Hear What They Want to Hear: This corollary to the previous point applies to everyone. Very few people hear the truth, especially managers. Gary Larson's "Ginger" cartoon is not about dogs; it is about people.

People Do What They Feel Like, Even When They Know Better: Steve McConnell writes that even when told what to do, "people just feel like doing something else." (Hallinan, pages 175 to 176) Part of the problem is that people are not robots, and they don't like being told exactly what to do. It is bad for motivation. Doctors know better, yet sloppy handwriting on prescriptions still causes many unnecessary deaths every year.

People Have Many Motives: People can want fairness, glory, credit, favoritism, success, ease, vindication, and so on. Customers can be cheap and whiny. Analysts and developers can be lazy or stubborn. People may not want to acknowledge these motives, they may not be aware of these motives, but they are real.

Conclusion

Much of human reality is unknown. In the 1630s, Rene Descarte wrote *Meditations* about how things can appear very different from how they really are. In the 2000s, Donald Rumsfeld said, "There are known knowns; there are things we know we know. We also know there are known unknowns; that is to say we know there are some things we do not know. But there are also unknown unknowns – the ones we don't know we don't know."

Unknownness lurks everywhere in software: in the intentions of the stakeholders, in the requirements that REs write, and in the architectures and codes that SEs create. What we don't know will cause trouble: bugs, misplaced and wasted effort, budget and schedule overruns, and so on. There is no way to avoid either unknownness or its consequences. No matter how hard anyone works to nail down perfect requirements and architectures, they will still be massively wrong. Everyone who strives to eliminate uncertainty or error within projects will fail, just like Sisyphus.

We tried to provide perspectives about unknownness so that REs and SEs can better appreciate the limits of what actually can be known. Much more could be said about unknownness, but unfortunately a full study is beyond our means. This chapter provides a foundation for upcoming chapters about the downsides of planning, how much error everyone should really expect, and how REs and SEs use and abuse unknownness.

Acknowledgements

We want to thank Andy Oram and Greg Wilson for their book *Making Software*, which provided tons of concrete evidence for unknownness in SE. Their book emboldened us to explore this topic more broadly.

Years ago, Jon Hall asked one of the authors how one might find requirement bugs more effectively. Even though we mostly dodge the question, this chapter is part of a belated reply. We now believe that it is impossible to find all requirements errors without predicting the future, making everyone rational, and so on, which will never happen.

Jon Hall also shared his perspective that RE differs from SE. Throughout this chapter, we discuss RE and SE issues separately to show that what the code does relative to users and how the code works relative to the requirements are essentially the same problems, even though RE and SE are very different fields. This distinction also applies to test and management, though we leave those details as exercises for the reader.

We want to thank our friends and colleagues who reviewed this chapter and contributed many ideas and caught many (but assuredly not all) mistakes. If only we knew how to do so, we would fix them all.

Bibliography

Dan Ariely, *Predictably Irrational*, Harper, 2009.

Alan Cooper, Robert Reimann, and David Cronin, *About Face 3*, Wiley, 2007.

David DiSalvo, *What Makes Your Brain Happy and Why You Should Do the Opposite*, Prometheus, 2011.

Paul Graham, *Hackers and Painters*, O'Reilly, 2010.

Joseph T. Hallinan, *Why We Make Mistakes*, Broadway, 2009.

Gary Hustwit, *Objectified*, movie, 2009.

John Kay, *Obliquity*, Penguin, 2010.

Thomas Kelley, *The Art of Innovation*, Profile, 2003.

Kevin Kelly, "How Technology Evolves," www.ted.com, 2005.

Panagiotis Louridas, "Rereading the Classics," in Spinellis and Gousios, *Beautiful Architecture*.

The Oatmeal, *5 Very Good Reasons to Punch a Dolphin in the Mouth*, Andrews McMeel, 2011.

Andy Oram and Greg Wilson (editors), *Making Software: What Really Works, and Why We Believe It*, O'Reilly, 2011.

L.B.S. Raccoon, "The Complexity Gap," in *Software Engineering Notes*, volume 20, issue 3, ACM, July 1995.

Rob Reiner, *This is Spinal Tap*, MGM, 1984.

Kathryn Schulz, *Being Wrong*, Harper Collins, 2010.

Nate Silver, *The Signal and the Noise*, Penguin, 2012.

Peter Sims, *Little Bets*, Free Press, 2011.

Diomidis Spinellis and Geogios Gousios, *Beautiful Architecture*, O'Reilly, 2009.

Duncan J. Watts, *Everything is Obvious: *Once You Know the Answer*, Random House, 2011.

4
Sponsoring Organizations versus Project Teams

Fully understanding software projects requires understanding both the insides and the outsides. The insides of projects seem well-understood because well-developed processes (like Scrum, Extreme Programming, Kanban, and Team Software Process) describe the specific responsibilities and activities of project teams. However, we know of no discussions of the outsides of projects (the sponsoring-organization sides) by software engineers. Yet like in a marriage, both sponsoring organizations and project teams need each other to successfully complete projects.

In the first section, we contrast sponsoring organizations with project teams to suss what the players on each side bring to projects. In the second section, we contrast project scopes with project details to suss how the choices of the various stakeholders differ. And in the third section, we make some observations about resources, behaviors, and transactions in organizations and about how projects catalyze progress.

Players – Sponsoring Organizations versus Project Teams

Contrasting the players in projects sheds light on the contributions that each makes and on the roles that each plays. Members of sponsoring organizations can only do the outside halves of projects (gathering purposes and resources) and only they can do so. Members of project teams can only do the inside halves of projects (writing programs) and only they can do so.

Table 1: Players – Sponsoring Organizations versus Project Teams		
Issues	**Sponsoring Organizations**	**Project Teams**
Examples	Microsoft, CNN, and Wikipedia	Staff, Consultants, and Volunteers
Key Contributions to Projects	Purposes and Resources	Technologies
Contexts of Change	Society	The Sponsoring Organization
Preferred Units of Progress	Projects	Commits
Preferred Statuses	Occasional Milestones and Done	Daily Standups and Progress
Preferred Coping Skills	Planning and Stubbornness	Adaptation and Responsiveness

Examples

Microsoft, CNN, and Wikipedia: Sponsoring organizations include software vendors like Microsoft, Google, Linux, and Eclipse; online retailers like EBay, Etsy, and Amazon; entertainment providers like CNN, Netflix, and Wikipedia; government agencies; and any organization that implements a CRM to help sales or support.

Staff, Consultants, and Volunteers: Project teams are groups of internal employees, external consultants, and volunteers.

Key Contributions to Projects

Purposes: Sponsoring organizations primarily care about how projects fulfill or improve their own missions, for example by selling better offices suites and video games or by improving the organization's customer support. Classically, requirement engineers divine purposes through discovery and analysis, but in many situations, sponsoring organizations divine purposes through politics. In CRM and consulting projects, analysts and other project-team members can facilitate, but only sponsoring organizations can actually resolve their own politics and set their own goals.

Resources: Sponsoring organizations understand and aggregate the resources that fuel projects, specifically time and money. Only sponsoring organizations can aggregate those resources. The managers and accountants in sponsoring organizations do not develop software themselves, rather they rely on project teams to do so. As a rule, sponsoring organizations do not care about technology, per se.

Technologies: Project-team members primarily take responsibility for technologies and more specifically for programming, which they care about deeply. They care less about purposes per se because they would do more or less the same kind of thing for any mission for any sponsoring organization. They don't care about resources, per se, in the same way that they don't care about air to breathe or water to drink, per se. They mostly just presume that adequate resources are available.

Contexts of Change

Society: Sponsoring organizations embody and carry out external, societal goals by delivering better software and services to society. Microsoft sponsors programs that make writers and businesspeople more productive and gamers more entertained. Etsy sponsors programs that help people to sell their arts and crafts. CNN sponsors programs that help the public to keep up with current events.

The Sponsoring Organization: Project teams write and improve programs that help sponsoring organizations to work better. For example, a project team may add features to a video game to make it more salable; they may improve a website to make it easier to use or more visually appealing; or they may add features to a CRM to help agents provide better support.

Preferred Units of Progress

Whole Projects: Projects are the primary units of progress or change by which organizations improve how they perform their missions. Process-driven organizations would prefer to never change again, but when necessary they prefer fewer and larger changes to maximize the feeling of progress and to minimize the number of disruptions.

Individual Commits: Commits are the primary units of progress or change by which teams improve programs. Project teams incrementalize large projects to minimize overload and to cope with the surprises (the unknowns, changes, and errors) that invariably arise. Small and frequent commits enable project teams to absorb changes as they go.

Preferred Statuses

Occasional Milestones and Done: When processes are mainly political, statuses can often be fudged trivially. Sponsoring organizations idealize crisp milestones. Managers and accountants like everything to be clear, simple, and done and they prefer to use milestones to detect problems. Milestones occur infrequently because the managers and accountants in sponsoring organizations often get busy doing other work in between.

Daily Standups and Progress: When processes are mainly technical, such as when writing software, statuses are harder to fudge. Yet, the statuses inside of projects remain murkier than anyone likes to admit. Project teams learn to live with the murk as they struggle to make forward progress day-by-day. Standup meetings occur frequently (like daily or every-other-day) to evoke personal commitments and peer pressure and thereby to encourage steady productivity.

Preferred Coping Skills

Planning and Stubbornness: Managers in sponsoring organizations want to create plans (such as requirements, architectures, budgets, and schedules) that predict the future before projects start and then they want everyone to stubbornly follow through on those plans without change after projects get going. We know of no managers or accountants in sponsoring organizations, who easily admit the possibility of unknowns, errors, or changes, though we have seen a number cope quite well when problems did occur.

Adaptation and Responsiveness: Project teams need to cope with the unknowns, errors, and changes that inevitably occur as they arise so that they can adapt to make useful programs. Project-team members don't necessarily want to adapt to change, but they can and do adapt continually as necessary, as reality unfolds.

Choices – Project Scopes versus Project Details

Project definitions embody specific decisions about both scopes and details. Budget managers in sponsoring organizations care mostly about project scopes. Users and project teams care mostly about project details. The scopes and details of projects are tightly and necessarily intertwined, so the choice of features should inform the choice of scope and vice versa, even though we separate them here.

Distinguishing between scopes and details enables consulting and outsourcing projects. Usually, contracts describe consulting and outsourcing projects in terms of fixed prices and goals. Distinguishing between scopes and details also enables Agile projects. In Agile projects, the details (for example in backlogs) can change significantly as users learn what they need and as developers figure out how to provide it, while the scope remains the same.

Table 2: Choices – Project Scopes versus Project Details		
Issues	**Project Scopes**	**Project Details**
Key Questions	How Much to Invest?	Which Features to Build?
Spectra of Choice	Minimum to Maximum	Element of Power Set
Why Choices Matter	Psychology of Price	Utility of the Program
Key Conflicts	Budget Managers versus Everyone Else	Among Users and Developers

Key Questions

How Much to Invest?: Those who represent a sponsoring organization need to decide how much to invest in each project. Scope concerns either the total number of features to implement or the total cost in terms of time and money. Sponsoring organizations only care about which specific features to implement in so far as the program does what users need.

Which Features to Build?: Users and project teams need to decide specifically which features each project should build. In other words, they need to distinguish which features to prioritize and implement now, in this release, and which to defer until later releases or forever.

Spectra of Choice

Minimum to Maximum: Every significant software project that we can think of has a broad spectrum of possible scopes from minimal to median to maximal, from quick-and-dirty to flowing-but-clunky to elegant-and-pretty, which need differing amounts of resources to implement. Haggling over scope means haggling over whether to make the project bigger or smaller. Scopes correspond to the growth sense of change.

Element of Power Set: Users often have a wide variety of desires and want a wide variety of features, so stakeholders must choose a subset of the possible features to implement that delivers the functionality that users need and fits within the negotiated scope. Haggling over details means making tradeoffs between different sets of features. Details correspond to the replacement sense of change.

Choices are usually arbitrary in that many different valid scopes and sets of details could work for each project. For example, an organization could sponsor more smaller projects or fewer larger projects to build the same set of features. Users can often be satisfied with a variety of different subsets of the possible features. Of course each organization, manager, user, and situation may favor different choices.

Why Choices Matter

Psychology of Price: Scope matters because of the psychology of price and the first estimate. In a negotiation, the first bid tends to set the price. (Hallinan, page 107) After a budget has been set, stakeholders may accept changes to the requirements, but only when the budget remains unchanged. In our experience, scope is the single most important decision in any project.

Utility of the Program: Details matter because the delivered features will determine the utility of the finished program, which is a key part of the success of every project. Choosing details resembles the knapsack optimization problem, even though the features should also work well together.

Key Conflicts

Budget Managers versus Everyone Else: Decisions about scope pit budget managers who generally want to spend fewer resources against everyone else (specifically users and developers) who generally want to build more and better features.

Among Users and Developers: Frequently, different users disagree about goals and want different combinations of features or different looks and feels. For example in many CRM projects, agents want more features while managers want more reports.

Frequently, developers have different goals than users. In many projects, developers can easily implement most of what users ask for but not everything. Developers often want to redefine the hardest requirements to make them easier to implement. Requirements may not quite fit a platform and developers may want to tweak the requirements to allow them either to use standard tools and platforms more consistently or else to use cool, new, innovative tools and platforms more consistently.

Resource limitations drive most of the conflicts among users and between users and developers. If the project scope accommodated everyone's desires, most likely they would have fewer conflicts. Of course, nobody can resolve contradictory goals with more resources.

Organizational Theory

Organizational theory and the resource, behavior, and transaction models reveal a variety of issues about the contexts of projects. (Wikipedia, "Organizational Theory") For example, organizations manage resources by aggregating and investing them; organizations crave waterfall and factory processes to imbue decisions with fairness and control; and projects catalyze change.

Resources – Organizations Manage Resources

Organizations use projects to transmute one kind of resources (time and money) into another (programs). Resources are always limited and sponsoring organizations must bound their investments or, in other words, must choose specific limits for each project.

Organizations Aggregate and Invest Resources

Time and Money: Time and money are the main resources that organizations aggregate and then invest into software projects. (Connor) Programs are the main resources that result from software projects. In turn, these programs should earn or save even more time and money later. Companies develop office suites and video games as resources to sell. Sales and service organizations develop CRMs as resources to help their agents do better and faster work.

Ongoing Investment: Large software programs require large amounts of resources invested over a long time, which in turn require large, enduring organizations to aggregate. So large, enduring programs cannot exist without large, enduring sponsoring-organizations and user-bases. To remain vital, all programs must evolve, which requires an ongoing investment of resources and so all enduring organizations that use software must continually aggregate resources to invest. No one should ever presume that a program can remain unchanged for long.

Commercial Examples: To evolve their programs, commercial software vendors pay salaries to their analysts, programmers, and testers. In turn, those programs support many normal users who each pay a little bit or else support some important users, who each pay a lot.

Open-Source Examples: To evolve their programs, open-source organizations (like Linux and Wikipedia) spend volunteer hours and donated money, which they aggregate. Millions of open-source projects are written via volunteer hours. Open-source organizations often need money to keep servers running or pay essential personnel.

Organizations Must Bound All Investments in Projects

Resources are Always Limited: Aggregating the resources necessary to create programs is always hard and resources are never unlimited. Limited resources force all organizations to deliberately bound how much they invest in and improve each feature, product, or system in any given project. Stakeholders allow many projects to overrun their initial budgets, but they never allow unlimited budgets. Organizations with unlimited resources wouldn't have any problems with outlandish user requests or exotic development practices because almost any approach would eventually succeed.

Commercial Examples: Online retailers (like Amazon and Etsy) would love to upgrade all of their software systems: the marketing portal, sales CRM, supply chain, support CRM, human resources, and so on. Software vendors (like Microsoft and Google) would love to improve all of their products, too. But, commercial organizations must recover all investments through future revenues and so they must bound all investments into projects by the expectations of those future revenues. If anyone expected to lose money, they should do nothing and just keep it in their pockets.

Open-Source Examples: Open-source organizations must recover all investments through the future enthusiasm of volunteers, who want to affect society as well as to engage in social networking and professional development. Many open-source projects allow seemingly unrestrained change, which can result in wasted effort (reducing impact) or frustration (reducing enthusiasm). Open-source projects that don't expect to meaningfully affect society or to meaningfully benefit volunteers should close and release their resources to contribute to other projects instead. (Lerner and Tirole)

Competition Encourages Efficiency, Sort of

Competition occurs down within organizations for resources as well as up between organizations for market-share. Resources and market-share often seem zero-sum and competition can become fierce. Competition encourages everyone to invest resources well. If invested poorly over time, resources will get squandered and organizations will eventually fall behind competitors. But, competition doesn't guide projects very well.

Not Always Motivating: Competition is not universally motivating, in part because not everyone is good at or interested in competing on any particular terms. Many people avoid competitive situations and seek cooperative situations instead.

Post-Facto: Competition is indirect and post-facto. One can only know how well a program meets the needs of users after they begin using it. One can only see how well a program competes in the market after it ships. Competition per se reveals little about what to do to create programs that will succeed.

Behaviors – Organizations Crave Processes

Sponsoring organizations crave rigid waterfall and factory processes to write programs. Organizations should attempt to allocate resources fairly when they decide who gets what or when they decide how many resources to invest into each project. When resource allocation seems unfair, morale may flag and stakeholders may slack off or quit. Processes encompass politics and technologies to deliberately and rationally set project goals and allocate work. Hopefully, processes imbue decisions about projects with consistency, fairness, and effectiveness.

Waterfall Processes – Requirements Express Shared Expectations

Waterfall processes concern fairness between projects. Sponsoring organizations naturally want to treat different projects fairly and so they want to cast requirements into bronze, which drives their desires for waterfall processes.

Everyone with a hand in a project wants to know what to expect and they want to know that their efforts will be productive rather than wasted. Requirements are essential for collaborations because they describe the goals or purposes that all stakeholders share; they describe the political compromises that everyone agrees to; and they distinguish between the features that will and won't get built in this project.

Users: Users want to know whether the project will solve their problems, i.e. whether to wait for the project to finish or to try something else like starting a different project or giving up in despair.

Managers and Accountants: Managers and accountants in sponsoring organizations want to ensure that their investments will solve real problems cost-effectively; that their investments in different projects are fair; and that they have the resources to allocate. So, they naturally want to know how many people should work on the project (1, 10, 100, 1000) and how long the project should take (1 hour, 1 day, 1 week, 1 month, 1 year). Without some such estimates, they cannot make rational decisions about which projects to support and to what degree. In order to make such estimates for a project, managers and accountants need clearly written-down goals that state what the stakeholders expect to accomplish.

Project Teams: Developers want to know what code to write. Testers want to know what problems to look for. Everyone else (marketers, trainers, and support personnel) also wants to know how to help.

Only a statement of shared purpose such as a specific set of requirements enables all stakeholders to ground their expectations about how the project will play out based on the same information. So, before any organization will commit to starting a large project, allocating resources, and so on, they demand requirements. Requirements have defined every substantial software project that we know of.

Casting in Bronze

Once set, people in sponsoring organizations demand that shared expectations remain unchanged, meaning that they cast the requirements into bronze.

Users: Users don't want to let their rivals change the expectations about the project independent of the consensus. For example, nobody may add their own features into or kick someone else's features out of the project without permission.

Managers and Accountants: Managers and accountants in sponsoring organizations naturally want to set fixed budgets and schedules (including milestones and delivery dates) for each project before it starts. Once projects begin, managers and accountants demand that requirements remain unchanged because changing the requirements risks changing the budgets and schedules. If sponsoring organizations let one project slip, then the next project will want to slip, too.

Project Teams: The people in project teams seem to tolerate changing requirements because they wrangle with change all the time and use incremental processes. However, they also work on behalf of sponsoring organizations and usually try to keep requirements as stable as possible.

All Fixed Requirements Entail Waterfalls: Rigid requirements define waterfalls with at least two steps: analysis transmutes stakeholder intentions into fixed requirements and programming transmutes fixed requirements into code. Requirements, architectures, budgets, and schedules invariably become commitments because they all embody political decisions about fairness within organizations.

Factory Processes – Local Productivity

Factory processes concern productivity and fairness within projects. Sponsoring organizations naturally want to do a lot of work and they historically emphasized individual productivity, which drives their desires for factory processes.

Managers and accountants in sponsoring organizations naturally, legitimately, and inevitably want to get the most out of each worker. Commercial organizations want to consistently guide their employees toward more productive work, so they naturally want to use deliberate processes to define and distribute work. Open-source organizations should also use deliberate processes to guide their volunteers.

Over a century ago, Max Weber argued that efficient bureaucratic organizations embody clearly-defined processes that have "rigid divisions of labor," "firmly established chains of command," and "regular and continuous execution of assigned duties." (Wikipedia, "Max Weber") Though often far from perfect, factory processes can efficiently make a lot of decisions and carry out a lot of work.

Scrum, Extreme Programming, Kanban, and Team Software Process are all factory processes for sustained productivity. They all work pretty well and parts of each seem destined to endure. However, factory processes can only do what they were designed to do – guiding low-level work in project teams. Note that factory processes cannot set effective goals for projects nor predict the future; that the downsides of factory processes include mistakes, boredom, and burnout; and that Lean manufacturing and development emphasize a more global or holistic sense of productivity.

Transactions

Ronald Coase used the transaction model in his "theory of the firm" to explain why organizations grow to specific sizes based on the relative costs of internal and external transactions. (Wikipedia, "Theory of the Firm")

The transaction model explains many aspects of software projects. Specifically, Coase's logic explains whether to insource or outsource software projects. Managers and accountants in sponsoring organizations often view projects in transactional terms because they primarily care about the exchange of what they get for what they pay. They boil managing projects down into making decisions about requirements, budgets, and schedules. They even reduce outsourcing and consulting projects to contracts.

However, we (the authors) mostly avoid transactions in this essay. Organizations of all sizes use CRMs in sales and support and they all use projects to tailor their CRMs, so transaction costs don't specifically define those projects. A following chapter concerns the obligations of sponsoring organizations to projects, which are primarily political and concern relationships more than transactions. Also, transactions feed the illusion that projects can transform organizations as cleanly and simply as moving a piece during a chess game, even though projects always turn out much messier.

Projects Catalyze Change

Organizations must either evolve or stagnate. Organizations sponsor projects to catalyze change by overcoming activation barriers. Without activation barriers, progress would occur spontaneously. Agency embodies the capabilities and mastery of the moment necessary to catalyze change.

Overcoming Inertia, Indecision, and Inaction

Inertia: Changing the momentum of an organization takes effort whenever sticking to the status quo is easy. In process-driven organizations (and all large, enduring organizations are process-driven), progress requires effort to break down old processes and more effort to build up new processes based on new software.

Creating Urgency: Inputs and negotiations invariably take longer than anyone wants, longer than the allotted time if tolerated. When stakeholders dawdle in giving their inputs, returning their reviews, or making their decisions, project managers must evoke urgency to counteract delay and must impose deadlines to cut off input and debate. We know of no alternatives. Bertrand Meyer described a virtual money trick to get users to prioritize tasks in meetings and we have seen variations on his trick used in many projects. (Meyer, page 61)

Overcoming Resource Allocation Problems

Resource allocation is a major activation barrier. Project managers must either gather adequate resources (time and money) or ensure failure. Projects that don't aggregate enough resources to implement all of the necessary features and quality are doomed. Ultimately, insufficient resources kills all projects that die because development stops when resources dry up.

Investment Constraints: All enduring software organizations should try to maximize the benefits of their investments, which means that they should avoid investing too much. Two key constraints on investments are direct and opportunity costs. Of course, stakeholders can only judge value heuristically.

Direct Cost: Do not invest more resources into projects than they merit.

Opportunity Cost: Do not invest resources into projects when those resources would be more productively invested elsewhere. Software is only one of many possible investments for organizations. In general, organizations would also like to spend resources on dividends or bonuses or marketing or other products. It takes additional political will to channel resources away from those other opportunities. Opportunity cost equals the value of the second-best option and it embodies the time-value of the opportunity as well as the relationship between scarcity and choice. (Wikipedia, "Opportunity Cost")

Overcoming Win-Loss Problems

Barry Boehm famously argued that projects should be win-win for all participants. (Boehm and Turner, appendix D) But in practice, projects of any size have win-loss elements for many participants. Authorities must often force users and developers to accept some decisions that they dislike, even if in trade for some decisions that they like. In our experience, whenever an executive must make extra efforts on behalf of a project, someone has a severe win-loss problem.

Internal Losses: Inside of projects, many users will lose their battles over goals and will not get the features that they want. The larger the user-base, the more users who will not get the features that they want. Many developers will also lose their battles over goals. Developers may dislike being limited to old technologies or being forced to use unfamiliar technologies outside of their expertise.

External Losses: People outside of projects often must handle many project tasks. When they do a lot of work yet get almost no credit or when they have other, higher-priority projects, their work all too often gets done more slowly or more poorly than desired or planned. People in the network department may delay fully testing and configuring the web-service interfaces for months. People in the test department may delay generating data for months. People in operations, support, training, and accounting often drag their heels for similar reasons. When the project isn't their main focus and they have plenty of other work to do, these people often get treated as support personnel, even though they should be treated as full-blown stakeholders.

Notes

V Model: The V Model distinguished between sponsoring organizations and project teams in 1991. (Forsberg and Mooz) However, Forsberg and Mooz only drew out a few distinctions between sponsoring organizations and project teams. This chapter expands on their work.

Project management differs from sponsoring organizations in that project managers usually embody the interfaces between sponsoring organizations and project teams. Project managers do occasionally discuss issues like alignment, risk, and resources in the context of sponsoring organizations, however usually with a strong, top-down emphasis when acting as proxies for sponsoring organizations.

Bibliography

Barry Boehm and Richard Turner, *Balancing Agility and Discipline*, Addison Wesley, 2003.

Kathleen R. Connor, "A Historical Comparison of Resource-Based Theory and Five Schools of Thought within Industrial Organization Economics," in *Journal of Management*, volume 17, number 1, pages 121 to 154, March 1, 1991.

Kevin Forsberg and Harold Mooz, "The Relationship of Systems Engineering to the Project Cycle," INCOSE International Symposium, October 1991.

Joseph T. Hallinan, *Why We Make Mistakes*, Broadway, 2010.

Josh Lerner and Jean Tirole, "Some Simple Economics of Open Sources," in *Journal of Industrial Economics*, volume 50, number 2, pages 197 to 234, June 2002.

Bertrand Meyer, *Agile!*, Springer, 2014.

5
Sponsoring-Organization Obligations

To make effective progress on large CRM projects, managers in sponsoring organizations must do a lot more than just write requirements, gather resources, and train users. Stakeholders must also work through and resolve their group goals, deal with change, and deal with each other. We believe that many problems in projects are caused by managers trying to oversimplify the politics or prevent change. "Bride-of-Agile" practices fulfill these obligations.

Setting Effective Group Goals: Conflict resolutions are necessary but not sufficient to guide successful projects. Two key techniques for resolving conflicts are bottom-up haggling and top-down authority. We also discuss debate, diversity, and speaking with one voice.

Working through Continual Change: Initial requirements tend to have many flaws and, in our experience, tend to be about half right. Stakeholders should winnow and refine requirements, both before and throughout projects. Managers and accountants in sponsoring organizations should set flexible budgets and schedules.

Dealing with Problem Stakeholders: Inexperienced stakeholders need training; hidden stakeholders need engaging early; and unhappy stakeholders need placating.

Setting Effective Group Goals

Setting group goals is a political activity, yet resolutions don't always lead to successful projects. Haggling and authority are two key techniques for resolving political conflicts. Debate and diversity tend to improve creativity in groups. Stakeholders should speak with one voice because otherwise they have not yet resolved their conflicts.

Resolutions are Necessary but Not Sufficient

The success of large projects depends on stakeholders resolving their political conflicts. Politics occur when groups argue with other groups. Sometimes compromises should balance the joy and sometimes they should balance the whining. But, compromises are not necessarily good enough. In our experience, unresolved conflicts cause problems for all large projects. If stakeholders don't want to or cannot resolve their conflicts, projects will remain at risk.

Compromise is a Prerequisite to Success: Compromise has a (perhaps undeservedly) bad reputation in societal politics, but compromise is essential to the success of large engineering projects. C.W. Miller drew a delightful cartoon about compromise in airplane design, showing the dream airplanes that different groups would prefer: maintenance, controls, armaments, stress, power plant, and so on. A complete airplane necessarily embodies a compromise between the desires of all of those different groups. (Hughes, page 121) (Miller) Similarly, a complete software program of any size must embody many compromises between the desires of different groups of stakeholders.

Gridlock Causes Failure: Gridlock is the alternative to compromise. Organizations need the discipline to eventually stop arguing, resolve their conflicts, and build consensuses around goals or else their projects will never actually start. In some sense, all project failures are really just political gridlocks: managers refuse to provide more time and money, users refuse to use programs without more and better features, and developers refuse to work for free. If anyone would relent, progress could continue. Note that developers comprise only a fraction of the problem in these gridlocks, even though they often bear most of the blame. Note also that managers providing more resources is the primary way forward.

Compromise is Not Sufficient for Success: Alas, the compromises that emerge don't always guarantee success. Many compromises are less than ideal and some are downright awful. Just because a requirement document exists, doesn't mean that enough stakeholders actually agree with it. Compromises don't need to work for all stakeholders, but they do need to work for "enough" stakeholders, as individuals and as groups. Compromises that help too few stakeholders will still lead to failure. Of course, changing circumstances, inept implementations, and other problems can also lead to failure.

Haggling and Authority

Bottom-up haggling and top-down authority are two key techniques for resolving conflicts between stakeholders. Both have benefits and detriments and many combinations thereof exist. In our experience, large projects must combine both.

Haggling Can Be Beneficial

Haggling occurs when individual stakeholders (specifically the affected users and developers) argue directly for the features that they need. Haggling occurs when they actively participate in resolving conflicts and deciding what should give, as opposed to leaving the outcome up to chance or delegating it to an authority. For example, users may accept deferring some requirements but not others. Users may accept some changes that make features easier to implement but not others. One can only find out which changes each stakeholder will accept by asking.

Haggling Can Be Detrimental

Unfortunately, haggling leads to unpredictable results that don't always give enough stakeholders what they need. The following problems obviously occur in CRM projects, but most likely also occur in a wide variety of software projects.

Uneven Clout: The fight among stakeholders never occurs on even ground. In most organizations, authority is explicitly hierarchical and uneven. In CRM projects, businesspeople wield more clout than support agents and developer clout lies somewhere in between depending on the issue. Managers may even discourage some stakeholders from participating by withholding the time or information necessary to do so, often when teams get busy or managers get annoyed. In the "The Best Laid Plans of Mice and Men" chapter, we note that haggling exaggerates power gradients within hierarchies.

Uneven Skills: Not everyone has equal haggling skills. Some stakeholders (such as support agents) may simply not know enough about software projects or corporate politics to know how to get what they need. Women often avoid competitive situations. Everyone who doesn't fight effectively may find that their opinions get pushed aside.

Never Ending: Haggling may never stop. When stakeholders have entrenched and conflicting desires, possibly no amount of haggling will ever resolve their conflicts. Hagglers frequently try to reopen resolved issues. For example, a feature deemed desirable but too expensive (or "beyond scope") may inspire every single user to try to change the decision, one by one. Projects may need "Decisions Made" documents that enumerate and explain the decisions that should remain settled.

Unfair: Haggling often seems unfair and many individuals distrust or dislike the haggling process. In her FSE keynote, Mandana Vaziri stated that haggling between users and developers is "unproductive." (Vaziri) We agree that users feel legitimate frustrations. However, the only alternatives are for users to solve their own problems, which only works for small projects like spreadsheets, or to delegate decisions to an authority or proxy, which can become even more unfair.

Authority Can Be Beneficial

Authorities simply impose their decisions on everyone else. Authority works well when decisions are obvious or arbitrary (such as the choices of algorithms in embedded programs) and when haggling stops working. Managers, designated users, and architects can all act as authorities. Boehm and Turner idealized authority for the efficiency of its unidirectional communication. (Boehm and Turner, pages 34 to 37)

Authority is a vital tool for breaking gridlocks and forcing some individuals to accept unpleasant win-loss realities so that the group as a whole can proceed. Within limits, everyone understands the need for authority when haggling stops working, even when they whine about the results afterwards. Authorities should act as win-win as they can, but in our experience, authorities who try to please everyone never succeed.

Authority Can Be Detrimental

Unfortunately, authority can be unpredictable and may not produce effective results that give enough stakeholders what they want. Because self-perception is so fraught with delusion, an authority may not realize when he or she makes mistakes or how abusive his or her actions come across to subordinates.

Mistakes: Authorities can make bad technical decisions. Without feedback channels, specifically haggling, low-level stakeholders have no means to fix the poor decisions that authorities make and to get the results that the group actually needs.

Abuse: Many managers work for their own benefits. Authorities can easily abuse their positions, which often seems unfair to subordinates. Ongoing problems with gender and racial bias and harassment in organizations show just how hard these sorts of problems are to perceive, let alone to fix. (Bielby) (SWE) Management has many more psychopaths than the general public, so always be wary.

Many Combinations of Haggling and Authority

In some projects, haggling proceeds in a democratic way until an authority cuts it off at some point defining the goals. In some CRM projects, users aggregate goals in a democratic way, then businesspeople winnow goals in an autocratic way, and then developers implement goals (as best they can) in a seemingly random way. In some projects, intermediaries (for example a group of team leads) act as authorities for their teams while haggling amongst themselves.

Additional Notes

Encourage Debate and Diversity

We take creativity as a proxy for making better programs. Both debate and diversity tend to improve creativity in groups, in part by helping to avoid making decisions too quickly. Yet, people often struggle to walk the line of enough but not too much debate and diversity. Both require additional efforts, which partly explains why so many groups prefer to avoid them.

Debate: Healthy debate helps people to make good decisions because it helps people to think things through, to avoid problems like groupthink, and to avoid getting lost in the weeds. Both too little debate (or acquiescence) and too much debate (or obstruction) can harm decisions. Adam Grant notes that ideally, devil's advocates would truly believe their dissenting opinions and that merely going through the motions of debate is suboptimal. (Grant, chapter 7)

Diversity: Diversity helps groups to make good decisions by more fully expressing the opinions of the whole group. Diversity encourages people to consider the needs of others upfront. Margaret Burnett and Denae Ford argued that gender and racial diversity in project teams and focus groups help them to understand and express the needs of diverse user-bases. (Burnett) (Ford, et al.) As CRMs become more widespread in the U.S., connecting to sales and support agents, they engage more women and racial minorities, whom homogeneous male development teams may not fully understand. Weiner notes that diversity can be uncomfortable and even difficult for participants, so everyone involved must apply extra effort to make it work. (Grant, page 190) (Weiner, pages 256 to 257 and 264) Thomas Hughes argued that interdisciplinary teams, which is a limited form of diversity, also help large system-engineering projects. (Hughes, epilogue) (Vedantam, "Edge Effect")

Speak with One Voice

"A servant with one master knows what to do, a servant with two masters is never sure." – Anon

Continuing to Fight: Everyone in a sponsoring organization or department needs to agree on the rules and goals and then speak with one voice. Speaking with one voice may sound authoritarian, but speaking with multiple voices means that stakeholders have not yet fully resolved their conflicts.

Picking and Choosing What They Hear: Different people, possibly from different departments within organizations or different groups within departments, often send different messages. When that occurs, analysts and programmers will pick and choose which messages they hear, which will assuredly differ from what the organization needs.

Avoid Splitting Responsibilities: Whenever possible, avoid splitting oversight across departments. When accounting pays for a CRM project, IT manages it, and support uses it, messages about priorities and governance easily become muddled. The IT department may prefer Agile processes because they keep up with contemporary software-engineering practices, but the accounting department may demand Waterfall processes because they always do. Developers often suggest improvements to requirements and members of support (who see the benefits) approve while members of IT (who see the cost) disapprove. When stakeholders don't communicate with each other regularly, they may not realize that others will disagree. For example, support agents may not realize that accountants will disagree.

Working through Continual Change

Requirements always have problems and so they must evolve both before and throughout projects. Before projects start, requirements change as stakeholders trawl and winnow their goals. Throughout projects, requirements change as stakeholders refine and integrate their goals. Managers and accountants in sponsoring organizations also need to go with the flow as reality unfolds over time and they should set flexible budgets and schedules.

Initial Requirements Tend to Be About Half Right

In spite of everyone's best intentions and efforts, many requirements are wrong, missing, or ambiguous and need to change. The only way to get perfect requirements would be to predict the future, but nobody knows how to do so – neither managers and accountants in sponsoring organizations nor members of project teams.

Inevitable Flaws

The initial requirements for large projects always contain flaws. In general, each stakeholder wants a different combination of outcomes, like adding new features or increasing his or her status within the group. Many stakeholders do not fully appreciate all of their options or even of all of their desires. Many users don't even need the features that they ask for.

Imagination is Flawed: When stakeholders write requirements, they imagine the future. When people imagine the future, they focus on a small number of important details and ignore the rest. Dan Gilbert stated, "You can't imagine every detail," and argued that people should think, "I'm only imagining one or two of the many pieces of the experience and, as a result, I should be humble about my predictions." (Vedantam and Gilbert, 9:26) But no. Many software people believe that they can imagine the outcomes of projects.

Unaware of Options: CRM users generally ask for features that will simplify their work. But, most CRM users don't know the technology very well because that isn't their area of expertise. They often don't know what is possible or effective, and so they make guesses about what features to ask for. They often ask for features that resemble what they need, but that have missing or extraneous details, or both.

Perception and Understanding: Stakeholders need to understand that the project will meet their needs, so users unfamiliar with software projects often ask for buttons. Users can see when a button gets put into a GUI and they can show it off to their colleagues. Perhaps the functionality would work better invisibly and automatically in the background, say via a database trigger. However, users may not appreciate features that they cannot see.

Social Goals: Some stakeholders feel driven to gain status, which often happens when men show off in front of support groups full of women. They may demand more features simply to keep talking and to remain in the spotlight. Some stakeholders feel driven to score points or defeat rivals, which often happens when multiple departments will use a program, but only one will pay for it. Stakeholders from the funding department may want to show their authority by demanding more features.

Specificity: Requirements should be as specific as necessary but no more. Stakeholders often try to keep requirements as vague as they can get away with because ambiguities simplify description. However, they invariably make mistakes, leaving some details overly ambiguous and others overly specific.

Premature: In our experience, large CRM projects invariably start before all political decisions get fully resolved. When this happens, everyone will argue that they should still get their way, either what had been promised verbally or in their own minds.

Poor Decisions: Meyer discusses a virtual money trick to evoke decisions in meetings. (Meyer, page 61) His trick gets decisions made quickly, but it doesn't necessarily produce good or lasting results. Deadlines tend to increase error and decrease quality because at the last minute, deciders may lack the time to detach from short-term emotions (such as the thrill of winning a point) or to think consequences through (such as considering all cases). Quick decisions (like all decisions) can be quite poor.

Cool, New Technologies: Developers often want to use cool, new technologies (such as a new graphics library) that users don't care about or even know about. But, such goals can be vital to developers for career advancement and, when appropriate, stakeholders should integrate those goals into projects.

Irrelevance: As negotiations continue, the requirements often change in ways that stakeholders don't understand. The emphasis naturally warps from tangible features that users do care about to features for administrators and managers that most users don't care about. The emphasis naturally warps from tangible features that developers can estimate and implement to ideals such as quality and ilities (like usability and security) that developers struggle to estimate and implement and users struggle to perceive.

Backlog Notes

At the end of a project, the backlog describes all of the desired but undelivered work, much of which got revealed only after the project started. In our experience, the initial requirements for mid-sized (5 to 10 man-year) CRM projects tend to be about half right, of course with huge variance. The number of unfinished requirements or the amount of unfinished work in the backlog approximately equals the number of the requirements that were initially requested or approximately equals the number of requirements that got delivered. This means that about half of what was hoped for throughout the life of the project got delivered. Note that we look at this fraction from the point of view of users.

At the end of a project, the backlog enumerates the features that someone wanted enough to make an official request for, yet lacked enough support from the whole group to get implemented. Backlogs include features that were dropped to make room for new requirements that fixed omissions, ambiguities, and errors. Backlogs also contain less-important ideas that arose during development.

When a project ends, the backlog contains the sum of all official disappointments. Many additional disappointments may exist that someone had hoped for yet did not officially document.

Boehm's diseconomy of scale probably affects the amount of disappointment in backlogs. Smaller projects generally have proportionally smaller backlogs. Larger projects generally have proportionally larger backlogs. Our scaling factor of half for mid-sized CRM projects is anecdotal, but certainly projects of all types and sizes end with large backlogs of unfulfilled requests.

The Chaos report states that many projects overrun their budgets by about 2/3, which we treat as in the ballpark of "half right." (Standish)

Requirements Continually Evolve Both Before and Throughout Projects

First, stakeholders should articulate and gather their desires into requirements through trawling. Then, the stakeholders should continually winnow and refine the requirements as development proceeds. They winnow requirements to shoehorn projects into tight budgets. They refine requirements to increase coherence and fix problems. At least some stakeholders and perhaps most will have to accept fewer or different features than they initially asked for.

Ideally, initial requirements would embody a prioritized and integrated design, but project teams can only develop such designs over the course of whole projects, which is what whole projects are for. The process of starting with independent requirements and then slowly merging them, resembles recent brainstorming practices. People should actually brainstorm independently and only gather their ideas together when they discuss them. (Cain, pages 87 to 92) (Lehrer, pages 158 to 161) Initial requirement documents and backlogs should start out as lists of random, independent features or, in other words, they should start out resembling the "blind men and the elephant." The features often mesh poorly at the start.

Trawling

"Trawling" means gathering the union of the desires of all stakeholders during discovery. Analysts in all kinds of organizations talk with members of their user-bases to gather their desires. Generally, the larger the user-base, the wider the variety of features that they want.

Commercial Examples: Consultants tailoring a CRM for a customer-support department may gather the desires of a thousand agents. Microsoft famously only works on products that have at least a million users. Some mobile-phone apps at Facebook have more than a billion users. In each case, analysts strive to understand what their user-bases as wholes want.

Open-Source Examples: Sharing source codes openly with many users only happens when the codes aggregate the purposes of all of those users. Linux and Wikipedia aggregate the needs of their respective stakeholders.

Start Out Independent: To minimize inappropriate biases, users should express what they want, independent of spin, independent of cost, and independent of what programmers want. During discovery, developers should avoid influencing the requirements to avoid driving solutions back toward their comfort zones, which they often do without realizing. Developers should join in later after users have had their full say. Developers can then add estimates of cost to enable stakeholders to prioritize the features based on relative value.

Winnowing

In general, people would like to get as much value or as many features as possible for what they spend. Optimization often leads to wanting more, but it can also lead to wanting more than the budget affords, more than what fits within the negotiated scope. In turn, optimization leads to conflicts whenever different stakeholders disagree on how to winnow enough features to make a project fit within its budget.

Groups of all sizes want more features than they can afford. The larger the stakeholder-base, the greater the likelihood that members collectively want too much. Pleasing one user in isolation may seem easy, but even individuals often want more features than their budgets allow. In groups of more than a handful of users, few decisions will please everyone. With thousands or millions or billions of users, no decisions will please everyone.

Whenever stakeholders want too many features for a given budget, then something must give. Stakeholders may tolerate deferring or cutting some of the features to fit the budget. Splitting some features out into a separate or upgrade project may make the rest more affordable.

Refining

Throughout the project, as developers slowly take over and as features get built one-by-one, the requirements should continue evolving. Design will reveal more requirements. (Brooks, page 191) Stakeholders should continually renegotiate and refine the requirements to resolve issues as they arise.

Increasing Design Coherence: As development proceeds, the requirements should slowly merge into a coherent, integrated program through structuring and organizing. Redefining disparate features can improve how they work together. For example, converting a set of independent, overlapping dialogs into a single generic dialog or workflow may improve usability.

Fixing Problems: As development proceeds, the errors, ambiguities, and omissions in the requirements will get revealed and stakeholders should fix them as they arise. These fixes generally cause requirements to change and grow.

Reducing Cost: Refining the requirements can help to reduce cost. If a feature turns out too hard or expensive to implement, users may accept a workaround that provides partial functionality more cheaply. For example, replacing a search system with a set of reports (or vice versa) may provide many of the same benefits more cheaply.

The Agilefall Spectrum of Change

Initial requirements, budgets, and schedules are at best heuristic guesses for how projects will unfold. The Agilefall spectrum of change extends from rock-steady stability to unfettered change.

Rock-Steady Stability: Project teams could stubbornly implement exactly what the initial requirements say, which by all precedent only works for the tiniest problems. This case isn't Agilefall in spirit, it is actually pure Waterfall, yet lies at one end of the spectrum.

Evolve: Project teams could use the initial requirements as a starting point and let the project evolve from there. Project teams almost always do this anyways as standard Agile practice, even though it leads to predictable conflicts with sponsoring organizations.

Unfettered Change: After a project starts, the project team could throw out the initial requirements and start over from scratch with new discovery using pure Agile. On one CRM project, the support team spent two years doing analysis before the project started and the requirements had became outdated and baroque, so they should have started over. But in general, this approach seems wasteful because most-likely many initial requirements are fine. This case isn't Agilefall in spirit either yet lies at the other end of the spectrum.

Stakeholders should not determine the combination of stability and change that their project follows, rather the farsightedness of the initial requirements and the rate of learning or context change should determine the combination. In other words, the actual situations or circumstances encountered should guide the way, rather than what anyone arbitrarily wants. Of course, everyone would rather have perfect and done.

We have heard that some consulting companies claim to turn down projects that are not pure Scrum. But, every pure Scrum project must start with a Waterfall to estimate the size of the project.

Flexible Budgets and Schedules

Sponsoring organizations crave stability, but circumstances invariably change beyond their control, so sponsoring organizations should adapt correspondingly. The question isn't whether requirements will change, but how to respond when they do. Everyone actually uses these strategies anyways, but sponsoring organizations should treat them as normal practices rather than as symptoms of failure. Anyone who disagrees with these spectra of strategies should not manage software projects.

The Spectrum of Budget Strategies

Table 4 lists three notable points on the broad spectrum of budget strategies. The table actually relates two different decisions: the initial guess about the actual cost and the means of coping with the inevitable change and growth of requirements.

Table 4: Points on the Spectrum of Budget Strategies		
Project Type	**Expected Cost**	**Coping Strategy**
Prototypes	50%	Cancel the project and try something else.
Upgrades	100%	Defer lower-priority features into the next release.
One-Offs	200%	Expand the budget to absorb problems.

Prototypes: For high-risk research projects and new products, invest 50% of the initial estimate or less. When projects have a high risk of failure, funders should minimize the cost. As soon as problems arise, cancel the project and try something else. The point is not to fail, but to learn as much as possible as quickly and cheaply as possible. If the prototype succeeds, then improve it later via upgrades. This strategy resembles finding the "minimum viable product" in Lean Startups. When startup companies build products that users don't even know that they want or need, they entail a lot of risk. Rapid prototyping forces stakeholders to make tough choices and to demonstrate value quickly and cheaply.

Upgrades: Commercial products (such as office suites and video games) often undergo long series of upgrade releases. The specific features of individual upgrade projects (or releases) often matter less than the long-term, sustained progress. Stakeholders can meet budgets and schedules (or keep them from slipping) by deferring lower-priority features from the current release into the next, so invest the initial estimate into each project. This strategy works well when users can live with ongoing, short-term progress and can live with getting only part of their initial request until the following release.

One-Offs: When an organization gets only one shot at a project, when users need all of the requirements, when stakeholders must succeed and must not fail, expect to invest double or more than the initial estimate. One-off projects have no follow-up or upgrade projects to defer features into, but requirements will still inevitably change and grow, so the budget must change and grow correspondingly. Don't just naively allocate twice the estimate. Initially, allocate the estimated value and only allocate more as understanding improves. Frank Lloyd Wright was known for always spending twice his initial budget.

Many combinations of these strategies exist. For example, a project could both defer some features and extend the budget a bit. Prototypes and upgrades often work together. An organization can use prototypes to create an initial program and then use upgrades to improve it.

An important difference between upgrades and one-offs concerns whether users can wait for the next upgrade. When the upgrade cycle takes longer than users will tolerate (perhaps the cycle is yearly, but users will only wait three months to get deferred features), then each upgrade effectively becomes a one-off. Facebook now upgrades their major apps weekly, to minimize the problems caused by deferments. (Savor)

The Spectrum of Schedule Strategies

Milestones are Time-Boxes: Sponsoring-organizations should treat milestones as Agile time-boxes. Each milestone encapsulates an attempt to make progress and then an opportunity to reconsider how to proceed by reevaluating the project and readjusting the goals. Stakeholders can narrow and defer goals to drive the project toward completion; they can continue with either the same or different goals at the same scope; or they can broaden the goals and make the project bigger. Sponsoring organizations should not use milestones as threats or straightjackets, even though milestones do tend to express adversarial distrust.

Dealing with Problem Stakeholders

Successful projects require adequate participation by each and every stakeholder, where "adequate" depends on the individual. We would like to discuss all stakeholders, but we have little to say about the happy and engaged except that managers should work to keep them that way. On the other hand, problem stakeholders need special efforts.

The managers in sponsoring organizations must deal with problem stakeholders because only those managers can do so. Project team members (especially external consultants, but also project managers) can negotiate, but cannot compel cooperation. Problem stakeholders live outside of the authority of project teams because otherwise they would be team members.

Problem stakeholders most likely cause fewer problems for organizations that write a lot of software (like Microsoft and Lockheed Martin), which have undoubtedly encountered these issues many times before and have evolved cultures for dealing with them. But CRM projects occur in all kinds of organizations that otherwise never write software. We have seen many problem stakeholders in real CRM projects.

Inexperienced Stakeholders Need Training

Stakeholders who live outside of development teams (for example, support agents and accountants) often misunderstand how software-development projects and processes work. When the previous CRM upgrade in the support department occurred 10 or 20 years prior, most likely few current agents will remember going through the process.

Don't Understand Requirements: Some stakeholders expect that they will get precisely what they ask for. For example, accountants may expect that analysis resembles making a shopping list for the office-supply store and that development resembles filling a basket at the store. Some stakeholders not knowing what else to ask for meticulously describe existing programs, but don't clarify what should change. Others not knowing the limits of the technology or the budget describe castles in the sky.

Don't Understand Quality: Some stakeholders expect that software in demos should be done. When they see all of the controls present on a GUI, but only half of them working, they may feel disappointed or even angered by the "deception." Other stakeholders unrealistically expect custom Salesforce webpages to have the same fit and finish as Microsoft Office.

Training about Software Development

Training everyone about software development can help to set more realistic expectations. Even so, many stakeholders may not fully understand until after their projects end.

Use Demo Projects: Whenever possible, use a demo project to train users. First, do something like the Custom Wallet exercise and, then, draw out the key observations about projects. The exercise could also make watches or hats or any other small item that everyone uses.

First discuss interview techniques for 10 minutes. Good questions evoke stories and emotions. "Tell me a story about how you got your current wallet." "Tell me a story about how you have used it." "What do you like?" "What do you dislike?" "What do you imagine?" Use active listening (Wikipedia, "Active Listening") and dig for underlying emotions. Then in pairs, each person interviews the other about their wallet needs for 10 minutes. Then everyone builds a custom wallet for their partner for 20 minutes. Provide construction paper, string, tape, glue, pens, scissors, hole punches, and any other desired arts-and-crafts materials.

Then participants should show some of the more interesting examples to the whole group and explain their decisions. Draw out the following points using the examples. Nobody can read minds, so users should communicate as clearly as possible. Even so, communication will never be perfect. Demos help to identify miscommunication and clarify goals and iterations enable refinement. Users know the status quo best and can often provide concrete examples, but describing the current solution doesn't clarify what should change. Imagined improvements may not work out, so describing them should only be part of requesting something new. And, different people have different skills and see different details clearly, so diversity often helps.

Don't Lecture: In lectures, everyone gets bored and nobody remembers anything afterwards. (Jeffries)

Hidden Users Need Engaging Early

"Out of sight, out of mind." – Anon

Users become hidden in many ways. Some are deliberately excluded and others are accidentally overlooked. Managers can exclude users from projects and users can hide from projects by remaining silent.

Regardless of the cause, silence differs from agreement. Holding one's tongue (whether because one doesn't know about the project, hopes to change it later, or just gives up) differs from agreeing with the project goals. Everyone interprets silence as tacit agreement because what else can anyone expect? But, programs that don't fulfill the needs of silent users can fail when those users later speak up or fight back. In our experience, too many CRM users silently disagree with goals as projects proceed obliviously.

Don't Have Any Cycles: Managers may exclude some busy or important users (for example support agents who specialize in legal or disability cases) from meetings to minimize distraction. But, their needs will either be omitted from the project or be shoehorned in at the last moment, disrupting everyone else.

Don't Have Any Interest: Software projects are often long and detail-laden. Some users simply lose interest and stop paying attention. They may attend meetings, but multitask using mobile devices to goof off or do other work instead, just tuning out. Repeating many questions twice reveals this problem.

Don't Trust the Process: Many CRM users distrust that they will get what they need. CRM agents rank low on corporate totem poles. Some users unused to having anyone ask for their input may not even realize that they can make a difference. People who feel disadvantaged in other situations (for example, racial and gender minorities) may also feel disadvantaged in software projects and may not try very hard. Those who expect to lose battles often turn away to avoid wasting their efforts, which is completely natural if undesirable.

Don't Feel Heard: Many users in support (and especially women) may not feel heard. Men in both user and developer groups with large personalities may dominate discussions during discovery and demo meetings. People who run meetings often like having a responsive representative speak for the whole group, but such individuals can drown out everyone else. Men often don't realize that they are blocking communication. Women do realize but don't know how to get through. For clarification, see any book by Deborah Tannen. (Tannen) Racial and other minorities may also feel unheard in mixed groups.

Manager Example: Managers sometimes add a slate of reports to a project at the last moment. They may have forgotten that they are part of the project; they may be trying to get the needs of their subordinates started first; or they may expect that their needs will be easy to satisfy. However, fixing these omissions often forces last-minute changes that will get implemented poorly or will disrupt everyone else.

Engaging Early

Threatening users that they won't get what they need if they don't speak up doesn't help. Everyone already knows this. Adam Grant delves into the challenges of engaging participants productively. (Grant, chapter 7) Engaging hidden users takes additional effort by everyone.

Dig for Hidden Users: Everyone must dig for hidden users. Find hidden users by comparing the total user-base with the participating user-base and keep asking about anyone who might remain hidden.

Engage Silent Users: Look for users who don't participate in meetings and follow up using different communication channels. Meeting in small groups or one-on-one enables and compels quieter, less-competitive stakeholders to participate. But, holding more meetings takes more effort by members of the project team during discovery and demos as well as more coordination on the organization side.

Hidden Colleagues Need Engaging Early

Collaborators on consulting projects need to build working relationships quickly. Many support employees are poorly integrated into projects, especially when projects get implemented by external consultants. For example, teams of consultants often treat employees in the network, test, and training departments as support personnel, rather than as full-blown stakeholders. Conversely, those employees usually give external consultants much lower priority than fellow employees. People who don't know each other often avoid making demands of each other, delaying shared work.

Salesforce Example: Consider a Salesforce project written by a team of consultants. IT employees must write the web-service configurations, which they can easily test behind corporate firewalls, but not from outside. Until the Salesforce prototype starts working, nobody can test the web-APIs through the firewalls. Testing becomes an imposition on IT personnel on the random day when the prototype finally starts working. As features incrementally get implemented and ready for demos, the development team incrementally needs data from the test group. They impose on the test team on seemingly random days.

DOD Example: In one DOD project, the internal team offered to help integrate a new program into an existing system, but the project team did not accept their help. Possibly, they thought integration would be easy. Possibly, they thought they could do it all themselves. Regardless, integration started late, failed later, and the project was eventually cancelled.

Engaging Early

People who don't yet know each other or trust each other still need to collaborate effectively. In large projects, senior managers or executives often step in to demand cooperation across department or corporate boundaries. Yet, everyone should wield authority as positively as possible.

Early Team Building: Introduce project-team members and internal-support employees as true colleagues early on, in person if at all possible. Dignitaries can help. Consultants may meet some stakeholders in person during discovery, but they often meet no one in test or IT. Even so, everyone needs to know how best to get each other's attention, how to make requests, expected turnaround times, and so on. Also, introduce consultants to internal managers so that the work that internal employees do for the project will be prioritized as normal work. Watts Humphrey wrote about ritual, off-site team building in government projects but, in our experience, adequate kickoffs rarely occur in outsourced CRM projects. (Humphrey, part II)

Early Integration Reviews: Schedule integration reviews with senior managers before trouble starts to reward accomplishment rather than to rebuke failure. Planning a high-ceremony demo of end-to-end functionality as early as possible (at say a third of the way through the project) will encourage everyone to work together constructively and quickly. Even if the demo is minimal or gets delayed multiple times, it will often coerce cooperation without negativity. Of course, the dignitaries must appreciate bare-bones demos and tolerate postponements.

Hidden Authorities Need Engaging Early

Authorities who never meet with users and developers imply that they won't cause problems later, which isn't always true. Users and developers sometimes change projects in unacceptable ways without realizing that they will provoke fights with those authorities later.

Accountant Example: We have seen whole projects (both users and consultants) get blindsided by accountants, who pop up at the end of the project saying, "You should have gotten my approval before making these changes." "But, we never even heard of you before." "Yet, I am the ultimate authority." He then stops all further payments, killing the project.

Engaging Early

Hidden authorities need to become visible. Send all arbiters of change, including executives and accountants, to some early meetings, so that everyone has a clue about their existence and powers. At the very least, introduce them to the project managers in person. Exposing hidden authorities takes effort and perhaps travel. Ideally hidden authorities would be sidelined, but if they could be sidelined, they wouldn't be authorities.

Unhappy Stakeholders Need Placating

In large projects, many stakeholders will inevitably lose battles over goals. Those who feel that they aren't getting what they need from a project (whatever that may mean) may become disappointed or angry and can exacerbate problems, especially when they have positions of authority. For example, hidden and quiet stakeholders can easily become passive-aggressive. Unfortunately, unhappy stakeholders put projects at risk. In our experience, perceived losses drive most of the problems.

Delay: Anyone who feels overwhelmed, unsure, ignored, or wronged can cause trouble by dragging their heels and providing information too slowly to meet project deadlines, which blocks progress or forces rework later.

Crypto-Requirements: Stakeholders who must give up requirements because the budget gets cut or another stakeholder gets shoehorned into the project, often weasel the game by finding ways to demand all of the same features with fewer official requirements. Heavily edited "crypto-requirements" are often jargon-filled or ambiguous and can be impossible to implement. For example, a requirement may say, "the page shall display and update the complaint codes." Everyone naively assumes that complaint codes are strings or numbers that will be implemented as text fields or drop-down lists, however they actually refer to sophisticated subsystems.

Bureaucracy: An authority (especially a manager) who feels dissed after being left out of a technical meeting may become a stickler for old bureaucratic rules. He or she may demand that all requirement changes get approved via individual change orders through both the business and accounting departments. However, the additional effort and delay will bog down the otherwise-supposedly Agile process, effectively prohibit all change, and may doom the project.

Attack: The internal project manager didn't get the contractor he wanted and circulated rumors to undermine the project.

Placating

Unhappy stakeholders can all too easily get stubborn, play dumb, and let the project fail. Ideally, managers would placate stakeholders before problems occur, but since nobody can predict the future, managers can only respond to problems as they arise. For example ideally, managers would remove stakeholders who will not get engaged in the project to avoid disruptions and wasting time and effort. But, identifying those stakeholders ahead of time is impossible.

Daniel Goleman argued that having a wide variety of emotional responses to people is a key to successfully resolving their problems. (Goleman) Effective managers can cajole, explain, command, distract, ignore, bribe, implore, intimidate, listen, commiserate, joke, or wait as appropriate. They can ask problem stakeholders to respond to the manager, the team, a colleague, the organization, the mission, the client, the project, or the situation as appropriate. A greater variety of tactics implies a greater likelihood of evoking cooperation. Weak managers have just one response, usually authority, which (while one valid tactic) often makes matters worse.

Consolation: Offering a small token (a mug, t-shirt, or responsibility on another project) to acknowledge the loss may work for some. Airlines routinely hand out gift baskets and frequent-flyer miles to mollify customers.

Time: Organizations may also need to provide time for frustrations and resentments to subside after projects end.

Notes

Bride-of-Agile Practices

If nobody articulates what projects need from sponsoring organizations, then nobody should expect to get it. In the software-engineering literature, we have found many discussions of the obligations that project managers have to projects (see any book on project management) but, so far, we haven't found any discussions of the higher-level obligations of sponsoring organizations. This chapter presents a first sketch based on our experiences in CRM projects. We expect that understandings of these obligations will improve significantly as the managers and accountants in sponsoring organizations begin to explicitly reconsider their own roles.

In the past, project managers often took on the responsibilities to set goals and to deal with stakeholders. But in general, the members of project teams shouldn't worry too much about these obligations because they can do little about them. Project teams are simply too small and powerless to address sponsoring-organization politics. Evoking cooperation from people who will not get what they need from a project lies outside of what analysts, developers, testers, and project managers can do.

Large CRM projects usually have internal project managers, who interface between members of the sponsoring organization and members of the project team, but we want to be clear about their responsibilities. They also need to push the members of the sponsoring organization to participate fully. The ratio of sponsoring organization effort to project team effort should be around 1:1, say somewhere between 2:1 and 1:2, which includes work on both requirements and integration.

Many of the obligations in this chapter and the corresponding coping skills are variations on classic parenting skills: speak with one voice, wield authority positively, and stay engaged. Barry Boehm would describe most of them as examples of Win-Win. Like Agile principles, these sponsoring-organization obligations are vague and general.

Two Kinds of Projects

In this chapter, we focus on consulting and outsourcing projects rather than on product-development projects. All software projects share many similar needs, for example management and financing. However, consulting projects and product-development projects differ in significant ways. Regardless, all projects should adopt Bride-of-Agile practices to one degree or another.

Consulting: In most consulting projects, users reside inside of the sponsoring organization; users set their own, mainly-political goals; and developers collaborate directly with users. Corporate choices about programs usually hold everyone captive and, for example, support agents cannot choose their own CRMs. CRM projects usually have infrequent upgrades at best. When the project results don't meet their needs, internal users can only whine because they have no other options.

Product-Development: In most product-development projects, users reside outside of the sponsoring organization, often among the general public; analysts set mainly-technical goals; and developers remain isolated from users, for example at Microsoft and Facebook. Commercial programs have no obvious organizations to encompass all users and so stakeholders in marketing, sales, and support act as proxies for users. When upgrades of commercial products take too long or provide too little benefit, users can often switch to competing products.

Bibliography

William T. Bielby, "The Challenge of Effective Interventions: Alternative Paths to Minimizing Workplace Gender Bias," http://www.hbs.edu/faculty/conferences/2013-w50-research-symposium/Documents/bielby.pdf, 2014.

Barry Boehm and Richard Turner, *Balancing Agility and Discipline*, Addison Wesley, 2003.

Frederick P. Brooks, Jr., *The Design of Design*, Addison Wesley, 2010.

Margaret Burnett, "'Womenomics' and Gender-Inclusive Software: What Software Engineers Need to Know," FSE 2016 keynote, ACM, November 2016.

Susan Cain, *Quiet*, Crown, 2012.

Denae Ford, Justin Smith, Philip J. Guo, and Chris Panini, "Paradise Unplugged: Identifying Barriers for Female Participation on Stack Overflow," FSE 2016, ACM, November 2016.

Daniel Goleman, *Emotional Intelligence*, Bantam, 2005.

Adam Grant, *Originals*, Penguin, 2016.

Thomas P. Hughes, *Rescuing Prometheus*, Vintage, 2000.

Watts S. Humphrey, *TSP: Leading a Development Team*, Addison Wesley, 2005.

William Jeffries, "Vermont Medical School Says Goodbye to Lectures," in NPR All Things Considered, August 3, 2017.

Tom Kelley, *The Art of Innovation*, Doubleday, 2001.

Jonah Lehrer, *Imagine*, Houghton Mifflin Harcourt, 2012.

Bertrand Meyer, *Agile!*, Springer, 2014.

C.W. Miller, search for online images using "dream airplanes cw miller".

Tony Savor, invited talk at FSE 2016.

Standish Group, www.standishgroup.com/outline/.

SWE, "What Drives Female Attrition in STEM Professions?," https://research.swe.org/wp-content/uploads/2016/08/16-SWE-029-Culture-Study-10_27_16-Final-CP.pdf, August 2016.

Deborah Tannen, *You Just Don't Understand*, William Morrow, 1990.

Mandana Vaziri, "Correct or Useable?," FSE 2016 keynote, ACM, November 2016.

Shankar Vedantam, "Edge Effect," on NPR Hidden Brain, July 2, 2018.

Shankar Vedantam and Dan Gilbert, "Why We're Bad at Predicting Our Own Happiness – And How We Can Get Better," on NPR Hidden Brain, August 21, 2017.

Eric Weiner, *The Geography of Genius*, Simon and Schuster, 2016.

Wikipedia, "Lean Startup," https://en.wikipedia.org/wiki/Lean_startup, September 7, 2017.

6
The Blob of Agile versus the Bride of Waterfall

Like Godzilla versus Mothra, the Blob of Agile and the Bride of Waterfall are slugging it out for world domination. The Blob of Agile has been attacking and devouring everything in sight. The Blob started small and as it grows it absorbs larger and larger projects as well as larger and larger chunks of organizations. The Bride of Waterfall has been fighting back in self-defense and revenge. Their 20-year battle seems destined to continue for decades to come.

Today, project teams mainly use Agile practices and sponsoring organizations mainly use Bride-of-Waterfall practices. But, Agile directly contradicts Bride of Waterfall and vice versa. As long as each side uses different practices, each side will continue causing untold trouble for the other.

The Revenge of the Bride of Waterfall

Our Story So Far: Agile won, CMM lost, and the Waterfall has been declared dead by constables. (Waterfall is Dead) But like any self-respecting monster from a movie, the Waterfall just won't stay dead – something keeps bringing it back to life. Waterfalls don't just spring from the labs of the mad bureaucrats in Pittsburgh, who delight in crossbreeding red tape to make tanglier and lethaler strains. Waterfalls also arise from graveyards and offices and classrooms everywhere: from Bangalore, Berlin, Johannesburg, Rio de Janeiro, San Francisco, Sydney, Tokyo, and even sleepy hamlets like Albuquerque. So in spite of the news reports, the Waterfall remains a technical nightmare, the terror of projects, the scourge and bane of programmers.

The Difficulties of Problems

In table 1, we describe four tiers of difficulties found in the broad spectrum of CRM problems. These tiers seem more than a bit arbitrary, yet they embody the main roles found in CRM projects. We think of these tiers as too easy, action, design, and too hard. These tiers also remind us of Chomsky's hierarchy.

Table 1: The Difficulties of CRM Problems		
Agents	**Problem Examples**	**Solution Processes**
Users	Tweak Configurations	Ad Hoc
Administrators	Add Users and Validation Rules	Customer Service
Developers	Add Webpages and Triggers	Agile
Researchers	Security	Ad Hoc

Problem Examples

Users: Users solve simple problems by configuration. GUIs often explain how to solve these problems in option dialogs or online search can find explanations. The solutions to these problems usually affect only individual users and they can often undo the changes.

Administrators: Administrators solve action problems like adding users, resetting passwords, adding fields to tables, adding validation rules, and tweaking permissions. Action problems tend to require special abilities, like super-user access; involve two or more related but far-apart steps; affect many users at once; or nobody can undo the changes. Administrators must also respond in a timely way.

Developers: Developers solve design problems like making database triggers, web pages, and batch jobs. Design problems usually involve programming, data, and page-description languages. Developers must also maintain the usability and performance of the system.

Researchers: Researchers solve the hardest problems, which have lots of unknowns. Everyone tries to avoid these problems as much as possible.

Solution Processes

    Users: Users tend to solve simple problems themselves, perhaps with some help from support. Users don't really use processes, rather they make ad hoc efforts and often blunder about ineffectively.

    Administrators: Administrators tend to solve action problems over and over, for example resetting passwords. The repeated work usually outweighs any amount of training by a lot. Administrators can usually describe large problems and break them into fixed series of steps, though of course some problems occur infrequently and others defy description. Administrators mainly use customer-service processes.

    Developers: Developers mainly struggle to figure out the user's real problems and how to solve them at a meta-level. Usually, the figuring out what to do takes much more effort than the actual typing of code. As development proceeds, the solution (or code) becomes known. If anyone could know or guess what code to write ahead of time, then he or she would just hire typists to do the programming. Developers mainly use Agile processes.

    Researchers: Researchers tend to use ad hoc processes because their problems defy planning and control. Research is the last resort because nobody can solve harder problems.

Everyone Should Know about All Tiers

    Most CRM people focus on their own tiers. Users mainly solve simple configuration problems; administrators mainly solve action problems; and developers mainly solve design problems. Researchers rarely work on CRM projects, though they occasionally work on the hardest problems.

    Many CRM people help out on adjacent tiers. Everyone can work on simpler, easier tasks on lower tiers if perhaps less proficiently because they practice less often. For example, developers routinely help to solve administration problems, especially for the new features that they create. Conversely, many CRM people work on harder tasks on higher tiers. For example, advanced administrators routinely solve design problems.

    Ideally, everyone would understand the full spectrum of tasks, so that they would know whether to handle and how to forward the curveball requests that users make. Ideally, everyone would understand research tasks so that they would know what to avoid.

Optimization

    Everyone would rather avoid work altogether, preferring that their tasks and projects were done. If a task remains unfinished, hopefully users, administrators, developers, or researchers (in that order) can solve it. Nobody wants to overpay, so less-expensive personnel should work on easier problems.

    User Examples: If a user can solve his or her own problems, maybe with some help from support, then nobody needs to engage administrators or developers.

    Developer Examples: Developers could help users in support or help administrators to tweak permissions, but that would cost more than having support personnel or administrators do those tasks. If an organization brings in developers, everyone presumes that they will work on design tasks. If the work were easier, the organization would have brought in less-expensive support personnel or administrators in the first place.

The Natures of Problems

    Both administrators and developers are software artisans. Both use processes – Customer Service and Agile, respectively. Waterfall processes just don't work for either of them, but they just don't work for completely different reasons. In table 2, we organize problems in two dimensions (knownness and change) to draw out an explanation. Of course, the categories in the table overlap.

Table 2: The Natures of Problems		
	Static	Dynamic
Knowns	Waterfall	Customer Service
Unknowns	Agile	Research

Knownness

    Knowns: "Known," "easy," "tame," or "navigation" problems resemble following a recipe to make cookies or following a map to a destination. Known problems tend to have minimal, well-understood, or forgiving variations. Nestle Toll House cookies have only 10 ingredients. If a batch has 20% too little sugar or 20% too many chocolate chips or omits the nuts, the cookies will still turn out edible.

Unknowns: "Unknown," "hard," "wicked," or "wayfinding" problems resemble making a new recipe or making a map of uncharted territory. Unknown problems tend to have many variations, many unknowns, or finicky variations, even when some parts are completely understood. If one function has 20% missing lines of code or another has 20% extra lines of code or one function is missing, the program may not work at all.

Change

Static: Requirement documents and blueprints describe static problems that remain unchanged for a long time. Once static problems become predictable, they remain predictable.

Dynamic: Dynamic problems change unpredictably within projects, sometimes from one day to the next.

The Natures of Problems

Waterfalls: Waterfall tasks mainly replicate existing, known, static products. Decomposition and long-term planning work well (even for large and complicated products) when one begins with a finished, working example. Factories can build 20k automobiles per year or 20m cell phones per year because they replicate existing, known objects that remain essentially the same from one month to the next. The key challenge is optimization.

Customer Service: Users tend to request administration tasks randomly, which makes them unpredictable. Nobody knows day-to-day or even hour-to-hour what help users will request next or what tasks administrators will work on next, so nobody can make specific, long-term plans. Administrators have found that customer-service processes based on queues and priorities work well. The key challenge is getting the work done.

Agile: Design tasks involve lots of variations and unknowns, making them unpredictable. Developers rarely repeat two tasks in exactly the same way. One task tweaks the GUI, the next tweaks the database, and the next tweaks a batch job. Even when a series of tasks edits the same file, each edit embodies a different purpose. One task adds a feature, the next refactors the code, and the next optimizes the performance. Developers can loosely plan their projects because they usually do know many things in general terms. But as development proceeds, problems and unknowns inevitably get exposed, so learning, refinement, and adaptation must follow. Developers can estimate design tasks, but their estimates often contain significant errors. The key challenges are understanding problems precisely and devising effective solutions.

Research: Research tasks defy solution. Nobody can solve them in controlled ways.

Problems are What They Are, Regardless of What Anyone Wants

What users actually ask for determines the natures of tasks and projects, rather than what anyone wants those tasks and projects to be. Nobody can control the nature of any given task or project in any other way.

Tasks: If users want to tweak page layouts, then users can often do the work themselves through configuration. If users want to keep database records in sync with external data sources, then they may need developers to write sophisticated triggers and prototypes may undergo many revisions to clarify murky intentions and hazy communications.

Projects: Large software projects have large groups of tasks that tend to come from all tiers of difficulty. A project may combine requests to both tweak page layouts and synchronize database records.

Solutions Should Match Problems

Ideally, everyone in project teams and sponsoring organizations alike would respond appropriately to whatever their tasks and projects actually are and to whatever problems actually arise.

Done if Possible: Nobody wants to use any processes at all. They would rather be done.

Waterfall if Possible: Only when a problem remains unfinished should anyone use waterfalls. Everyone wants projects to have fixed and precise requirements, which enables administrators and developers to plan out exactly what work they will need to do to finish the project. Knowing exactly what will happen over the course of a project reduces confusions, mistakes, and rework.

Customer Service or Agile if Necessary: Only when Waterfall processes cannot solve a task or project, should anyone use anything else. Customer service is not what anyone wants – it is just the best that anyone can do when tasks arise dynamically. Agile is not what anyone wants – it is just the best that anyone can do when projects contain significant unknowns. The reason to use Customer Service or Agile processes is not because anyone wants to, but because problems inherently require them to.

The Revenge of the Bride of Waterfall

Due to their natural desires, people in sponsoring organizations resurrect waterfalls whenever possible.

Natural Desires

The analysts, developers, and testers in project teams must cope with the unknowns and surprises that invariably arise during projects. They prefer using Agile practices, which easily encompass Waterfall and Action tasks with minimal overhead. They also prefer to avoid making plans and commitments in the presence of uncertainties and unknowns. By inspection, project-team members are naturally pragmatic and cavalier.

The managers and accountants in sponsoring organizations naturally want all software tasks to be simple and routine. They prefer to impose Waterfall practices on projects, hoping to improve productivity, quality, and control in ways that they understand. They demand plans (specifically, requirements, budgets, and schedules) in order to make rational and fair decisions about projects. Managers and accountants then want project teams to follow those plans exactly. By inspection, sponsoring-organization members are naturally idealistic and willful.

Productive Debate

People often perceive the problems of others much more easily than they perceive their own problems via introspection because they have fewer self-delusions about others. Conversely, people can often solve their own problems much more effectively than they can solve other people's problems because they more-fully understand their own situations. Debate between sponsoring-organization members and project-team members about how the other side should improve benefits everyone when each side honestly digs for truth and respects the other.

In the 1970s and '80s, Watts Humphrey saw that many developers worked in ad-hoc ways and that they seldom used consistent and transferable processes. Unfortunately, his solution (the CMM) was a manager's pipedream – only developers could figure out Agile and solve their own problems. Members of sponsoring organizations should push for planning and processes when projects benefit and members of project teams should push back whenever managers get carried away.

Today, we (the authors) see that managers and accountants continue to engage in wishful, magical, delusional thinking about projects. We suggest that they use Bride-of-Agile practices. But we cannot solve their problems – only managers and accountants can solve their own problems. Members of project teams should push for progress and flexibility when projects benefit and members of sponsoring organizations should push back whenever developers get carried away.

Resurrecting Waterfalls

Asymmetric Power: As a rule, the managers and accountants in sponsoring organizations have a lot more power than members of project teams and, as a rule, software engineers have no power over anyone in sponsoring organizations. This reflects their statuses within hierarchical organizations based on the Golden Rule, "whoever has the gold makes the rules."

Transmogrification: Unfortunately, whenever possible and especially on consulting and outsourcing projects, the managers and accountants in sponsoring organizations use their powers to transmogrify initial plans (or best-guess requirements, budgets, and schedules) into rigid commitments. In other words, the Bride of Waterfall resurrects her husband whenever she can.

Blaming Down: Managers and accountants usually blame down (or blame developers) whenever projects deviate from those initial plans. Forcing project teams to make their own commitments provides political cover for blaming down, but it doesn't actually improve the plans. Blaming down is human nature, but is also abuse. Initial plans remain guesses about the future and the real problem remains everyone's inability to predict the future. (Hallinan, page 191) (Dilbert)

The Attack of the Blob of Agile

The attack of the Blob of Agile occurs as two transitions between the Pure-Waterfall era and the Pure-Agile era. During the first transition, by the mid-2010s, the Blob of Agile had devoured most software projects. In other words, most project teams have already shifted from Waterfall to Agile practices. The Blob of Agile routinely bumps into sponsoring organizations and during the second transition, it will break through to devour them as well. In other words, sponsoring organizations are just starting to shift from Bride-of-Waterfall to Bride-of-Agile practices.

Table 3: Evolution of Practices			
Era	Years	Development Team	Sponsoring Organization
Pure-Waterfall Era	1968?-2001?	Waterfall	Bride of Waterfall
Agilefall Transition	2001?-2018?	Agilefall	Bride of Waterfall
Bride-of-Agilefall Transition	2018?-	Agile	Bride of Agilefall
Pure-Agile Era		Agile	Bride of Agile

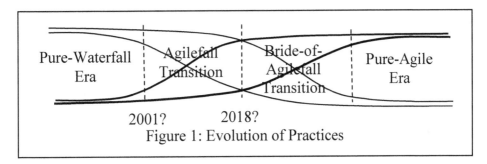

Figure 1: Evolution of Practices

The Pure-Waterfall Era

During the Pure-Waterfall era, from around 1968 when the first NATO conference on software engineering was held to around 2001, waterfalls made huge inroads into projects. By the mid-1980s, almost everyone aspired to combine Waterfall practices in project teams with Bride-of-Waterfall practices in sponsoring organizations. People tried to make these practices work for larger and larger projects, and they partially succeeded. Everyone just presumed that uncertainties and unknowns would not cause problems and that managers and accountants could easily impose budgets and schedules.

During this era, the Waterfall and the Bride of Waterfall rampaged together over projects. The Bride of Waterfall was always present, but she lurked invisibly, hiding in the shadows behind her husband. Nobody even considered the duties of sponsoring organizations to projects.

Royce: In his classic paper on the Waterfall from 1970, Winston Royce argued that pure waterfalls don't quite work well enough for software projects and he proposed several refinements. He encouraged project teams to do more technical work, specifically more design, inspection, test, and project management. (Royce, page 335) Royce's suggestions probably helped project teams to write better code and provide better service, but they didn't help organizations to write better requirements or cope with change. But, nobody cared about that. Royce attempted to make life easier for everyone in sponsoring organizations by staying out of their way, showing that he feared the Bride.

Humphrey: In *Managing the Software Process* and in *Winning with Software*, Watts Humphrey made many suggestions directly to the managers in sponsoring organizations. But, he didn't tell managers to be better managers, rather he told them to micromanage programmers with processes and metrics. He spent so much effort bossing programmers around that he never noticed that sponsoring organizations have their own obligations to projects and need guidance lest they remain dysfunctional.

Forsberg and Mooz: The V model from 1991 was the first system model to describe the dichotomy between project teams and sponsoring organizations. (Forsberg and Mooz) It put sponsoring organizations at the top of the diagram, project teams at the bottom of the diagram, and a waterfall in between. Forsberg and Mooz linked project definition and system operation with sponsoring organizations and linked implementations with project teams. The V model refined our understanding of how development teams contribute to projects; and it identified the stages where sponsoring organizations contribute to projects; yet it still glossed over what members of sponsoring organizations should actually do.

The Agilefall Transition

Throughout the Agilefall transition, more and more projects combined Agile practices in project teams with Bride-of-Waterfall practices in sponsoring organizations. Project teams took decades (from the mid-1990s to the mid-2010s) to chase Waterfalls away from most software projects. Sponsoring organizations continue to prefer Bride-of-Waterfall practices that have rigid requirements, budgets, and schedules.

The Bride of Waterfall continued to rampage over projects throughout the Agilefall transition. She fought the Blob of Agile whenever she could. As conflicts between sponsoring organizations and project teams have become more visible, the Bride of Waterfall has become more visible, too.

Classic Agile: In 2001 at the dawn of the Agilefall transition, project teams used a wide variety of classic Agile practices including DSDM, Scrum, and Extreme Programming and soon thereafter Lean and Kanban. These classic practices focused on the activities within project teams and (without overtly saying so) stayed out of the way of sponsoring organizations.

Boehm and Turner: In their 2003 book, *Balancing Agility and Discipline*, Boehm and Turner attempted to mesh Agile in project teams with the Bride of Waterfall in sponsoring organizations. Their word "discipline" meant respecting the requirements, budgets, and schedules that sponsoring organizations set. In other words, "discipline" refers to cooperating with the Bride.

Cote and Fred: Cote used the term "Wagilefall" as a pejorative in 2006. (Cote) Ann Marie Fred used the term "Agilefall" as a pejorative in 2010. (Fred) Both Cote and Fred despaired over using Agile on a small scale within development while using Waterfall on a large scale, for example, by doing all requirements up front and doing all testing at the end.

Redkite: Pain points often become opportunities for learning and growth. Redkite, a New York City consultancy, recognized the need for using both Waterfall practices in sponsoring organizations and Agile practices in project teams, and they called the combination "Agilefall" in a complementary way in 2013, though they spelled out few details.

Scaled Agile: Both Scaled-Agile Framework (SAFE) and Large Scale Scrum (LESS) have opposite principles that embody the Agilefall dichotomy. SAFE combines principle 4 (the bottom-up, Agile concerns of project teams) with principle 5 (the top-down, Bride-of-Waterfall, Milestone concerns of sponsoring organizations). LESS combines bottom-up Agile with top-down awareness of the full delivery lifecycle and goal-driven, enterprise-aware projects. Both SAFE and LESS embody a paradox: they recognize the needs for both Agile and Bride of Waterfall, but they don't actually reconcile them.

Interlude

By the mid-2010s, almost everyone presumed that project teams should use Agile practices. Agile practices will probably never go away because the needs to deal with errors, ambiguities, and changes in goals will probably never go away.

In 2018, Agile is used far beyond software. Lean is widely used throughout manufacturing. Agile is widely used throughout business projects. (Rigby, Sutherland, Takeuchi) Traditional engineers increasingly use Agile practices, for example in maintenance projects on the Alyeska Pipeline and in chip design projects at Intel. Ed Catmull and Amy Wallace described using Agile-like processes to make movies at Pixar. (Catmull and Wallace) Bruce Feiler advocated using Agile practices for happy families. (Feiler)

Even so, Agile has a long way to go. In 2017, David Jones wrote that two-thirds of all companies wanted to use Agile in more projects, even though only 12% were on their way to doing so. (Jones)

The Bride-of-Agilefall Transition

Throughout the Bride-of-Agilefall transition, sponsoring organizations will slowly change from using Bride-of-Waterfall practices to using Bride-of-Agile practices. Managers and accountants in sponsoring organizations will eventually need to accept that they cannot predict the future either. They will eventually need to think about uncertainties and unknowns in realistic and effective ways.

Chasing the Bride of Waterfall away from sponsoring organizations will probably take decades, at least. Until the Bride of Waterfall reforms, she will continue battling the Blob of Agile and rampaging over projects.

Scaled Agile: In the decade before 2018, a new generation of scaled-Agile practices combined the concerns of project teams and sponsoring organizations, including Scaled Agile Framework (SAFE), Large-Scale Scrum (LESS), and Disciplined Agile Delivery (DAD). (Larman and Vodde) They all touch on the responsibilities of sponsoring organizations, but they are only initial sketches. DAD discusses the Disciplined Agile Enterprise, delving into what IT departments should do. But, it still ignores the rest of what sponsoring organizations should do. (DAE) (Ambler)

The Authors: Our chapter "Sponsoring-Organization Obligations" describes some practices that sponsoring organizations could adopt to help CRM projects succeed. But, that is only an initial sketch.

Traditional Accountants: Traditional accounting practices conflict with Agile software-development practices. Traditional accounting works best in retail trade, real estate, and banking because widgets on a shelf and rental properties sit still and easily abstract into accounting concepts. But, software projects simply don't behave like that and they won't in the foreseeable future. One accountant of our acquaintance from a real-estate company commented about the prospect of overseeing an Agile software project, "that would make me crazy." (personal communication 2017)

Software Accountants: Sponsoring organizations that thrive on software (like Microsoft, Google, and Facebook) have had to accept that they cannot write sophisticated programs in one project and that changes and surprises arise continually. They have had to create new business models to manage and finance their software projects, in addition to the new software development practices that everyone knows about. These new management and finance models enable them to incrementally rationalize and pay for their programs. Brian Randell commented that only the third versions of many programs are good enough to use, showing just how hard it is to develop good software. (Randell) Long-lived programs like GCC, Windows 10, Office, Google search, and Facebook have benefitted from decades of polish.

Entrepreneuring Organizations: Entrepreneurs roll with the punches and go with the flow. They have done so for as long as anyone knows. But, established organizations have only accepted their techniques as valid in recent decades, based on role-models from Silicon Valley.

Other Organizations: Organizations throughout the economy (including ones that only write CRM software) should also adopt Bride-of-Agile practices. Jeff Gothelf argued that some human-resource and accounting departments have already begun to do so. (Gothelf)

The Pure-Agile Era

We speculate that a Pure-Agile era will arise someday when both sponsoring organizations and projects teams honestly face up to uncertainties and unknowns and accept that nobody can predict the future. But, that will only happen when the Bride reforms.

Notes

"Normal" practices occur in project teams and "bride" practices occur in sponsoring organizations. We also think about the Blob of Agile in terms of Katamari.

This chapter was inspired by questions from Robert Schaefer about reconciling Agile with Waterfall, specifically "how Agile fits within the context of plans, budgets, and schedules." Our response emerged from thinking about Redkite's Agilefall.

We include accountants in the discussion because of Jodi Bockenek's observation, "accountants are the sources of all information in organizations."

In terms of marriage counselling, project teams have already undergone analysis and change and sponsoring organizations should now reciprocate.

Both Agile and Bride-of-Agile practices will continue evolving for many decades to come.

Rethinking Waterfalls

Rereading SEMAT Essence 1.1 after finishing this essay led us to rethink waterfalls. Essence 1.1 says that stakeholders in sponsoring organizations follow Waterfall processes to exploit opportunities. Their stakeholder waterfall has six states: recognized, represented, involved, in agreement, satisfied for deployment, and satisfied in use. (SEMAT, page 25) Their opportunity waterfall has six states: identified, solution needed, value established, viable, addressed, and benefit accrued. (SEMAT, page 29)

Essence 1.1 presumes that small groups of representatives can speak for large groups of stakeholders (it falls for the law-of-small-numbers delusion), that waterfalls work at the sponsoring-organization level, that sponsoring organizations can predict the future, and that problems (such as unknowns and uncertainties) won't arise. But, if sponsoring organizations could predict the future, then they should just share their wisdom with project teams and nobody would need Agile.

By inspection, Waterfalls and Brides of Waterfalls (such as Essence 1.1) are "happy paths" or best-case scenarios. They usefully document what sponsoring organizations and project teams hope for. But, Waterfalls and Brides of Waterfalls deny the possibility of problems and provide no mechanisms for coping with any problems that do arise. They are idealistic and oblivious.

By inspection, Agile and Bride of Agile admit that problems can occur and they provide mechanisms for coping. Nobody wants problems to occur, but Agile and Bride of Agile provide rational mechanisms to cope with whatever problems do arise. They are pragmatic and aware.

Bibliography

Scott Ambler, "The Disciplined Agile Enterprise: Harmonizing Agile and Lean," www.youtube.com/watch?v=QyHWeiBIOoY/, 2016.

Barry Boehm and Richard Turner, *Balancing Agility and Discipline*, Addison Wesley, 2003.

Ed Catmull and Amy Wallace, *Creativity, Inc.*, Random House, 2014.

Cote, "Cote's People Over Process," redmonk.com/cote/2006/05/31/agile-rebellion/.

DAE, www.disciplinedagiledelivery.com/dae/, 2017.

Dilbert, http://dilbert.com/strip/2017-11-12, November 12, 2017.

Bruce Feiler, *The Secrets of Happy Families*, William Morrow, 2013.

Ann Marie Fred, "What is Agilefall?" agile-fall.blogspot.com/2010/03/introduction.html, March 3, 2010.

Ann Marie Fred, "Struggling with the Product Backlog," agile-fall.blogspot.com/2010/03/what-is-agilefall.html, April 7, 2010.

Ann Marie Fred, "When is a Story 'Done Done'?" agile-fall.blogspot.com/2010/03/when-is-story-done-done.html, March 8, 2010.

Kevin Forsberg and Harold Mooz, "The Relationship of Systems Engineering to the Project Cycle," INCOSE International Symposium, October 1991.

Jeff Gothelf, "Bring Agile to the Whole Organization," in, *Harvard Business Review*, November, 2014.

Joseph T. Hallinan, *Why We Make Mistakes*, Broadway, 2010.

Watts S. Humphrey, *Managing the Software Process*, Addison Wesley, 1989.

Watts S. Humphrey, *Winning with Software*, Addison Wesley, 2001.

David Jones, "Most Businesses Want Agility but Few Have It" www.ecommercetimes.com/story/84731.html, Aug 8, 2017.

Craig Larman and Bas Vodde, *Scaling Lean and Agile Development*, Addison Wesley, 2009.

Brian Randell, keynote at ICSE 2018.

Darrell K. Rigby, Jeff Sutherland, Hirotaka Takeuchi, "Embracing Agile," in *Harvard Business Review*, May 2016.

Winston W. Royce, "Managing the Development of Large Software Systems," in *Proceedings of IEEE WESCON*, pages 328 to 338, August 1970.

Ken Schwaber, "SCRUM Development Process," in Business Object Design and Implementation Workshop at OOPSLA 1995, www.jeffsutherland.org/ooplsa/schwaber.html, April 27, 1995.

SEMAT, *Essence 1.1*, http://semat.org/essence-1.1/, December 2015.

Waterfall is Dead, search online for "waterfall model is dead."

7

Determinism versus Emergence

On one hand, there have always been hints that the universe is inherently unpredictable, full of earthquakes and hurricanes and other "acts of God." On the other hand, as Duncan Watts recently stated "we like deterministic stories" and as Daniel Kahneman recently stated "stories about the past are so good that they create an illusion that life is understandable – that you can predict the future." (Rosin and Watts) (Vedantam and Kahneman, 19:50)

Debates over determinism and emergence have raged within philosophy and science for thousands of years. And, software engineering seems to be repeating these same debates at it evolves from Waterfall to Agile, from idealizing determinism and dismissing emergence to combining both.

In the first section, we note that determinism and emergence are loosely coherent within themselves and completely incompatible with each other. We note that different contexts and different people naturally favor different concepts of reality – everyone favors whichever concept gives them what they want. Increasingly, software engineers say "do both," although nobody actually explains how to do so.

Throughout most of the remaining sections, we delve into the individual facets of determinism and emergence as detailed by the rows of table 1. In each section, we describe both ends of a facet and then argue that everyone needs both. And in the last section, we add some final notes.

Table 1: Facets of Determinism and Emergence		
Facet	**Determinism**	**Emergence**
Philosophy	Determinism	Emergence
Mechanics	Clockwork	Quantum
Statistics	Frequentist	Bayesian
Geometry	Euclidean	Fractal
Knowledge	Bounded	Unbounded
Motivations	Rational Behaviorism	Irrational Humanism
Program Contexts	Isolated Machines	Networks and Users
Program Descriptions	Specifications and Algorithms	Requirements and Scripts
Tools	Tools	Skills
Practices	Rules	Judgements
Organizations	Factories	Workshops
Management	Scientific	Lean
Design	Reductionism	Holism

Bifurcated Concepts of Reality

The deterministic and emergent concepts of reality or worldviews are detailed in the columns of table 1. They are both loosely coherent within themselves and completely incompatible with each other. Despite the looseness, we believe that the bifurcation sheds light on some of the conflicts within contemporary software engineering, for example why some people love planning and others hate it.

A wide variety of biases affect what people consider normal, what they aspire to, and how they actually respond in specific situations. Some biases come from contexts (such as tools and practices) and others come from roles (such as managers and programmers). All of these biases are completely natural and understandable. However, all of these biases can lead people astray. In the past, many idealists strove to impose whichever concept of reality they preferred on everyone else. Increasingly, pragmatists say "do both," even though nobody actually explains how to do so.

Loosely Coherent

Coherent

The facets of each concept of reality (the cells in each column of table 1) act as loose metaphors for each other and reinforce each other.

Within Determinism: Clockwork mechanics and rational behaviorism imply that physical objects and people are inherently predictable and controllable, and so metaphorically software projects should be, too. Tools, rules, factories, and Waterfalls fit together and reinforce each other because they all emphasize repetition of knowns, especially when writing machine-oriented programs such as embedded systems. Factories, Scientific management, and reductionism all concern (or require) fixed sets of parts and tasks.

Within Emergence: Quantum mechanics and irrational humanism imply that physical objects and people are inherently unpredictable and uncontrollable, and so metaphorically software projects should be, too. Skills, judgements, artisanship, and Agile fit together and reinforce each other because they all emphasize original responses to unknowns and surprises, especially when writing user-oriented programs such as games and social media. Workshops, Lean management, and holism all tolerate evolving sets of parts and tasks.

Loose

However, the facets of each concept of reality (the cells in each column of table 1) align imperfectly. We have found mismatches between every pair of facets that we looked at.

Within Determinism: Determinism differs from knowns because fractals can be both deterministic and impossible to predict. Determinism differs from reductionism because fractals can be deterministic as well as infinite. Some machine-oriented programs (such as operating systems) are enormous, complicated, and effectively emergent. And factory employees also use skills and judgements.

Within Emergence: Emergence differs from unknowns because electrons and photons move unpredictably even though computers and networks use them to create determinism. Some user-oriented programs (such as business-card apps for smart phones) are small, simple, and effectively deterministic. And workshop employees also use tools and rules.

Completely Incompatible

Determinism and emergence seem completely incompatible, bicameral rather than spectral. We know of no ways to describe or understand either concept of reality in terms of the other. This bifurcation reminds us of the optical illusion shown in figure 1. Each end makes sense in isolation, even though the whole figure is impossible.

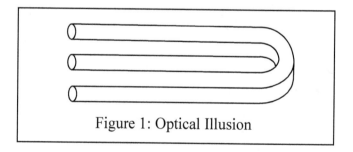

Figure 1: Optical Illusion

Flip Sides of the Same Coin – Good and Evil Twins

The ends of some facets begin at the same place and then head off in opposite directions.

Statistics Example: Both Frequentist and Bayesian statistics start with the laws of probability, but each uses them in different ways to deduce different things. Frequentist statistics makes more sense when looking at the past where lots of Gaussian data exists and it strives for objectivity. Bayesian statistics makes more sense when predicting the future where little Gaussian data exists and it tolerates subjectivity.

Program-Orientation Example: All kinds of programs are built from similar lines of C or Java, but machine-oriented and user-oriented programs embody different ideals. Embedded systems and operating systems make machines more powerful and they can endure as long as the underlying hardware endures, often for decades. Video games and social media make users more productive or entertained and they are often fad-driven, sometimes enduring for a year or two at most.

Having or Knowing versus Doing

The ends of some facets differ in the sense of having or knowing versus doing. Certification differs from skill.

Knowledge Example: Owning a tool differs from using a tool. For example, owning a piano differs from playing piano. Reading about a skill differs from practicing the skill. For example, reading biographies about pianists and books about music theory differs from practicing piano.

Tools and Practices Example: Programmers use and read about a variety of tools and practices, including compilers, linters, coding standards, and inspections. Even so, writing lousy code in C and Java remains all too easy. Programmers must also develop and apply skills and judgements to write excellent and enduring code.

Scale and Composition

The ends of some facets differ by scale, especially when one is composed of the other.

Mechanics Example: Clockwork mechanics describe the predictable behaviors of large objects, like cannonballs and planets. Quantum mechanics describe the unpredictable behaviors of small objects, like electrons and photons. Large objects are composed of many, many small objects.

Program-Description Example: Most programs are composed of many algorithms and scripts glue those algorithms together. However, the concepts and activities needed to create algorithms differ completely from those needed to create scripts. Algorithms embody mathematical truths that are objectively and deductively correct; they address common problems that can be studied and solved in isolation; and algorithmists share their results widely. Scripts embody user opinions that are subjectively and inductively correct at best; they solve situation-specific problems; each project gets implemented once; and sponsoring organizations usually treat the results as private intellectual property.

Degeneration

The ends of some facets differ in that one is a degenerate form of the other.

Geometry Example: Euclidean geometry can be thought of as a degenerate form of Fractal geometry. In figure 2, expansions with a kink of 0 degrees produce Euclidean spaces while expansions with a kink of any other angle (such as 90 degrees) produce Fractal spaces. Each geometry leads to a radically different understanding of what dimension and distance mean.

Design Example: Reductionism (where the whole equals the sum of the parts) can viewed as a degenerate form of holism (where the whole differs from the sum of the parts). Each case enables and requires a different approach. Projects that easily decompose into parts and tasks can use deterministic Waterfall and Factory processes. Projects that do not easily decompose into parts and tasks need emergent Agile and Workshop processes.

Visibility

The ends of some facets differ by their visibility. Deterministic concepts can usually be observed or experienced directly. Emergent concepts often remain invisible.

Mechanics Example: Seeing deterministic planets and cannonballs is much easier than seeing emergent electrons and photons. (That sentence contains an irony.)

Software Example: Deterministic tools, rules, certifications, and contracts are much easier to see than emergent skills, judgements, expertise, drive, and relationships. When project statuses are visible and crisp, trust is unnecessary and Waterfall and Factory processes work well. When project statuses are invisible or murky, trust becomes essential and Agile and Workshop processes work better.

Leap of Faith: Accepting that invisible or emergent concepts exist often requires a leap of faith that not everyone willingly takes. From our position on the ground, the sun appears to move through the sky. Accepting that the earth moves around the sun requires a leap of faith. Accepting that electrons and photons exist and move unpredictably requires a leap of faith. Accepting that Agile works better than Waterfall for many software projects requires a leap of faith. Unknown unknowns are invisible by definition and accepting that they exist requires a leap of faith.

Contextual Biases

Different tools, practices, and ideals naturally favor different concepts of reality.

Toward Determinism

Program Descriptions, Tools, and Practices: Program descriptions, tools, and practices favor determinism. Algorithms, tools, and rules are reliable and efficient when they work, but they don't always work. For example, no algorithms efficiently solve large NP-complete problems and most programs are much larger, more arbitrary, and more complicated than any algorithm. IDEs help developers to write code, but IDEs cannot write code for developers. Developers should use deterministic (or existing) algorithms, tools, and rules whenever possible and use emergent (or new) scripts, skills, and judgements as necessary.

Planning: Planning favors determinism. Planning increases understanding and reduces risk when it works, but it doesn't work in the presence of unknowns. Projects should use plans and Waterfalls whenever possible and should use experiments and Agile as necessary.

Simplicity: Simplicity favors determinism. Transactional management (based on contracts) that exchanges work for money is simple and easy. Enlightened management that builds relationships remains vague and requires a lot of effort. So from a simplicity point of view, everyone should prefer work relationships to be as transactional as possible and as emergent as necessary.

Productivity and Quality: Productivity and quality favor determinism. When parts and tasks are fully known ahead of time, workers can prepare and then do the work quickly and correctly. So, from productivity and quality perspectives, everyone should prefer work to be as deterministic (or known) as possible and as emergent (or unknown) as necessary.

Toward Emergence

Motivation: Motivation favors emergence. People respond much better to peers and clients than to managers and they do much better work with enlightened management. Transactions and contracts that trade work for money actually demotivate most workers. Even so, workers still need salaries and project assignments. So from a motivation perspective, everyone should prefer work relationships to be as enlightened as possible and as transactional as necessary.

Role Biases

Different roles naturally favor different concepts of reality.

Toward Determinism

Purchasing Managers: Purchasing managers who spend money (often millions of dollars or more) on software projects would prefer to spend less. They would prefer to buy software once and never again. They naturally want guarantees about results: about cost, quality, and deliverables.

Project Managers: Project managers naturally want to set accurate expectations about goals, budgets, schedules, and deliverables upfront and they want to minimize the changes and errors that will occur throughout the project. They want to increase transparency and objectivity as well as to decrease hand-waving and guessing.

Architects: In order to accelerate the progress on projects and to predict and control the evolution of programs, designers want to create enduring software architectures.

Educators and Students: Certifications test for specific knowledge. Educators want to teach to the test and students want to study for the test, so both educators and students want stable, bounded bodies of knowledge. The committee members who write the standards for education (like SWEBOK) want them to be complete and enduring.

Regulators: Regulators at the FAA and FDA naturally want aerospace and medical software to be perfect. Psychologists have shown that obsessing over perfection or minimizing mistakes leads to a fixed mindset that emphasizes states of being.

Many of these individuals are high-status authorities who personify projects, organizations, and ideals. They naturally want to be able to predict the future, to control projects, and to minimize changes and errors. They tend to idealize stability and outcomes, specifically finished programs. They want software engineering to be bounded and deterministic. Emergence contradicts their heartfelt desires.

Toward Emergence

Programmers: Programmers write features and fix bugs day-by-day, so they create emergence day-by-day. When working on upgrades, they naturally want to make their marks on those programs, so they naturally argue that architectures must change. They want to increase the value of their individual experiences, skills, and judgements and they want ongoing opportunities to write new programs that will affect the world.

Researchers: Researchers want to think about software in new ways, so they want new concepts within software engineering to arise continually.

Many of these individuals are low-status workers who actually do stuff. They naturally want change to occur continually. They tend to idealize possibility and opportunities to write the programs of the future. They want software engineering to be unbounded and emergent. Determinism contradicts their heartfelt desires.

Historically, Idealists Tried to Impose Their Preferences on Everyone Else

We would like to urge everyone (managers and developers, alike) to see the world as it is and to embrace the full spectrum of possibility of what could or should happen during a project. But, doing so asks for way too much. Psychologists have shown that heartfelt desires influence rational thoughts, which is called the "self-serving bias." People naturally favor the concepts of reality that will give them what they want, based on their circumstances and worldviews, regardless of what the situation calls for, regardless of what they might otherwise rationally believe. Everyone actually sees what they want or expect to see. They tend to be unaware of their own biases and oblivious to anyone else's needs.

As long as nobody gets carried away, all of the biases listed above really are just fine. In fact, everyone really should want what they want. Questions like "how to lower the cost and raise the quality of software programs?" are useful and important. Questions like "what are the programs and technologies of the future?" are also useful and important. Someone needs to work on cost and quality and someone else need to write new programs.

Unfortunately, fans of one worldview often act as if their concept of reality will work for everyone else, too, and they tend to dismiss all other worldviews whenever it suits their purposes. Over the past 30 some odd years, the IEEE and the SEI have advocated for deterministic practices (CMM, SCAMPI), certifications (PSP, CSDP), and standards (SWEBOK). Over the past 20 some odd years, we (the authors) have advocated for emergent practices (Agile), improvisation, and subjective judgement (Chaos model and Chaos strategy). But, software engineering really is much larger than either side alone.

Today, Pragmatists Say "Do Both," even though Nobody Says How

Everyone Actually Needs Both

We have come to believe that everyone needs both determinism and emergence and that everyone already mixes them naturally if ad-hocly. In our experience, all projects and most tasks combine determinism (knowns) and emergence (unknowns).

Toward Emergence: Most projects have some core functionality that is known precisely, upfront. Projects to write embedded systems and operating systems obviously emphasize determinism. However, projects to write video games and social media also have machine-oriented tasks that emphasize determinism, such as improving performance via better algorithms and query optimization or accessing new data sources via translation of representations.

Toward Emergence: Most projects have many unknowns and encounter many surprises. Projects to write cool video games and social media that respond to the whims of users obviously emphasize emergence. However, projects to write low-level operating systems and embedded systems often have tasks that emphasize emergence. Users routinely think of new features and most low-level programs must get some information out to users at some point, so developers must also improve user interfaces with better information, controls, and dashboards.

More and More Pragmatists Encourage Both

More and more software engineers urge everyone to use both concepts of reality. However, saying "use both" is easy, while effectively using both remains hard. The ends of each facet mix more like a tossed salad than like a roux (gravy). We don't know of anyone who explains how to synthesize or unify both ends of any facet into a coherent whole and we now suspect that nobody will ever do so. Regardless of what anyone aspires to do in any given situation, it seems that he or she must actually use one extreme or the other.

Mechanics Example: Nearly a century after physicists understood both relativity and quantum mechanics, they continue to use each theory independently. Stephen Hawking combined both theories to explain how black holes evaporate. But even so, no well-accepted theory of quantum gravity exists.

Statistics Example: In the 1980s, Joe Hill helped to unify Frequentist and Bayesian statistics into Empirical Bayes. Hill described Empirical Bayes with "be as Frequentist as you can and as Bayesian as you must," which alas still really means doing one or the other.

Boehm and Turner Example: Barry Boehm and Richard Turner wrote about combining agility and discipline, but in every example, they ended up arguing for either one or the other at a broad-brush level. For example, they wrote that everyone should scale Agile by doing more planning. (Boehm and Turner, pages 84+) So, they still advocate doing one or the other. We note that they used the term "balance" rather than "synthesis," suggesting that they understood the difficulty of combining them.

SAFE Example: Scaled Agile Framework (SAFE) combines both determinism and emergence. Principle 4 is "agile" or the emergent, bottom-up work that developers do. Principle 5 is "milestones" or the deterministic, top-down planning that managers do. So, SAFE says do both Agile and Waterfall, but it doesn't actually say how to combine them.

LESS Example: Large-Scale Scrum (LESS) says do both systems thinking and lean thinking, both managing and coaching, both architecture and structure and continuous improvement. So, LESS says do both determinism and emergence at a finer grain, but it still doesn't actually say how to combine them.

Larman and Vodde Example: Craig Larman and Bas Vodde argued that gymnasts and Navy Seals are both agile and disciplined and so synthesis might seem possible. (Larman and Vodde, pages 125 to 126) We totally agree with their point. But in their example, agility and discipline actually occur on independent dimensions and so remain distinct rather than unified concepts.

The Authors Example: Throughout this chapter, we (the authors) urge software engineers to use both determinism and emergence appropriately. We now believe that determinism and emergence should matter equally, half and half, more or less. Unfortunately, we cannot describe how to synthesize both ends of any facet into a coherent, unified whole because we haven't figured out how to do so.

Doing both ends together, half and half, is a reasonable start. Combining both determinism and emergence means mixing them person-by-person, task-by-task, detail-by-detail as appropriate to each specific situation. Choices matter because the approach that actually handles each task affects expectations about planning, control, optimization, and outcomes.

Philosophy

Determinism

People have always wanted to predict and control their fates and they have always striven to overcome the randomness of the world. Their desires for a deterministic universe are natural and will never end. In particular, those with wealth or status won't want to lose the advantages that they have gained.

In a deterministic world, everything can be known, so surprises should never occur. In a deterministic world, smart and attentive people can predict the future, even when it isn't easy. They shouldn't have to handle cases that they don't know about because such cases should not exist. Surprises mean that someone didn't pay close enough attention or didn't think hard enough. Statisticians can analyze known, existing data using Frequentism because the future merely repeats the past.

Software Example: Many software problems, today, have deterministic solutions, specifically those that are solved by existing algorithms, tools, and practices. In particular, many small, embedded, signal-processing (DSP), cryptography, and networking programs have deterministic solutions, especially when someone can write a code generator or compiler for it. Computers provide stable platforms for programs and programs extend computers. The small, machine-oriented, algorithm-based, tool-based, and practice-based parts of projects are often deterministic.

History

Ancient China: Around 2500 years ago, some Chinese philosophers emphasized determinism and rules. Confucius (551 BC – 479 BC) developed rituals to respond to the situations that arose repeatedly in everyday life (for example, greeting friends or playing songs on flutes) and in government (resolving disputes between neighbors). Practicing rituals makes them natural and easy. Confucius said "If you don't know li (rituals), you cannot take your stand." Mencius (372 BC – 289 BC) refined that philosophy, saying "there is nothing that is not destined." Han Feizi (280 BC – 233 BC) and other legalists attempted to impose fa (rules or patterns) on the world. (Puett and Gross-Loh) (Slingerland)

Ancient Greece: Around 2300 years ago, some Greek philosophers emphasized determinism. Zeno of Citium (374 BC – 262 BC) founded Stoicism, saying "fate is the endless chain of causation." Cicero (106 BC – 43 BC) expressed Stoic principles, saying "All things happen through antecedent causes." Both men were wealthy and had every reason to want to sustain the status quo.

At the time, both China and Greece were becoming literary societies, but lots of things remained unwritten. Drill and ritual remained essential to acting consistently, whether hanging out with friends or working in the government. Ancients used drills and rituals where moderns might use training manuals and checklists.

Newtonian Mechanics: Around three hundred years ago, during the Enlightenment, Newtonian mechanics inspired a new wave of deterministic philosophy. Clockwork mechanics suggests that predicting the future is possible and, as a consequence, accurately predicting and controlling the future are also possible.

Computation: The first generations of electronic computers, from the 1940s through the 1970s, inspired another wave of deterministic philosophy. Almost everything that can be reliably solved by computers, algorithms, and programs is deterministic, though there are also a variety of probabilistic and heuristic techniques. One could even argue that computer science is the study of what can be known or achieved deterministically. Computation seems to have inspired governments and businesses to emphasize deterministic processes for workers and customers.

Popular-Culture Example: Determinism has become enshrined in popular culture. For example in 2017, Sherlock Holmes said, "I have theorized before that if one could attenuate to every available data stream in the world simultaneously, it would be possible to anticipate and deduce almost anything." Late-20th-century Americans tend to believe that they are (or should be) in control of their fates. (Silver, page 453)

Emergence

Emergence has been around forever. Humans have always dealt with whatever random events actually happen, even when they don't want to or like to. Nobody has ever been able to reliably predict the future out very far. Nobody has yet been able to prevent the world from changing for very long.

In an emergent world, the future will continue to change in unpredictable and surprising ways and it will increasingly diverge from the past. The future will routinely surprise even the smartest and most attentive people. When changes occur, data and models about the past will lead everyone astray, so statisticians can only predict the future using Bayesian approaches.

Social Change Examples: Scientists, product developers, entrepreneurs, and social activists all attempt to do things that have never been done before, to do the unexpected or innovative. They all attempt to reveal previously unknown opportunities and then to change the expectations and behaviors of people in society. Technologists don't try to change society directly, but books, electricity, cars, and smart phones have affected society profoundly. Entrepreneurs do not use the past to predict the future – they fail until they succeed.

Software Examples: To the extent that any program was not predicted in the past, it embodies emergence. Every software project deliberately tries to create chunks of change or emergence that benefit the sponsoring organization. Software has always had emergent, user-oriented, artisan niches, for example in new markets and in research. User-oriented software is annoyingly emergent because whenever users see a finished program, they raise their expectations and move the goals again. Users will continue changing their minds and asking for more and better features for the foreseeable future.

Terminology: Philosophers prefer the term "indeterminism" to contrast with "determinism." But that term is consistent with purely random change where positive and negative changes can occur more-or-less equally and cancel each other out. Software engineering seems to have some form of ratchet based on comparison or learning that drives the field in a positive direction, so we prefer the term "emergence."

Free Will: Emergence in philosophy is usually associated with free will. In a deterministic world, nobody would actually need to live their lives out to find out what will happen. So, emergence makes living each life out essential.

History

Ancient China: Around 2500 years ago, some Chinese philosophers emphasized emergence. Laozi (604 BC – 531 BC) advised responding to change, saying "Life is a series of natural and spontaneous changes. Let things flow naturally." Chuangzi (370 BC – 287 BC) refined that philosophy, saying "Flow with whatever is happening. Let your mind be free." Each encouraged people to appropriately accept and respond to the surprises that inevitably arise. (Puett and Gross-Loh) (Slingerland)

Ancient Greece: Around 2300 years ago, some Greek philosophers emphasized chance and change. Aristotle (384 BC – 322 BC) discussed emergence saying "fortune and chance are said to be in the number of causes."

Quantum Mechanics: Nearly 100 years ago, quantum mechanics inspired a new wave of emergent philosophy. In 1931, only a handful of years after the Uncertainty principle was defined, Arthur Compton suggested that predicting the future is impossible and so the best anyone can do is to respond as the future unfolds.

Both

In general, software engineers need both some determinism and some emergence. In a world with some of each, software often merits writing, but few guarantees exist. A combined world is neither fully determined nor fully random.

Determinism: If the world were totally random, without stability, then nothing would ever be planned or built because doing so would provide no advantages and the only ways to succeed would stem from luck. Without a reasonably stable foundation on which to predict the future, nobody would ever invest in new software.

Emergence: If the world were purely deterministic, predicting the future based on the past would be possible and so there would be no unforeseen changes, no surprises, and no new opportunities; the first mover or the biggest, richest organization would always win; all attempts to change the status quo would easily be predicted and thwarted; and the status quo would continue forever. Without some emergence, writing new software would make no meaningful difference, so nobody would bother.

Mechanics

Clockwork

Ever since Copernicus, Kepler, and Newton sparked the Scientific Revolution, researchers have been trying to make nature predictable in earnest. David Hand notes that between the seventeenth and twentieth centuries, scientists discovered the deterministic laws of nature. The improving clockwork mechanics made nature appear increasingly predictable. By using Newton's laws, Maxwell's equations, and other rules, one can predict and even manipulate nature. (Hand, 39 and 40)

According to Newtonian science, nothing is unpredictable in principle. In 1814, Pierre Simon Laplace wrote that if a supreme intelligence could know the position and velocity of all particles accurately enough, it could predict the future. This supreme intelligence, known as Laplace's Demon, became the mascot of scientific determinism. The main limit to knowledge about the future is the precision of measurements and whoever can measure their reality accurately enough will predict their fates. In 1943, Albert Einstein famously argued, "God does not play dice."

History

In the 300s BC, Aristotle believed that the earth was the center of the universe and that the sun and planets orbited the earth. Most Europeans accepted this theory as scientific truth for nearly two millennia. In 1543, Nicolaus Copernicus's *De Revolutionibus Orbium Coelestium* was published, which explained the heliocentric model of the planets. His model unified the motion of the Sun with the seasons and provided a foundation for the Gregorian calendar. Between 1615 and 1621, Johannes Kepler's *Epitome Astronomiae Copernicanae* was published, which described the elliptical orbits of the planets. In 1687, Isaac Newton's

Philosophiæ Naturalis Principia Mathematica was published, which unified the motion of heavenly and terrestrial bodies, specifically planets and cannonballs. In 1915, Albert Einstein published the General Theory of Relativity, which refined Newton's equations.

Quantum

Quantum mechanics has been undermining determinism ever since the late 1920s. Two important phenomena are Heisenberg's Uncertainty principle and particle-wave duality. The first states that nobody can know the position and momentum of a particle to an accuracy greater than Planck's constant, which explicitly limits what Laplace's Demon can know. The second states that electrons behave like particles when observed as particles and like waves when observed as waves. Both phenomena imply that particles move unpredictably at least part of the time.

Quantum effects are tiny, mostly contained within atoms, so originally they were ignored in the macro world. More recently, scientists have shown particle-wave duality for objects with the mass of 10,000 hydrogen atoms. (Eibenberger, Gerlich, Arndt, Mayor, Tüxen) Even cows would exhibit particle-wave duality, if one could build large-enough accelerators. When combined with the Butterfly effect (that under the right conditions, the flap of a butterfly wing can cause a hurricane), the uncertainty caused by quantum mechanics can escape into the macro world and affect us all. So at its core, the universe is unpredictable and emergent.

History

In 1877, Ludwig Boltzmann suggested that physical systems (later called molecules) have discrete levels of energy. In 1897, Joseph Thomson discovered the electron. In 1900, Max Planck solved Black Body radiation by presuming that energy is released in quantized packets. In 1905, Albert Einstein argued that energy quanta (later called photons) are absorbed and generated as wholes. In 1923, Louis de Broglie proposed that particles can behave like waves and vice versa, which Clifton Davisson and Lester Germer showed experimentally in 1927. And in 1927, Werner Heisenberg proposed the Uncertainty principle.

Both

In general, software engineers need both clockwork and quantum mechanics.

Clockwork: All of the clockwork mechanics remain valid, today. The concept of day remains geocentric and Aristotelian. Scheduling an appointment with a colleague about a software project for next week concerns the motion of the Sun through the sky. The concept of year remains heliocentric and essentially Copernican. Tossing a ball to a dog remains Newtonian.

Quantum: All contemporary high-speed computers and networks tame electrons and photons.

Statistics

Frequentist

Determinism in science depends on probability and especially on Frequentist statistics. David Hand notes that randomness seems incompatible with determinism, but they complement each other and they evolved together. "The idea that chance could be quantified arose at the same time as the view that the universe was intrinsically deterministic." (Hand, page 50) Determinists needed a rug to sweep the messiness of nature under and probability is that rug.

Software Examples: Many people believe that they can understand all questions by gathering and analyzing a lot of data and that when they have gathered a lot of data, useful information must exist. These beliefs provide rationales for aggregating large databases of software projects or consumer purchases and then using machine learning. Such efforts routinely uncover useful insights.

History

Classical Statistics: Classical statistics concerns gambling and emphasizes crisply defined games of chance, such as those based on cards or dice. Around 1564, Gerolamo Cardano wrote *Liber de Ludo Alae*, which for the first time correctly defined odds. In 1654, Pierre de Fermat and Blaise Pascal exchanged letters solving the Problem of Points and defining the expected value of an incomplete game. In

1657, Cristiaan Hyugens published *De Ratiociniis in Ludo Aleae*, the first treatise on probability. In 1713, Jacob Bernoulli published *Ars Conjectandi*, which proved the Law of Large Numbers. And in 1812, Pierre Simon Laplace published *Theorie Analytique des Probabilites*, the second treatise, which defined the field of probability.

Frequentist Statistics: In the early 1900s, Ronald Fisher developed analysis of variance and hypothesis testing, which form the basis of Frequentist statistics. In Frequentism, models come from data. For example, an average and a standard deviation can describe a set of data points. When statisticians gather enough Gaussian data, meaning that the Law of Large Numbers applies, Frequentist models are simple and strong.

Bayesian

Statisticians know that data and models are often incomplete and that Frequentists cannot predict anything that remains absent from the data or the model. For example, Frequentists cannot predict anything about a series of events before the first event has occurred, before they have sampled enough events for a valid model, or when the data is not Gaussian. Bayesian models can express rational uncertainties about a much wider range of situations than Frequentist models can. For example, Bayesian Belief Networks can support rational decisions when one lacks enough data for valid Frequentist models.

Bayesian deductions span the gamut from purely subjective to purely objective by combining arbitrary priors, personal opinions, and empirical samples. When nobody knows anything about the actual probability of an event, one can start by presuming it is *50-50* or *1/n*. Whenever someone believes that he or she has a better personal opinion or subjective estimate, he or she can use that. Whenever someone has objective data, he or she should use that. Bayes' law shows how to incrementally improve models as better evidence becomes available.

Innovation: It has been argued that all innovation requires a Bayesian point of view because valid Frequentist models simply don't exist until after an experiment has been repeated many times. Requiring a valid Frequentist model before doing anything new precludes ever doing anything new. For example, valid Frequentist models of how a new product will sell in a market don't exist because one can only gather such data and develop such models after the product already sells in the market.

Note that if big data and Frequentists could discover everything worth learning, scientific research would be unnecessary. Note also that Bayesian statistics can analyze known, Gaussian data.

History

In 1763, Richard Price published Thomas Bayes' paper about inverse probability or reasoning from effect to cause. Then everyone totally ignored it for a century and then mostly ignored for another century.

Computation: Sharon Bertsch McGrayne argued that computation explains why Bayesian statistics did not break through until the 1980s. (McGrayne, pages 177 and 178) Bayesian models are usually much larger than Frequentist models, so updating Bayesian models requires a lot more computation. When computations were done by hand, meaning slow and error-prone, small Frequentist models were the best that anyone could reliably compute in practice. As inexpensive computers became available in the 1970s and '80s, Bayesian statistics took off.

Arbitrary and Subjective: Many people (and especially Frequentists) disdained the arbitrary and subjective elements of Bayesian statistics. Frequentists disparaged subjectivity throughout most of the 1900s. However, various mavericks championed Bayesian statistics off and on for over a century, including Vilfredo Pareto, Richard Price, Frank Ramsey, Bruno de Finetti, Richard Jeffreys, Irving Good, and Leonard Savage.

Both

In general, software engineers need both Frequentist and Bayesian statistics. The following example is absurd but suggestive. Consider a company that wants to develop a new consumer product, one out of the enormous possibilities.

Frequentism: Frequentist models better predict the past. Frequentist statistics can reveal how the experiments turn out or how the products actually perform in the market.

Bayesian: Bayesian models better predict the future. Bayesian statistics can use opinions and incomplete data to decide which experiments to run or which products to prototype.

Statistics is a modest technique for seeing the invisible, which is why so many managers love metrics. But, laymen are remarkably superstitious about statistics because it can only reveal limited aspects of the future.

Geometry

Euclidean

Math was initially developed to understand the past and predict the future. Accountants want to add up bills in restaurants and stores in the same predictable ways. Bankers want to reliably compute compound interest. Soldiers want to reliably compute the arcs of cannonballs.

Euclidean geometry concerns the relationships between independent dimensions. In Euclidean geometry, dimensions are separate and they scale in the ways that one learns in high-school classes.

Fractal

There are many non-Euclidean geometries, but Fractal geometry is particularly interesting. The complexity, catastrophe, and bifurcation theories explain how tiny differences in initial conditions and paths can affect outcomes.

Butterfly Effect: Perhaps the best-known example of complexity theory is the Butterfly effect. Most butterflies don't affect the atmosphere whatsoever, but under the right conditions, the flap of a butterfly wing can cause a hurricane. This resembles the "for want of a nail the war was lost" proverb. Most nails have no effect on the outcome of any war whatsoever, but on rare occasions under the right conditions, a nail can change the course of history. Living plants and animals as well as electro-mechanical systems can all amplify change (whether random or deliberate) to foster emergence.

Initial Conditions and Unpredictable Outcomes: Complex systems that are purely deterministic can appear either completely predictable or completely random or anything in between, depending on the initial conditions. Big differences in initial conditions can lead to essentially identical outcomes. Miniscule differences in initial conditions can lead to radically different outcomes. Lorenz's strange attractor, Feigenbaum's logistic map, and Mandelbrot's set all show that some initial conditions produce predictable results and others produce seemingly random results. Any error in the measurement of initial conditions, no matter how small, can potentially grow to overwhelm the signal.

Paths and Unpredictable Outcomes: Complex systems that contain any randomness or variations in paths can appear totally predictable or totally random or anything in between, depending on the sequences of events or actions. Bifurcation theory provides models where some sequences of events lead to predictable results and other similar sequences don't. The Swallowtail, Cusp, and Butterfly equations from Catastrophe theory show this sensitivity to paths. Everyday games, like Chess and Go, do so too. The rules are very simple, yet the games are very complicated; there are many ways to win and many ways to lose; some moves will change an outcome significantly and others won't; minute variations in a path may or may not matter; and few people play either game well.

Complexity May or May Not Undermine Induction: Herbert Simon noted that for some systems, complexity may be manageable. For example, all airplanes manage the turbulence of air during flight. (Simon, page 179) On the other hand for other systems, understanding chaos does not give one the ability to predict. (Simon, page 178) Sensitivities to initial conditions or paths and the resulting differences in outcomes can show up either quickly or after a long, long time, which undermines induction or predicting the future based on the past. Since only perfect measurements of a complex system can reliably predict the future, nobody can trust finite sequences of empirical measurements to reveal truth. Stability in complex systems can lull people into false confidences.

Mechanics Example: Most orbits of a planet like Mercury are stable. But, for perhaps 1% of the orbits, the planet will move predictably for billions of years and then crash into the sun or into another planet against all prior expectations. (Laskar and Gastineau)

Software Examples: In numerical computations, round-off errors can either cancel each other out or accumulate and overwhelm computations. (Denning and Martell, page ix) Software architects often discuss "the set of decisions that are hard to change." Every argument that architects should do Big Design Up Front (BDUF) to avoid problems later implies that those parts of software projects are sensitive to initial conditions. (Fairbanks, page 330) Barry Boehm's COCOMO equation and the concept of "diseconomy of scale" are also fractals.

History

The public became aware of fractals and chaos theory in 1982 when Benoit Mandelbrot published *The Fractal Geometry of Nature*, which contained many pretty pictures. Mandelbrot documented examples from hundreds of years in math, physics, biology, economics, meteorology, and the arts.

Math Example: In the late 1600s, Gottfried Leibnitz noticed the self-similarities of line segments, but didn't know how to generalize the observation. In 1890, Giuseppe Peano showed the first of the monster curves, lines that could interleave dimensions to fill planes and volumes. The traditional concept of physical dimension became amorphous and the differences between lines, planes, and volumes became murky. In the 1970s, Mitchell Feigenbaum developed his logistic map and Benoit Mandelbrot developed his set.

Three-Body Example: In the mid-1890s, Henri Poincaré became possibly the first to understand Chaos theory when he "solved" the Three Body problem. The Two Body problem (for example, the sun and the earth) can be solved easily. The Three Body problem (for example the sun, the earth, and the moon) may or may not be solvable. Some initial conditions lead to predictable outcomes and others lead to seemingly random outcomes.

Turbulence Example: In 1963, Edward Lorenz published "Deterministic Nonperiodic Flow," describing his "strange attractor," which models turbulence in the atmosphere, dynamos, and motors.

Brownian-Motion Example: Small particles in calm air or liquid move in jagged curves called Brownian motion. These curves have been studied for millennia, from Lucretius in 60 BC to Jan Ingenhousz in 1785 to Robert Brown in 1827 to Albert Einstein in 1905.

Biology Examples: Many biological systems have fractal shapes, including the shapes of lungs, the shapes of circulatory systems, the shapes of trees, the locations of trees in forests, predator-prey cycles, and on and on.

Table 2: Complex Systems		
System	**Equations**	**Year**
Lorentz's Strange Attractor	$dx/dt \leftarrow \sigma(y-x)$, $dy/dt \leftarrow x(\rho-z)-y$, $dz/dt \leftarrow xy-\beta z$	1963
Feigenbaum's Logistic Map	$x_{i+1} \leftarrow r\, x_i(1-x_i)$	1976
Mandelbrot's Set	$z_{i+1} \leftarrow z_i^2+c$	1979

Both

In general, software engineers need both Euclidean and Fractal geometries. In our experience, most software projects include both some independent or new features as well as some interdependent or improved features. Figure 2 contrasts four expansions of Euclidean and Fractal (dragon) curves, which model these features.

Euclidean: Each Euclidean expansion goes twice as far as the previous one. Euclidean curves model going farther to get more independent or new features, in other words to get more productivity.

Fractal: Each Fractal expansion goes from the same starting-point to the same ending-point by a route that is twice as intricate. Fractal curves model going deeper to get interdependent or improved features, in other words to get higher quality. Every feature could always be better. Refining each part of a program by one level doubles the cost of the whole program, so quality is anything but free.

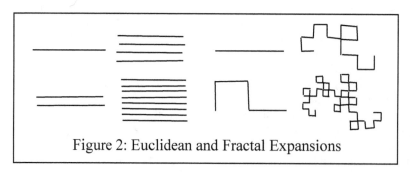

Figure 2: Euclidean and Fractal Expansions

Knowledge

Bounded

For most of human history, knowledge was bounded because good, generalizable information was hard to acquire and expensive to share. Before the printing press, scholars shared knowledge through lectures and hand-written scrolls. People had to live in cities with academies and libraries (like Athens, Alexandria, Fez, or Bologna) to become educated. Very few people had the opportunity (time and resources) to do so. Only after the printing press could encyclopedias cost-effectively document and share large swaths of knowledge. In a bounded world, all important knowledge can be captured and expressed in encyclopedias.

Encyclopedism

Bounded: In a bounded world, encyclopedias can describe the truth, the whole truth, and nothing but the truth. When knowledge is effectively finite and enumerable, encyclopedias work. Due to the difficulties and costs of gathering knowledge and printing it, encyclopedias had to be bounded.

Gatekeepers: Because of the cost of generating and sharing knowledge, gatekeepers controlled the flow of resources and therefore the flow of knowledge within society. Experts wrote articles and acted as gatekeepers for what gets shared. They tend to prefer conservative information that will remain stable for longer.

Software Examples: Mary Shaw recently argued that menus in a website can describe all relevant software architectures. (Shaw) The IEEE claims that SWEBOK describes everything that anyone needs to know about software engineering. Editors and committees at SigSoft and TCSE act as gatekeepers for the software engineering community.

History

In the 300s BC, Aristotle developed an early compendium of human knowledge about physics, biology, math, and so on. It was not called an "Encyclopedia" because that term referred to the knowledge needed for a general education. The first book titled "encyclopedia" was published in 1559 by Pavao Skalić. The first books to embody the modern notion of "compendia of all knowledge" were *Cyclopaedia* by Ephraim Chambers in 1728 and *Encyclopédie* by Denis Diderot and Jen le Rond d'Alembert in 1751. More recently, *Encyclopedia Britannica* and then Wikipedia have taken over as the repositories of all that anyone needs to know.

Deduction

Deduction enables people to generalize and make full use of existing knowledge.

The ancient Greeks were among the first (who we know about) to aspire to perfectly rational human discourse. They developed rhetoric and simple rules of inference like modus ponens and modus tollens. In the late 1600s, Gottfried Wilhelm Leibnitz wanted to resolve human conflicts using logical deduction, famously writing "calculemus" or "let us calculate." He developed an early propositional calculus and a knowledge-representation scheme. In 1854, George Boole published *The Laws of Thought*, which described a complete propositional logic. In 1879, Gottlob Frege published *Begriffsschrift*, which described logical quantifiers.

Making math rigorous turned out much easier than making human discourse rigorous. Between 1910 and 1913, Bertrand Russell and Alfred Whitehead published *Principia Mathematica*, which formally derived set theory and arithmetic. They combined Gottlob Frege's logic, Giuseppe Peano's axioms from 1889, and a new type system to remove paradoxes. Throughout the twentieth century, mathematicians sought to deterministically evaluate the truth of all expressions and to enumerate all of math and make it rigorous. The drive for completeness and rigor eventually led to mechanical proof checkers. Matti Tedre argued that verificationism nearly fulfilled Leibnitz's dream. (Tedre, page 26) In 2015, Donald Knuth documented ongoing progress in knowledge representation using Boolean logic and deduction using satisfiability solvers. (Knuth, *Fascicle 6*)

Unbounded

In recent years, the infinite and error-laden nature of human knowledge has become better understood. In an unbounded world, knowledge is too large for any person or group of people to understand everything. Encyclopedias simply cannot describe everything that one needs to know and deduction cannot fill in all of the gaps. The glut of fake news exacerbates these problems. So every year, all encyclopedias become more overwhelming, more incomplete, and more error-laden. In an unbounded world, many things remain unknown: a lot of important knowledge has not yet been and never will be expressed.

Anti-Encyclopedism

Infinite: In an unbounded world, encyclopedias are finite approximations of the infinite and evolving truth. In *Too Big to Know*, David Weinberger showed that way too much information exists for anyone or any group to know everything, and so knowledge has become effectively infinite. In particular, the Internet contains so much information that it overwhelms everyone.

Error-Laden: In *The Half-Life of Facts*, Samuel Arbesman showed that knowledge expires in predictable patterns, much like radioactive decay, even when the expirations of individual facts remain unpredictable. In general, half of all scientific papers expire within a couple years and half of all scientific books expire within a decade. (Arbesman) This notion was originally published by the IEEE.

Encyclopedias have the same problems. Some ideas are not yet expressed articulately. Some ideas are wrong and should be deleted. Many ideas are off by a bit and should be refined. The problem is that nobody knows what and where the problems are, i.e. can distinguish between which ideas are right and which are wrong. If anyone did know, they would just fix the problems. So, editors must continually maintain encyclopedias to keep them up-to-date as understanding improves.

No Gatekeepers: Fake information has been around a long time. There has always been propaganda. In the 1960s, Trurl and Klapaucius defeated Pirate Pugg using a random information generator. (Lem, "Sixth Sally") The Internet has few gatekeepers, which allows everyone to share new information, but it also allows them to share fake information. Distinguishing between real and fake information is hard, in part because fake news often tells people what they most want to hear while real news often tells people what they don't want to hear. On the web, fake information can easily undermine or drown out real information.

History

Awareness of the limits of human knowledge has been around for a long time. In 1887, Sherlock Holmes said, "There comes a time when for every addition of knowledge you forget something that you knew before. It is of the highest importance, therefore, not to have useless facts elbowing out the useful ones." In 1972, Edsger Dijkstra wrote a chapter in *Structured Programming* about the limits of the human brain titled "On Our Inability to Do Much." In 2005, Niklaus Wirth wrote about the limits of intellectual capability in regard to the design of Modula 2 and Oberon. (Tedre, page 131) (Daylight, page 122) (Wirth)

Anti-Deduction

The ancient Greeks knew that $\sqrt{2}$ is irrational and cannot be written out, even though it can be constructed using ideal calipers and straightedges. But for millennia, that limitation mainly concerned precision and knowing all other mathematical truths seemed possible.

Incompleteness: In 1931, Kurt Gödel showed that nobody can know everything that is true in mathematics. In 1936, Alonzo Church and Alan Turing independently showed that nobody can solve the Halting problem. For the first time, mathematicians became aware of specific hard limits to mathematical deduction.

Intractability: In the early 1970s, Stephen Cook and Richard Karp showed that many well-defined problems, like Satisfiability and Traveling Salesman, are NP-complete. Nobody knows how to solve the general cases of these problems without exponential algorithms.

Most likely, many additional problems exist that will remain unsolvable for other reasons or are less crisply defined. Truth emerges slowly because mathematicians and computer scientists can always discover more and more truths, yet nobody can ever know them all.

Matti Tedre argued that formal verification ran out of steam in the 1980s and that software engineering stepped in to fill the void. (Tedre, page 60) Tedre noted that math differs from programming, that computers differ from the real world, and that the physical world is uncertain. Daniel Jackson and Mandana Vaziri gave verificationism another boost in the early 2000s by harnessing the rapidly improving satisfiability solvers. (Jackson and Vaziri) But, verification seems to have lapsed again since then. (Knuth, *Fascicle 6*)

Both

In general, software engineers need both bounded and unbounded concepts of knowledge.

Bounded: Software engineers know a lot of algorithms, tools, and practices. SWEBOK documents a useful baseline of knowledge that practitioners should start with.

Unbounded: If software engineering were bounded, then programmers would eventually write the last program and a standard committee could just enumerate them all and close the profession. In an unbounded world, both new software problems and new software technologies will continue to arise forever.

Motivation

Rational Behaviorism

Rational

When John von Neumann founded economic game theory in 1944, he treated people as rational players who maximize their personal rewards. The Chicago School of Economics emphasized monetarism, based on rational, game-theory models of economic behavior. Mutual Assured Destruction (MAD) provided a game-theory rationalization for the nuclear arms race during the Cold War.

In 1970, Nathan Leites and Charles Wolf argued that people make rational decisions, so authorities should define the costs and benefits to motivate people in society to behave in desired ways. Leites and Wolf's ideas were used to justify Draconian punishments when attempting to solve the "political troubles" in Northern Ireland and to deter crime in the U.S. with "three strikes" laws. (Gladwell, page 201)

Sometimes, such as with MAD, treating people as rational seemed to work. Other times, such as with Northern Ireland and Three Strikes, things went horribly wrong.

Behaviorism – Motivated by Carrots and Sticks

Using rewards and punishments to train, educate, and manipulate animals and people has been around for at least thousands of years. "Spare the rod and spoil the child," is an ancient proverb. In 1937, B.F. Skinner began developing Behaviorism, refining the notion that animals can be trained and controlled through rewards and punishments. His ideas were widely adopted by managers. Behaviorists used to think of leadership in similar terms, of motivating workers through carrots and sticks. (Fowler, page 6)

Susan Fowler notes that Skinnerism seemed to work. (Fowler, page 7) Management after World War 2 was full of gamification, rewarding and punishing workers based on metrics. "Complex schemes [motivated] workers with compensation systems, rewards, contests, tokens, badges, prizes, and formal recognition programs." (Fowler, page 7) The SEI fully espouses behaviorism when they use processes and metrics in the CMM and SCAMPI to judge and motivate programmers.

Logical and Robotic

Computers affect expectations of who people are and what people should become. In the 1950s, those with a narrow focus on technology were referred to as "computerniks," meaning something like "idiot savants." (Tedre, page 43) In the 1960s, as the prospect of computers and robots loomed, Spock became the ultimate or ideal "human" being. Spock embodied a hybrid of human and robot behaviors, fulfilling the dreams of Socrates, More, Boole, Putnam, and others, of perfectly rational humans. The original *Star Trek* ran from 1966 to '68, before the public understood what computers are and could do. Autism is now becoming in important ideal in pop culture, for example on the TV series *Elementary* and in the book *The Curious Incident of the Dog in the Night-time*. (Haddon) Some companies now specifically hire autistic programmers, believing they provide competitive advantages. (Noguchi)

Programmers are Inconsistent and Unreliable: In a deterministic world, people (and especially programmers) are compared with perfection and they often fail to be as robot-like (or as productive and perfect) as managers desire. Managers seem to view programmers as lazy and error-prone.

Transactional Management

In a deterministic world, the division of labor between managers and developers is mainly transactional – managers give workers paychecks in exchange for bossing them around forty hours per week. Managers motivate teams and track projects using processes, rules, metrics, carrots and sticks, challenges, money, power, and fear. These practices endure because of tradition, but are justified by rational economics and behaviorism. Managers naturally prefer transactional relationships because it simplifies the work for managers and exaggerates class distinctions between managers and workers. Transactions enable managers to turn their attention away from coaching their teams and toward other duties.

It Does Work: Behaviorism and transactions work for routine and assembly-line tasks like dishwashing, which tend to pay poorly; career software engineers work in exchange for salaries; and many top athletes and actors perform best for large prizes and fees.

Irrational Humanism

In the 1800s and early 1900s, psychology focused primarily on mental illness, but over the last 75 years or so, psychologists and sociologists have begun focusing on normal people. In the 1940s, led by Abraham Maslow, they began asking "how do normal people actually behave?" and "how can normal people do better work and live better lives?" (Maslow)

Irrational

People are irrational in many ways.

Blind-Spots: Psychologists have learned that normal people have many cognitive blind-spots, including the Confirmation, Self-Serving, and Hindsight biases, the Gambler's Fallacy, and the Law of Small Numbers. (Lewis, pages 158+) The Confirmation bias describes the tendency of people to notice data that confirms their beliefs and to ignore data that contradicts their beliefs. So, providing better data or examples rarely changes anyone's mind and may even provoke stubbornness. The Gambler's Fallacy is the belief that in a 50-50 game, wins and losses will even out, so if a gambler keeps playing, he or she will eventually recover from a loss. Most people blatantly misunderstand randomness. The Law of Small Numbers is the belief that small samples actually do represent large populations. These blind-spots are part of the brain and *nobody* can avoid them completely, not even statisticians and psychologists who should know better. (Lewis, pages 157+) Matthew Hutson argued that these biases were useful in human evolution, but can cause problems in modern society. (Hutson, page 5)

Charity: Millions of programmers work on open-source projects for free. Probably billions of people donate to charity. Charity contradicts all rational economic theory.

Behavioral Economics: As behavioral economics emerged in the 1980s and '90s, mainstream economists slowly accepted that people make many irrational decisions. Daniel Kahneman and Richard Thaler won the 2002 and 2017 Nobel prizes in economics for revealing these irrationalities. Thaler argued that the rational humans or "homo economicus" that John von Neumann presumed occur as rarely as unicorns. (Vedantam and Thaler) Everyone struggles with temptation, causing too many people to fail to exercise and too many to fail to save for retirement. Resisting temptation turns out to be hard work and people need help doing so. (Vedantam, "Predictably Unpredictable")

Motivated by Autonomy, Relatedness, and Mastery

Psychologists have learned that people do not primarily maximize their personal rewards and that people who excel are not primarily driven by greed and fear. Abraham Maslow, Edward Deci, Carol Dweck, Anders Ericson, and many others showed that intrinsic and peer motivation work much better than extrinsic or manager motivation. Daniel Pink summarized their results with the principles of autonomy, mastery, and purpose. (*Drive*, part 2) Susan Fowler summarized them as autonomy, relatedness, and competence. (Fowler, page 32+) It takes all three to excel. (Fowler, page 46)

Autonomy: People need to have choices and they need to believe that their work is of their own volition, that they are the cause of their own actions. (Fowler, page 33) As a rule, software engineers hate being told how to do their work, just like everyone else. Everyone dislikes rigid processes.

Relatedness: Most people like to help and please and work with others. Adults want to produce something of value, to give something back to the world as an act of gratitude. (*Why Grow Up?*, page 173) Generativity means giving back and nurturing the young. (*Why Grow Up?*, page 190) Developers like to deliver treats to users and to get thankyou in return. Workers also want to be part of an effective team, in other words to have a group of peers who understand and appreciate their efforts.

Competence and Mastery: People need to feel competent and effective. (Fowler, page 42) They like to demonstrate their mastery of skills by working on and solving truly hard problems. Software developers like to build interesting, innovative features and applications. They also dislike feeling stupid when they get thrown curveball tasks or must work on parts of a code base that they don't know.

Emotional and Human

As PCs and smart phones became widely used throughout society, everyone began to understand that people are not and should not be robots.

People are Emotional: Increasingly, people realize that software engineers are emotional creatures. Brene Brown argued that vulnerability is the essence of courage and that killing emotional lows also kills emotional highs. (Brown) So, healthy people should experience a broad range of emotions. Software problems (such as struggling with a difficult bug) can lead to disappointment, frustration, and even anger. Finding solutions is fun and builds pride. Successful software engineers must learn to work through their emotional highs and lows.

Ideal People: As Spock became understood, everyone realized that humans cannot and should not emulate him; nobody is as knowledgeable or disciplined as Spock – nobody can be; and Spock eventually stopped being a human ideal.

Enlightened Management

In general, enlightened management seems to work much better for sustained productivity and contemporary software processes increasingly urge enlightened management.

Enlightened management combines a lot of good ideas. Bertrand Meyer argued that "guru managers" should establish a productive environment, champion the team, and handle resources. (Meyer, page 79) Both Large Scale Scrum (LESS) and Disciplined Agile Delivery (DAD) encourage teams to have coaches rather than bosses. Desi Brown argued that leaders should tell stories to workers to explain why their efforts matter. (personal communication) We believe that truer stories work better. Daniel Kahneman argued that leaders should generally express more praise than criticism to workers because of the "regression-to-mean" illusion. (Lewis, page 126) In *Management 3.0*, Jurgen Appelo provides many suggestions about motivation, purpose, and communication. (Appelo, chapters 5, 8, 12)

Unfortunately, in our opinion, enlightened management remains a poorly-defined, ad-hoc collection of ideas and it remains far from clear what guru managers should actually do. We believe that enlightened management is not yet a coherent and teachable concept. This makes sense because a finite number of enlightened rules cannot cover the infinite possibilities that could arise. In our experience, most managers still seem lost without their carrots and sticks and action items and spreadsheets, and enlightened management remains far from the norm.

Note that happy programmers can still write bad software, but surely, unhappy programmers would write worse software. Note that we mean "happy in their work" rather than "happy go lucky." And note that "humanism" is not quite the right word, but we have not found a better one.

Both

In general, software engineers need both some rational behaviorism and some irrational humanism.

Rational Behavioralism: Software engineers pride themselves on being rational, especially whenever they puzzle out complex software logic or fix bugs. Not every task is inspiring or motivating and yet they all must get done. So, managers must often assign unpleasant tasks to someone, even though that contradicts autonomy and may make the selected individuals feel picked on. And, workers need salaries.

Irrational Humanism: On the other hand, Behaviorism and transactions demotivate and demoralize most people. Managers should evoke autonomy, relatedness, and mastery whenever possible. For example, daily standup meetings encourage developers to make personal commitments to colleagues and provide opportunities to share their challenges and victories with their peers.

Yet how best to combine rational behaviorism with irrational humanism remains unclear. Giving commands reduces autonomy, but we don't know how managers can direct work without giving at least some commands. Merely mentioning money lowers productivity, but we don't know how managers can pay workers without ever discussing money. The defined processes and coding standards that organizations impose can raise the level of quality, even though they also undermine volition. Of course, many other social conventions (like wearing clothes) both have benefits and undermine volition.

Program Contexts

Isolated Machines

Originally, program contexts were small – programs were written for standalone computers and operators served programs. From the 1940s through the '60s, programs (such as operating systems and embedded systems) ran close to machines and extended the capabilities of machines. Programs were often thought of as shells, layers, or virtual machines, like in the THE operating system.

Standalone Computers: From the dawn of computing into the 1970s, computers largely stood alone. Human operators moved programs and data between computers using "sneaker net" and physical media like punch cards, magnetic tapes, and floppy disks.

On Behalf of Machines: Originally, all programs were of the computer, by the computer and for the computer. Into the 1970s, mainframe computers resided in cold-rooms and were cared for by operators who manually adjusted programs for the computers and manually adjusted data for the programs. Programs did not interact with users, only with trained operators, who acted as intermediaries. Into the 1970s, input and output required physical devices like line-printers, punch cards, and magnetic tapes, which limited user interaction. In other words, computers resided in temples and were worshipped by acolytes. Programs ignored users because of circumstance and awareness rather than mal-intent.

Stable Contexts Entail Enduring Programs: Hardware tends to remain stable because it doesn't spontaneously grow new abilities or expectations. When contexts (like technologies and markets) are stable products can endure and companies can take their time to create great products. Both Bell Telephone phone lines and General Electric lightbulbs endured for a century nearly unchanged. With upwardly-compatible computers (for example x86-based), hardware-oriented programs can potentially endure unchanged for many decades. With upwardly-compatible virtual platforms (for example, hardware emulators, Java, and .Net), programs can potentially endure forever.

Networks and Users

More recently, program contexts have grown enormously – programs communicate directly with each other across networks and with users through graphical user interfaces. Matti Tedre wrote that computers and programs are not isolated, "they are part of a complex socio technical system." (Tedre, pages 116 to 117)

Networked Computers: Since the 1970s, networks, and especially the Internet, have enabled programs to interact directly with each other and to access data in shared databases on remote machines. Increasingly, programs communicate directly with remote devices (such as pedometers and thermostats) in the Internet of Things and with remote servers in the Cloud. Networked programs must implement communication protocols, understand representations of remote data, and tolerate asynchrony, so networks increase program size and complexity.

On Behalf of People: Today, most programs are of the people, by the people, and for the people. Since the arrival of the Mac and Windows 3.0, many programs have emphasized user interactions. Computers come with keyboards, mice, graphical displays, game consoles, touch screens, microphones, and speakers to promote user interaction. Programs run at a high level and extend the capabilities of people. Different users have different skills and training and need different functionality and information. Programs serve these users in diverse ways – spoon feeding novices and presenting deep and subtle analysis to experts, so user interactions increase program size and complexity.

Ephemeral Contexts Entail Ephemeral Programs: Hardware and software engineers continue to build new computers that have new capabilities and use new protocols. Users have insatiable cravings for novelty and they continue to want more features and quality. When contexts (peer computers and user expectations) evolve continually, programs are ephemeral: they must continually be upgraded or replaced and they can only provide short-term solutions. Today, fewer and fewer consumer products remain relevant for long. The fashion retailer Zara avoids planning and predicting altogether, striving to respond continually to the fashion on the street. (Holmes, chapter 6) Phone and tablet apps compete in fad-driven markets, where being on top for a month, or even a week, can be major success.

Both

In general, programs relate to both machines and users.

Toward Machines: Some programs emphasize machines and ignore users, especially operating system kernels, embedded systems, physics and chemistry simulations, tools for training neural networks, and satisfiability solvers. Yet, many user-oriented programs also need to use computer hardware efficiently, for example when rendering 3D graphics for games and movies and when querying databases. And, programmers only write one line of code at a time, so as Niklaus Wirth noted, "Programming is extending a given system." (Daylight, page 116)

Toward Users: Some programs emphasize users and ignore machines, especially webpages and mobile apps. Yet, embedded programs can also be huge, containing all of the complexities and speculations of user programs. And, most embedded programs must eventually get some information out to humans, for example status, so that when things go wrong the device can get fixed.

Programs in autonomous cars must address both machines and people. Controlling the motions of a car is machine-oriented while interacting with the environment includes dealing with other human drivers and pedestrians.

Program Descriptions

Specifications and Algorithms

Algorithms are possibly the highest achievements of computer science and so people naturally want to think of their programs as either algorithms or representations of algorithms. For example, Peter Denning and Craig Martell recently wrote "a program is an expression of an algorithm, encoded for execution on a machine." (Denning and Martell, page 84)

Specifications Describe Common, Stable Problems: Problems that occur over and over in many different contexts merit taking the time and effort to solve well. Both sort and discrete Fourier transform describe problems that are widely encountered and have endured unchanged for centuries.

Specifications are Simple and Precise: Ideally, specifications are simple, precise, and even minimal. The postcondition for sort could be $\forall 0<i<N\ y_{i-1} \leq y_i$ (elements are ordered) and $\forall e\ |\sigma_e\ y| = |\sigma_e\ x|$ (elements are otherwise unchanged). The postcondition for discrete Fourier transform could be $\forall 0 \leq j < N$ $y_j = [\sum 0 \leq k < N\ x_k e^{-i2\pi jk/N}]$. These postconditions are trivial, even though very few people understand them.

Specifications Generally Have Pseudo Code Solutions: Most algorithm solutions are described by pseudo codes that spell out all of the important and sometimes tricky details. For example, Quicksort, Cooley-Tukey, and Secure Hash Algorithm 1 (SHA1) all describe specific solutions using pseudo codes. However, some algorithm solutions are more vague. Donald Knuth uses prose descriptions, so transliterating his algorithms into source code tends to be harder, though it remains straightforward. (Knuth, *The Art of Computer Programming*) Recent algorithms for max flow by James Orlin and for matrix multiplication by Virginia Williams provide only the sketchiest of pseudo codes, so transliterating them into source code can be truly difficult. (Orlin) (Williams)

Specifications often have Many Different Solutions: Sort has Quick, Merge, Insertion, Shell, and thousands of other variations. Donald Knuth published a tome on the subject in 1972 and much has been learned since then. Discrete Fourier transform has literal, matrix multiply, Cooley-Tukey, Bruun, and many other variations.

Pseudo Code Solutions can take a Long Time: It took the brightest minds in computer science 59 years to go from Ted Harris and Frank Ross's 1954 specification of max flow to James Orlin's 2013 O(VE) solution. Rudrata solved the Knight's Tour problem in the 800s; Leonhard Euler solved the Königsberg Bridge problem in 1736; and Stephen Cook and Leonid Levin laid the foundation for NP Completeness around 1971; yet after more than a millennium, Hamiltonian Cycle remains effectively unsolved.

Pseudo Code Solutions are Eternal: Because specifications remain valid forever, pseudo code solutions also remain valid forever. Anyone who wants their programs to endure eternally will naturally want them to be thought of as algorithms or representations of algorithms.

Pseudo Code Validation is Objective and Deductive: Pseudo codes are objectively and deductively correct when algorithmists use mathematics to show that a pseudo code implements a specification. Even so, validations can be tricky. Algorithms often embody a lot of opaque mathematical (or contextual) knowledge. For example, Fast Fourier transforms (such as Cooley-Tukey and Bruun) presume knowledge of advanced if 250-year-old mathematics that very few programmers know and is not even mentioned in SWEBOK. Few programmers understand matrix multiplication using FFTs.

Algorithms Hide Complexity: Algorithms tend to combine simple, short, abstract specifications with tricky, long, detailed pseudo codes. In every algorithm that we know of, the specification is far shorter and far more abstract than the pseudo code.

History

Until 1977, the best minds in computer science and software engineering equated algorithms with programs. In the late 1940s and early '50s, programs computed logarithm, trigonometry, and ballistic tables and were almost pure algorithm. Donald Knuth published the first volume of *The Art of Computer Programming* in 1968, proclaiming in the title that the finest programs are algorithms. Edsger Dijkstra published *Structured Programming* in 1972 and *A Discipline of Programming* in 1976, which used the terms "program" and "algorithm" interchangeably. All of his example programs were actually small algorithms, the most complex being Eight Queens and Convex Hull. In 1975, Fred Brooks published the *Mythical Man-Month* in which his example of good code transliterated a published sorting algorithm into PL/1. (Brooks, page 173) And in 1976, Niklaus Wirth, published the book titled *Algorithms + Data Structures = Programs*. (Wirth)

These luminaries naturally thought of programs as algorithms because they all started their careers when tiny programs ran on tiny computers. In the academic world, small problems were discussed in one lecture and examined in one test. Though much less often today, luminaries continue to argue that programs are either algorithms or expressions of algorithms. Denning and Martell recently wrote that the design process transfers the idea of each algorithm from our heads into code patterns or "the design of the machine." (Denning and Martell, page 50)

Requirements and Scripts

Requirements are written in natural languages or technical shorthands and describe the goals of software projects.

Requirements Describe Unique, Ephemeral Problems: Requirements describe what should change during this project from the status quo toward the as-yet-unknown future. Analysts usually develop requirements uniquely for each project and, in general, requirements differ for every project. Nobody ever practices rewriting the requirements for the same project over and over, rather they move on to the next project.

Requirements are Arbitrary: What users want is arbitrary and often murky. Users could want to improve existing features or to create whole new features or any combination thereof. No guarantees exist that the users won't change their minds halfway through the project. No guarantees exist that different users won't want totally different requirements.

Requirements usually have Script Solutions: Whether written in C, Java, Python, or Ada, most source codes are actually ad-hoc scripts that glue together and invoke known algorithms. For example the requirement, "The button shall use the text in the input box as the key to fetch the remote data," describes the glue that will eventually invoke a series of algorithms to compress, transmit, error-correct, parse, and display data.

Requirements usually have One Solution: In general, only one project (script or body of code) will ever get built for any set of requirements. An analyst might occasionally copy some requirements from one project to another, but he or she runs the risks of making the usual copy-and-paste errors. Nobody ever spends decades reimplementing the same requirements over and over, looking for better solutions. Rather, all problems in the results of one project become new requirements for upgrade projects.

Script Solutions must be Timely: Requirements express priorities by describing the features that should be worked on now in this project, as opposed to later or never. Rarely will anyone wait for years for a program to get written. No requirement should ever presume a solution to an unsolved problem, such as Satisfiability, which remains open-ended research.

Script Solutions are Ephemeral: A script only endures as long as users need the requirements that define the script. When users change platforms (for example when users upgrade from MS-DOS to Windows or Android), older programs (scripts) become irrelevant and eventually die. So, quality for script solutions emphasizes short-term utility rather than eternal correctness.

Requirement Validation is Inductive and Subjective: In practice, requirements are often quite horrible, having many erroneous, missing, and ambiguous details. • Validation attempts to improve a set of requirements by showing that they describe a future program that will satisfy the future needs of users. Analysts can survey users about whether a specific set of requirements expresses their needs, but such surveys produce inductive truth. Nobody can ever prove that requirements describe what users will actually need because inductive truth can never become deductive truth. Such surveys are fraught because humans have many systemic biases, such as the availability and self-serving biases and humans all-too-often make mistakes, even if unintentionally. • Requirements are subjectively correct at best. Putting a validation check on one button and not on another has everything to do with what users say they want via the requirements and nothing to do with any objective concept like hardware, operating systems, libraries, pseudo codes, or mathematics.

Programs Expose Complexity: Analysts should express every important, visible detail of the project clearly in the requirements and should avoid compression and implication. Otherwise, programmers might overlook or forget the hidden and implied details. This makes requirements large. Requirements often unintentionally leave many details unstated, such as the interconnections between requirements, but such omissions all-too-often cause problems later. Similarly, source codes must express every important and visible detail needed to make the program work properly.

History

Since 1977, people have argued that programs (or scripts) differ from algorithms in fundamental ways. In 1977, Richard De Millo, Richard Lipton, and Alan Perlis published "Social Processes and Proofs of Theorems and Programs" about the differences between mathematics and programming. In 1988, James Fetzer published "Program Verification: the Very Idea" about the differences between the logical structure of an algorithm and the physical control of a program. In 1996, Brian Smith published *On the Origin of Objects* about the differences between models and things. Matti Tedre elaborates on this history. (Tedre, chapter 4)

Today, almost everyone (outside of the formal-specification and model-driven communities) accepts that programs differ from algorithms. But researchers will forever attempt to shift the boundary between programs and algorithms because that is part of their jobs.

Both

Programs have always combined algorithms with scripts and they always will.

All Projects Need Specifications and Algorithms: Small embedded programs (for signal processing and secure communication) are often nearly pure algorithm. Large programs usually invoke many algorithms. For example, sort is used all over the place in most large programs. Libraries of string and matrix functions contain many algorithms. Even programs that do pure arbitrary interaction, such as "hello world," use algorithms for input and output. Users and programmers are often unaware of the algorithms that get invoked, for example when they use secure communication.

All Projects Need Requirements and Scripts: Someone needs to define the goals of each project, even when the result is essentially pure algorithm. For example, when users want to compute Fourier transforms, someone needs to state clearly that the program should compute Fourier transforms rather than say Cosine or Wavelet transforms. Requirements describe how scripts should glue algorithms together, how to move data from one algorithm to the next, under what conditions to invoke each algorithm, and so on.

Most algorithms are already shared in libraries, so software engineers rarely implement algorithms anymore. As time goes on, less of programming relates to algorithms and more relates to scripts.

Tools

Tools

Tools are Powerful and Consistent: Tools have a lot of "power under the hood" and can consistently apply sophisticated algorithms, optimizations, and searches, managing enormous quantities of detail and complexity that human brains simply cannot keep up with. Compilers and optimizers are imperfect, yet they consistently outperform humans at generating correct and fast assembly code. IDEs can search through and refactor enormous code bases flawlessly. Repositories can store and retrieve the history of large code bases more swiftly and accurately than developers could ever remember or imagine.

Tools Counter Human Flaws: Many software tools counter the flaws in developers. For example, high-level languages and IDEs enable developers to do more work, improving productivity; type checkers and linters catch many routine mistakes, improving quality; and metrics encourage developers to work steadily and overtly, improving accountability.

The SE Profession is Defined by Tools: Tools have always driven progress in computing and everyone more or less defines software engineering in terms of tools. For example, Denning and Martell argue that people define computing by the core technologies of algorithms, programming languages, databases, graphics, and so on. (Denning and Martell, pages 10 to 11)

SE Jobs are Defined by Tools: Today, HR departments mainly define developer jobs by tools. Job descriptions usually list the languages and tools that new hires will need to use. For example, "candidates should know Rust, Rails, containers, block chain, and Eclipse." HR personnel emphasize tools because they can trivially compare keywords on resumes and cannot otherwise evaluate the skills of unknown candidates.

Limits of Tools

Tools Only Do Repetitive, Well-Defined Work: Increasingly, software engineers realize that tools automate the common, easy, well-defined, repetitive, algorithmic (read deterministic) tasks like compiling, type-checking, building, storing, and searching. Tasks that get done only once or cannot be defined precisely (such as "solve the user's problem") don't get built into tools.

Tools Don't Understand Intention: Tools cannot create value on their own because they do not understand human intentions and cannot guess the purposes behind the changes to code. Requirement and estimation tools do not know which details are missing, wrong, ambiguous, or destined to change because they do not know what users actually want. IDEs cannot do the typing for programmers because they have never been able to guess user or programmer intentions. Predictive typing on smart phones is still only 10% accurate. Compilers cannot generate the assembly code that users actually want because they cannot deduce what programmers meant to write. Repository tools cannot reliably merge changes on their own because they do not know the intentions behind the changes to source codes. Testing tools for GUIs and webpages help, but do not actually know whether a program does what the users want.

Tools are Overwhelming: Software engineers don't understand most of their tools. Few practitioners truly understand branching and merging in repositories; they often use repository tools in ad hoc ways and often do lots of unnecessary work. Updating Eclipse packages too often becomes a nightmare of bizarre dependencies. Microsoft Word can do anything, but it is so huge that many simple tasks remain beyond understanding, such as page headers and footers for books.

General Purpose Languages are Overwhelming: C++ is now infinitely large and nobody understands it all anymore. Java is getting that way.

Skills

Programmers Understand the Needs of Users: Only software engineers can interpret (or figure out) the needs of users and write the appropriate code. Software engineers create value by spanning the gap from intention to code and by applying tools on behalf of users.

Programmers Do Bespoke, Problem-Specific Work: Humans have always picked up where tools leave off, filling in for the limitations of tools. Tasks that are hard (such as solving NP) or poorly defined (such as figuring out what users actually need and then writing the random code to implement it) won't get automated by tools because that remains impossible.

The SE Profession should be Defined by Human Skill: Today, the most important resource in software development is the mind, its knowledge, experience, attention span, and so on, all of which are limited.

SE Jobs should be Defined by Human Skills: Before the 1980s, before software tools became so specialized and elaborate, job requirements for programmers were primarily "experienced," "driven," and "willing to learn." Those attributes will always remain essential, even though nobody knows how to evaluate them effectively.

Both

In general, software engineers need both tools and skills.

Tools: Tools are vital and have always supported developers. In general, developers write more and higher-quality code using Java and Eclipse than using Assembler and card punchers. Type checkers and linters can quickly and reliably verify type-safety, which is an important first step toward making useful programs. Practitioners should know the concepts behind core tools (like languages and IDEs) very well and the concepts behind many other tools (like repositories) at least tolerably.

Skills: Tools are not enough on their own – they must also be applied effectively, even artistically. Developers must use their experience and drive to pick up where tools leave off, to write the useful code that solves actual user problems. Software engineers should also use at least some tools (like IDEs and languages) with ease to avoid digging out the manual for every task. And, they should type proficiently.

Practices

Rules

In a deterministic world, rules keep developers on the straight and narrow to improve productivity and quality. Rules document fixed units of human activity as processes and fixed units of knowledge as scripts. Organizations benefit both from documenting common problem-solution pairs and from responding to similar problems consistently.

Repetitive Processes: Bertrand Meyer argued that the term "practice" refers to "repeated activities." (Meyer, page 89) Most processes focus on what analysts, developers, and testers routinely do. Task-level loops (for example, Beck's Extreme Programming) include get the next task, implement it using test-driven development, inspect it, check it in, and do the "paperwork." Iteration-level loops (for example, Sutherland and Schwaber's Scrum) include plan the iteration, do the work, retrospect the iteration, and improve the process. Quarterly-release loops (for example, Boehm's Spiral model) include plan the release, do risk analysis, do the work, test the results, retrospect the release, and improve the process.

Ad-Hoc Processes: Many development tasks occur infrequently (such as quarterly versioning of DLLs) or even just once (such individual process improvements and one-off customizations). Documenting tasks that occur infrequently helps to ensure that solutions don't get forgotten, but everyone should remain skeptical that such tasks ever get documented accurately or carried out with ease.

History

Processes: In the early days of computing, say before 1968, practices came from personal experience and individuals applied them inconsistently. The NATO conferences on software engineering inspired immediate progress on processes. Winston Royce wrote about improving Waterfalls in 1970. (Royce) The Cap Gemini SDM from Pandata in 1970 might be the first true software development process. Structured Analysis and Design Method (SADM) was initially developed in the late 1960s and was published around 1980. And, the Capability Maturity Model was published in 1989.

Processes are Software: Leon Osterweil published a classic paper in 1987, arguing that processes are software, too. (Osterweil) His metaphor has a bright side. Documented processes reveal the current state of practice and they can be incrementally improved like programs. But his metaphor also has a dark side. It implies that programmers are robots who merely do what they are told and that their work can be defined deterministically. He reinforced the rational behaviorism view of people.

Patterns: Kent Beck and Ward Cunningham started the software patterns movement when they presented "Using Pattern Languages for Object-Oriented Programs" in 1987. (Beck and Cunningham) The *Design Patterns* book from 1994 documented the common substructures that occur inside of large objects or classes, especially ones that occur in GUIs. (Gamma, Helm, Johnson, Vlissides) The patterns movement reinforced the scripts movement.

Scripts: Scripts can describe anything worth remembering and often contain flowcharts or programs that treat people like programmable computers. Boehm and Turner give example scripts for a "quality/process manager role" and an "inspection process." (Boehm and Turner, pages 63 and 67 to 68) Barry Boehm and Richard Turner argued that bright and well-intentioned but inexperienced people can merely follow scripts and write great software. (Boehm and Turner, page 47)

Many organizations strive to document all of their institutional knowledge, building enormous databases of scripts. IBM was renowned for its comprehensive documentation in the 1950s, which led the U.S. military to select them to build SAGE. (Hughes, pages 48 to 52) Script databases have become more and more common since the Internet made them widely-sharable. Scripts remain widely used in sales and support organizations.

Limits of Rules

Increasingly, everyone realizes that processes and scripts have severe limits. Process and script databases fail for essentially the same reasons that encyclopedias fail.

Gaps: Many rules are missing or contain gaps. In real projects in rapidly changing and complex fields, new situations and special cases arise all the time. More prosaically, the situation anyone is experiencing right now has all-too-often never occurred to him or her before and surprisingly-often has never occurred to anyone he or she knows. Historically, IBMers joked about their "Great Oral Tradition," all of the corporate knowledge that remained undocumented.

Errors: Scripts all-too-often contain contradictory, out-of-date, wrong, or vague details. Maintaining large sets of scripts takes a lot of work, which rarely occurs.

Overwhelming: Rules easily become overwhelming. Ideally, everyone would consider all of the rules in the corporate knowledgebase, IEEE standards, and their personal experience before making each decision or typing each line of code. But they cannot. When these knowledge sources have thousands or tens of thousands of rules, nobody can know them all, let alone take time to consider them all. Daniel Kahneman argued that people should only ever consider five to seven rules at a time because that is the limit of human working memory. (Ariel) When too many processes and scripts get documented, they just add noise and sow confusion.

Demotivating: Psychologists have shown that nobody has ever, ever, ever been motivated to excellence by a three-ring binder or database full of rules. The processes inspired by CMM, ISO 9001, and TQM were often just put on shelves and forgotten. (Boehm and Turner, page 6) On the other hand, people are inspired by things like cultures and goals.

Hard: Documenting processes and knowledge well is really hard because good documentation takes more time and effort than almost anyone has patience for. While most software engineers can type, in our experience, very few take the time and energy to write well.

Judgements

Since rules cannot document all of the problem-solution pairs for coping with the actual situations and surprises that will occur in the next project, everyone also needs judgement. Judgements both fill in the gaps between rules and work around the errors within rules.

Technical Examples: Bertrand Meyer wrote "sometimes it is better to fix each problem and sometimes it is better to move on." (Meyer, page 76) But, choosing which is best in each specific situation requires judgement. To fix bug "abc," one could type line of code x here or line of code y there, but deciding which is best requires judgement.

Social Examples: Susan Neiman writes "deciding how to treat someone is enormously complicated." (Neiman, page 193) As programs become more user-oriented, social interactions with end users matter more and developers need better social judgement. But, developers often do social work much more poorly than technical work. For example in CRM projects, talking with users in the sales and support departments differs greatly from talking with colleagues in the IT department. The conversation skills that put users at ease and evoke meaningful information won't ever come from scripts.

Think for Yourself: Susan Neiman writes "How do you use good judgement? Think for yourself." (Neiman, page 199) "Without judgement, you don't know how to apply the principles you know." Good judgement is common sense and stupidity is lack of judgement. (Neiman, pages 192 to 198) When decisions matter, everyone should use their judgements and best guesses. They should also be aware and honest that they do so and perhaps should also get colleagues to collaborate on or review their work.

History

Throughout history, many people have argued that judgement matters more than rules. In *Phaedrus*, Plato said "if men learn [writing], it will implant forgetfulness in their souls. What you have discovered is a recipe not for memory, but for reminder. And it is no true wisdom that you offer your disciples, but only its semblance. For the most part, they know nothing." In the 1700s, Emmanuel Kant wrote that judgement is what links general principles with specific situations, i.e. theory with practice. (Neiman, pages 192 to 198) Charles McCabe wrote, "Any clod can have the facts; having opinions is an art." The pattern and script movements have created tsunamis of rules and practitioners increasingly feel overwhelmed and recognize the need for judgement.

Both

In general, software engineers need both rules and judgements.

Rules: Rules remain essential for sharing knowledge and training. A searchable database of scripts can provide hints for coping with new situations, when someone else has encountered similar problems in the past. Neiman argued that examples are crucial for developing judgement and script databases document many such examples. (Neiman, pages 192 to 198) Daniel Kahneman and Amos Tversky noted that human judgement is fraught with systemic bias, and so everyone should use rules whenever they can. (Lewis, pages 174 to 176)

Judgements: Judgements must always override rules and scripts. Software engineers must always decide whether and when to apply each rule, which requires judgement. Many situations encountered in typical projects lie beyond the documented rules and judgement enables analysts, programmers, and testers to cope.

Organizations

Factories

Structure: Factory processes (like Cleanroom and Rational Unified Process) attempt to improve productivity, quality, and control within projects by imposing structure on both the workers and the work.

Offices: Factories embed workers within large, office-based organizations. Before the Internet, offices were essential for making software because people went to offices to access shared computers and to communicate with colleagues. Offices also enabled people to separate work and home life.

Capital: From the dawn of computing through the 1990s, computers and software tools (and especially CASE tools) were expensive. Factories provided these expensive tools to workers, which was capitalism at its finest. Even today, Google and Microsoft build their own supercomputers for analyzing web data and training neural networks.

Workers are Cogs: Bertrand Meyer noted that cross-functional teams can be difficult for managers, who would rather have the flexibility to assign workers wherever they want. (Meyer, page 81) Managers and HR personnel hate the "purple squirrel" problem of having to find a different worker for each distinct, unique position. Defining ideal workers as interchangeable cogs simplifies the work for managers and HR personnel.

Certifications Reinforce the Status Quo: Boehm and Turner note that training, certifications, and professionalism concern developing and proving proficiency at the common skills that everyone should know, which enables managers to assign workers to tasks freely. (Boehm and Turner, page 12) Certifications and professionalism reinforce the presumption that workers are interchangeable cogs.

Metrics Reveal Reality: In meritocracies, people want to distinguish between those who do good work and those who are merely pals with the boss. Metrics (like SCAMPI) attempt to reveal the truth of productivity and quality objectively.

Rigid Class Distinctions: Distinguishing between those who control a factory and those who work in a factory exaggerates class distinctions between managers and developers, and so managers naturally prefer factories to enhance their statuses.

Leaders Plan: In a deterministic world, the future is predictable, so plans and estimates can be and should be accurate. Leaders at the upper levels of projects and organizations use plans and architectures to predict and control the future.

Workers Follow: In a deterministic world, workers resemble actors following scripts by William Shakespeare, musicians following scores by Ludwig von Beethoven, or construction workers following blueprints by Philip Johnson. Ideal workers strive to follow the lead of managers and architects and to meet expectations and standards.

Workshops

Flexibility: Workshops provide flexible spaces for artisans to collaborate and to respond to whatever challenges arise. Denning and Martell recently wrote, "Good programming is an artisan skill developed with good training and years of practice." (Denning and Martell, page 97)

Gigs: As inexpensive high-speed internet access and software tools have become widely available, programmers can work independently of factories. They can work remotely from almost anywhere in the world, increasingly from coffee shops or home offices. In the gig economy, practitioners increasingly work project to project. Everyone takes their phones and computers home, so separating work and home life becomes more difficult.

No Capital: Today, everyone uses tools and practices for nearly free. As the prices of computers and software tools have plummeted, more and more practitioners can afford to acquire their own toolkits. In the late-1970s, $2000 bought a personal computer – much less today. Free and inexpensive software tools, such as the GNU toolchain, Java, Eclipse, and Github, are available to everyone and they facilitate open-source projects. Documentation about contemporary practices is widely available online. In many projects today, developers provide their own resources, often called Bring Your Own Device (BYOD). However, artisans remain unable to do capital intensive projects on their own.

Workers are Snowflakes: Every worker has unique strengths that should be exploited by cross-functional teams. As each practitioner gains experience in his or her own situation-specific ways, those skills slowly become more specialized and idiosyncratic. (Ambler) Ideal workers differ for each project. Skill at the current project, which matters most, cannot be measured by metrics or proven by credentials.

Experience and Enthusiasm: Humans are limited by their abilities to learn what they need to learn to adapt and overcome new situations that they do not yet understand. Both experience and enthusiasm contribute to effective solutions. Unfortunately, resumes and certifications cannot reveal whether anyone has the experience and drive necessary to contribute effectively to any given project.

Metrics Distort Reality: No metric has ever inspired anyone to excellence, not even SCAMPI. All metrics must be gamed because anyone who doesn't play the game gives their rivals a leg up. Metrics distort reality because the artificial game becomes the new reality. One problem is that the same people tend to excel at playing each particular game, and so the same people always appear to perform best when judged by any given metric. Within each organization, performance awards tend to reinforce the status quo, which can seem unfair and demoralize everyone else. Tweaking metrics to give other people a chance increases the politics and tends to make everyone mad.

Murky Class Distinctions: In artisan workshops, the divisions of labor and class distinctions between managers and workers are murky and fluid, so programmers naturally prefer workshops to enhance their statuses.

Everyone Engages: In an emergent reality, everyone struggles to keep their feet as the ever-changing world tries to shake them loose. During projects, they strive to deal with the changes that get revealed as ongoing and seemingly-random surprises. Project team members resemble actors in improv theaters, musicians in jazz bands, athletes on basketball courts, or rafters on rapids. Everyone tries to contribute to the group and to solo in turn. Even working on a single task resembles surfers riding waves or cowboys riding broncos. Constraints always exist, but individual choices matter and they add up fast. Ideal workers strive for appropriateness and timeliness.

Both

Everyone wants practitioners to focus on the work and so, in general, software-development organizations should function both as factories and as workshops.

Factories: Everyone wants the large-scale division of labor of factories for project assignments and payroll. For example in CRM projects, team members want to avoid the politics of defining projects and to avoid the sales and business aspects of acquiring resources. In addition, capital remains essential for paying salaries.

Workshops: Within most projects, team members behave as workshop artisans to do the work. Artisans bring their experiences and enthusiasms to each project, filling in and helping each other to do whatever needs to be done.

Management

Scientific

Scientific management works better for projects that are primarily opportunity-bound and have ample resources. It emphasizes reductionistic and fully-funded projects.

Reproducing Existing Products: Scientific management seems most effective when reproducing existing products, such as when expanding from making one copy of a product to making many copies. The only way to accurately plan projects is to do them twice so that the second time around, everyone can start with reasonable expectations. For example, industrial engineers can have reasonable expectations when they expand from making one car to making many cars. Software administrators can have reasonable expectations when they expand from installing a program on one computer to installing it on many computers. Scientific management primarily sustains the status quo.

Perfecting means Doing Everything: Scientific management judges quality relative to perfection. Ideally, projects would give all users everything that they want and make them totally happy. Omitting even one feature lowers satisfaction. Ideally, analysts, developers, and testers would do all possible activities (planning, designing, inspecting, tracing, testing, and so on) for every single detail, regardless of size or risk, tracking down and fixing every last possible flaw. Omitting even one step (like requirements tracing or regression testing) opens up opportunities for error.

Top-Dog Strategy: Top dogs strive to use their resources as entry barriers to block competitors from succeeding. They strive to convince competitors to play the same resource-driven game. The SEI persuaded Europe to fund the ESI for a while, but they were unable to hoodwink Japan. Only India (Tata) had enough low-cost manpower and experience with bureaucracy to beat the SEI at their own game.

Quality is Free: Capers Jones and Watts Humphrey were both inspired by Philip Crosby's book *Quality is Free*. Jones argued that improving quality would lower cost, which works in deterministic contexts, like factories.

History

The concept of Scientific management came most notably from the United States. After World War 2, the U.S. had the only developed economy whose industry remained intact. For decades thereafter, it maintained a huge resource advantage compared to all other economies.

Frederick Taylor was an American mechanical engineer and steel-plant manager interested in industrial efficiency who advocated for scientific management in the late 1800s. Henry Ford applied the factory model to automobile production in the early 1900s, which succeeded because the reasons for putting the engine and seats into each car are mostly alike. Watts Humphrey applied the factory model to software development in the late 1900s, which failed because the reasons for putting each line of code into a program are mostly different.

Lean

Lean management works better for projects that are primarily resource-bound and yet have ample opportunities, for example where many different solutions could work. When limited resources must satisfy vague aspirations or enormous expectations, projects are effectively resource-bound and they can only provide partial or short-term solutions.

Creating New Projects: Lean management seems most effective when creating innovative or new products, such as when expanding from zero copies of a product to one copy. Resource limitations occur frequently in startup companies that struggle to create new products, so many entrepreneurs use variations on the Lean Startup methodology. (Wikipedia, "Lean Startup") Lean management primarily facilitates emergence.

Satisficing means Doing Only the Most Important Things: Lean management judges quality relative to failure and emphasizes the pragmatics of satisficing or doing good enough work for now, for this specific situation. For example, satisficers may provide partial solutions; they may address the symptoms rather than the underlying problems; or they may provide cheaper short-term solutions rather than more expensive long-term solutions. When problems are resource-bound, managers and developers must continually make hard choices – to solve the highest-priority, most-important issues now and to defer or cancel everything else.

Satisficing contradicts many of the ideals of perfection and correctness. Users always want as many features and as much quality as they can get, which means more than developers can possibly deliver. Users will grumble about all finished programs because no matter when development stops, someone will still want more. Dropping any feature reduces functionality. Dropping any step increases opportunities for error. For example, developers may only do tracing and regression testing on the most critical components. But, resource-bound projects simply cannot afford to do everything and so projects necessarily drop a lot of features and steps. Projects are abandoned when resources run out, rather like proverbial novels and movie scripts.

Underdog Strategy: Underdogs rarely have many resources and often have little more than determination. To succeed and upset the status quo, they must endure and strive to exploit the opportunities that arise. Toyota proves that Lean can also work as a top-dog strategy.

Quality is Expensive: Software quality corresponds to more features and fewer bugs. The ongoing maintenance that improves quality, invariably costs a lot. Brian Randell has noted that many software applications are only usable after the third release, such as Windows or Office or Salesforce, which shows just how hard and expensive quality really is. (Randell)

History

The concept of Lean management came most notably from Japan when resources were scarce. Before World War 2, the Japanese economy was still developing rapidly and, after World War 2, it was devastated. Throughout the mid-twentieth century, Japanese companies needed to find their own ways to compete and they learned to thrive by using pragmatic, flexible, opportunistic processes.

Lean may have started as early as 1934 when Toyota produced its first car, though Lean was most famously used in the decades after World War 2. Lean started as a manufacturing practice more than half a century before it started as a software practice. • In 1986, Hirotaka Takeuchi and Ikujiro Nonaka (two Japanese business professors working the United States) shared their concept of Scrum processes in *Harvard Business Review*. (Takeuchi and Nonaka) Scrum started as a business practice for product development nearly a decade before it started as a software practice.

Both

In general, everyone wants quality, but depending on their specific situations, they want or can tolerate different combinations of perfection and good enough. In other words, most projects need both some Scientific and some Lean quality.

Scientific: In our experience, all software projects have some core functionalities that must get implemented exactly right in the Scientific sense. Web-API callouts usually must work exactly right to work at all. And, developers should close all major security holes.

Lean: In our experience, all software projects encounter hidden expectations, changes in goals, mistakes in planning, and so on. In effect, users and managers always want more features and quality than their initial budgets and schedules allow. In our experience, all software projects have at least some flexibility in the requirements that should be delivered. Everyone should satisfice appropriately and use their limited resources as well as they can to maximize the benefits to users.

Design

Reductionism

In a deterministic and non-fractal world, reductionistic approaches to design often work. In reductionistic systems, the whole equals the sum of the parts and so project plans can fully describe a fixed series of known, discrete tasks that encompass all of the work. Plans and estimates based on decomposition into parts should be accurate.

Small, Robust, Known: Reductionism requires that projects and systems be relatively small, i.e. that they have relatively few and relatively large parts. It requires that interfaces are stable and robust so that changes and errors can be localized. It requires that no unknown unknowns exist, so that significant surprises cannot occur. These conditions occur most often in small systems with few top-level parts, like toys, or in enduring systems that have the well-developed internal structures, like cars.

Toy Examples: Toys and activities for children are usually reductionistic. Paint-by-number sets, Lego blocks, and jigsaw puzzles all constrain the possibilities for success and for failure by restricting the top-level to few and large parts.

Automobile Example: Automobile factories are reductionistic. Automobile factories are more than a century old and cars have well-developed and stable internal structures. The steps of an assembly line that build whole cars include welding the frame; painting the sheet metal; and adding the engine, seats, and tires. Automobile factories have a couple hundred steps at most. Engines, tires, and seats are relatively large components that have stable and robust interfaces and that get built in other, simpler factories. Factories can now easily swap out paints, engines, and tires from one car to the next. Opportunities for error are limited on an assembly line yet, even so, automobile factories have stations to detect and fix problems.

Software Example: Factory and Waterfall processes embody reductionism by breaking projects into discrete stages or steps that fully encompass all work. Machine-oriented and embedded programs that do encryption, signal processing, and compiling have small and stable interfaces. Compilers have well-understood components (like lexers, parsers, symbol tables, and code generators) as documented in the Dragon books. (Aho, Lam, Sethi, Ullman)

Stable Contexts: Determinism and reductionism idealize shopping or selecting among existing parts. Component-based development idealizes assembling programs from a catalog of parts, like Erector sets.

Holism

In an emergent world, reductionistic approaches to design don't work. Kurt Koffka defined holistic systems with "the whole is different than [or more than] the sum of the parts." Taking a holistic system apart changes something important. When goals are vague or missing or cannot be reduced to a small number of discrete, existing parts, then plans and estimates cannot be accurate.

Large, Sensitive, Unknown: Holism tends to occur for relatively large systems, i.e. systems that have relatively many or relatively small parts. It tends to occur when using new components that lack robust and stable interfaces, so changes and errors can easily ripple throughout the system. (Hughes, page 7) It tends to occur when many unknown unknowns exist. Until these unknown unknowns are revealed, developers cannot deliberately set out to solve them. These conditions occur most often for large systems that have many top-level parts and for new systems that have poorly-defined internal structures.

Tool Examples: Tools and activities for adults are often holistic. Artists confronted with a blank canvas and a palette of oils could paint almost anything. Writers confronted with a blank page and a word processor could type almost anything. Adult tools and activities expand the possibilities for success and failure as far as possible.

Software Example: Most programs have many, many lines of code and each line of code must work exactly right. In 10k-line programs, lines of code are relatively small compared to whole programs. There are many, many ways that source codes can go wrong. In almost all software projects, requirements and architectures are sketches that have many unstated, ambiguous, or misstated details, in other words many unknown unknowns. Large programs are actually large systems that have too many potential problems to guarantee avoiding or fixing them all.

History: Herbert Simon noted that after World War 1, gestalt, holism, and creative evolution were developed. After World War 2, feedback and general systems theory were developed. More recently, in the 1980s, chaos and adaptive systems were developed. (Simon, page 169)

Evolving Contexts: Refinement and holism work best for programs that respond to evolving contexts, such as competitive markets and customizations. Customization means doing new work that does not already exist in the code-base. The new work is often used just once.

Both

In general, software projects should have both reductionistic and holistic elements.

Reductionism: Reductionism means that developers can effectively organize large source codes into semi-independent pieces. Without some reductionism, large software projects would be "big balls of mud," too complicated and expensive to attempt.

Holism: Holism means that programs are more than the sum of their parts and that the synergy between different parts provides emergent benefits to users. If software were completely reductionistic, there would be few benefits to building large programs and small Unix programs combined with pipes could solve all problems.

Notes

The Lamppost Problem

The IEEE SWEBOK and CSDP (or PSEM), like all standards and certifications in complex fields, suffer from the Lamppost problem. One searches for one's lost car keys near a lamppost because everything near the lamppost is visible in the light and known and everything else is invisible in the dark and unknown. Everything described in SWEBOK and tested by CSDP is correct and important and everything else does not exist or, in other words, is effectively wrong or unimportant.

Emphasizing Determinism: SWEBOK links professionalism, accreditation, and licensing with determinism. (SWEBOK, section 11.1) All topics in a body of knowledge must have known and correct answers so that someone can document, teach, and test them, which is why SWEBOK focusses on existing tools and rules. SWEBOK states that everything important about software engineering is already known and enumerated in SWEBOK and other IEEE standards. (SWEBOK, appendix B)

Ignoring Emergence: SWEBOK and CSDP effectively deny that emergent concepts (such as skills and judgements) matter. Since CDSP never expires, it effectively claims to tests for all knowledge that will ever be needed by anyone on the project. But, emergent concepts cannot be documented, taught, or certified because nobody knows what they are, yet. The editors cannot acknowledge that emergent concepts matter because that would mean that SWEBOK and CSDP do not reveal everything that professionals need to know.

Developer Questions: How should one cope with the vagaries of real projects? What will change during a project? What errors will occur during a project? What new technologies will arise? What should one do when users cannot articulate their needs? What should one do when users are unrealistically demanding? What should one do when project funding gets cut in half or overruns get revealed?

Manager Questions: How should one motivate team members? Do you challenge, demand, ignore, engage, bust chops, bribe, plead, what? What should one do if a team member has spring fever? What should one do if a team member is going through a divorce? What should one do if two or more developers want the same promotion, given that the losers often quit?

The answers to all of these questions are "it depends on the specific situation and the specific people involved" and the solutions are simply impossible to document, teach, or certify. Skills, judgments, enlightened management, and dealing with unknowns are deemed unimportant in SWEBOK and are untested in CSDP. They effectively deny that hard problems, unknown unknowns, and emergence exist.

SWEBOK and CSDP Cannot Predict the Future

The Future of Individuals: Certifications presume that tests from the past do signify whether someone will contribute to the successful projects of the future. "Professional certification also can verify the holders' ability to meet professional standards and to apply professional judgement." (SWEBOK, page 11-3) Professional judgement is defined by an exam about the contents of SWEBOK.

The Future of Projects: In fact, certifications like CSDP do reveal that someone did a lot of work in the past, which can be an excellent heuristic that they will also do well in the future, but it doesn't actually reveal what will happen on any given project because nothing can do so. CSDP doesn't reveal whether anyone will have the necessary flexibility, imagination, enthusiasm, and grace under pressure. SWEBOK actually claims that people can resolve all uncertainties by consulting textbooks, journals, colleagues, and stakeholders, or through some magical form of "risk management." (SWEBOK, page 11-10)

The Future of the Profession: The authors of SWEBOK describe ideas that were true in the past and they presume that those ideas will accurately describe software engineering until the next update, usually ten years later.

The authors of SWEBOK should be proud of their efforts because it took a lot of work and it usefully describes a large chunk of software engineering. But they should not be too proud because SWEBOK ignores the emergent half of the profession and, on average, half of what they do describe is wrong because it expires in half-life patterns. We find it interesting that ancient Chinese civil service exams had open-ended essay questions to evoke judgement while CSDP and PSEM exams are multiple guess to minimize judgement.

Perception is Reality

Whether determinism and emergence are "realities" or "concepts of reality" is actually irrelevant to this chapter. In the first draft, we described determinism and emergence as "realities," however almost every reviewer gave us grief. So in this draft, we describe determinism and emergence as "concepts of reality" because that seems the easiest way to avoid those objections.

However, we actually believe that determinism and emergence are "realities" rather than "concepts of reality" because we believe that "perception is reality." According to psychologists, people perceive the world through their mental models, so beliefs are tools like telescopes and microscopes that enable people to perceive and to manipulate their environments. Beliefs influence what people expect is possible and what they believe should be done.

One reviewer argued that "factories and agile are ideas and ideas are there to serve purposes." We would agree, except that those ideas influence perceptions and expectations and so those ideas also define realities. Too many conflicting ideas about software engineering are floating around for anyone to coherently wrap their minds around all of them at once. The subset of possible ideas that anyone actually believes defines his or her reality, so every software engineer effectively lives in his or her own unique reality. The folks at the SEI value managers and architects and planning. We (the authors) value programmers and coping. They value different things than we do and so they live in different realities than we do.

A common ground state that underlies both determinism and emergence may actually exist, like a computer that can underlie both an embedded system and a video game. However, we didn't bother looking for it. Philosophers and scientists have been debating determinism and emergence for at least two and a half millennia and they haven't found such a ground state yet, so we wouldn't expect to find one either.

People Don't Only Believe One Thing

We use quotes to show that at one point or another someone articulated each specific idea. We do not mean to imply that anyone held only that single point of view. All quotes are taken out of context and may not accurately express the intentions of the authors.

Most Believe in Both: Most people seem to believe in both determinism and emergence. Confucius emphasized determinism in his rituals and yet he also supposedly said, "study the past if you would define the future," which some have been interpreted as support for emergence, though we do not. Laozi emphasized emergence, but his observations about accepting change also apply to accepting one's fate in a deterministic world. Aristotle believed in a deterministic universe driven by clockwork mechanics and also in an emergent universe driven by chance events. Tony Hoare is mostly known for his work on algorithms and formal verification, which align with determinism. Yet, he also wrote, "the most important property of a program is whether it accomplishes the intentions of its user," which aligns with emergence. (Tedre, page 72)

Most Change Their Minds: Most everyone changes their minds from time to time. For example while writing the first draft of this chapter, we associated patterns with emergence because they were developed at around the same time and by the same people who developed early Agile processes. But after hearing a researcher at Microsoft comment on some of the problems with patterns, we came to associate patterns with determinism. In the first draft of this chapter, we argued that Agile and emergence had vanquished Waterfall and determinism. But, Robert Schaefer and Will Tracz pointed out the continuing value of Waterfalls and determinism. After getting their feedback and reading the books *The Path* and *Trying Not to Try*, we changed our minds. (Puett and Gross-Loh) (Slingerland) In the second draft, we attempt to support both equally. We suspect that many others change their minds on occasion, too.

As Determinism Grows, Emergence Also Grows

The Basic Level Rises Continually: The basic level is the relationship between analysts, developers, and testers and their algorithms, tools, and practices. Since the mid-1940s, the basic level for programming has risen steadily. Programmers changed from using cables and switches on the ENIAC to using machine code on the SSEM to using Fortran on the IBM 704 to using Java on Android. Programmers developed algorithms, data structures, abstract data types, operating systems, libraries, patterns, IDEs, code repositories, processes, and reuse. The basic level will continue to rise as long as algorithms, tools, and practices continue to improve.

Shallow Technologies: As software technologies rise in level and mature, they become shallower. Shallow technologies in CRM projects enable administrators and developers to focus more on what the users want rather than on how the software works. In contrast, classic government and commercial projects often do deeper and trickier things with technologies.

Some Existing Programs Become Easier: As the basic level rises, some programs that solve older, known problems should get simpler and easier. New algorithms and commonly-used components slowly migrate into standard libraries. As these libraries improve, developers can rely on them, rather than rolling their own. Programs should slowly evolve to contain less algorithm and more glue. As databases improve, programs should slowly evolve to rely more on dynamic query optimizers. Suzanne Sluizer noted that contemporary programmers do more integration than innovation. • Denning and Martell wrote "The best methods [of design] have been encoded into the structures of languages and operating systems" (Denning and Martell, page 198) We would add that the best methods are also encoded into practices like processes and scripts.

Some Existing Programs Become More Complete: As the basic level rises, many improvements in technology enable developers to change from doing things inconsistently in emergent ways to doing them consistently in deterministic ways, even when the total work increases. • GUI programs tend to be much larger than command-line programs because they enable flexible interactions and meaningful visual expressions. Quality improves as these programs become more useful and complete and handle more errors more effectively. As the basic level rises, user-oriented programs tend to get larger.

More Emergence Become Possible: However, improving tools and practices (i.e. making existing programs easier and more complete) differs from getting closer to knowing everything. As the basic level rises, the emergent possibilities of software engineering also continue to increase and the power and scope of programs continue to rise. More improvements to programs are possible today than ever before. For example, sponsoring organizations have always found new opportunities to write bigger, more powerful programs that integrate on larger and larger scales. We expect that bigger and bigger programs will always get written. We believe that current CRM systems could not even be envisioned if programmers were still struggling to write machine code.

The improving-tools-and-practices fallacy occurs whenever someone thinks that solving an outstanding problem (such as improving tools or standards) will reduce the problems that remain. As the basic level rises, our concepts of reality and of software engineering rise. As expectations of science and society change, expectations of programs also rise.

Odds and Ends

Inspiration: The panel "The Algorithmic View of the Universe" in the *Alan Turing Centennial Conference* inspired our epiphany that deterministic concepts from computation had already strongly influenced society with processes and metrics.

Eurocentric: The history in this chapter is mainly Eurocentric. Alas, we don't know enough about the history of philosophy and technology in the Middle East, India, and China to broaden the references. We hope that software engineers from those regions will do so.

Irony: Using a reductionistic, facet-by-facet analysis to describe emergence is ironic and wrong. This chapter merely contains a list of observations about emergence.

Boehm: Working on this chapter has increased our respect for Barry Boehm's work. Barry Boehm and Richard Turner wrote the first book about combining agility and discipline. (Boehm and Turner) Barry Boehm also presaged aspects of Agile with the Spiral model.

Dialectical: Each section resembles Georg Hegel's Dialectical method of thesis, antithesis, and synthesis, except that we don't actually synthesize anything into unified wholes.

Vocabulary: Three words used in this chapter have multiple meanings, which may confuse some readers. The word "script" means both "code that glues algorithms together" in the Scripts Program Description section and "article about knowledge" in the Rules Practices section. The word "complexity" means both "fractals and chaos" in the Fractal Geometry section and the computer science concept of "inherent difficulty" in the Unbounded Knowledge section. The word "induction" means both "generalizing from examples" (or more specifically "generalizing from statistical truth") and "a proof technique used in mathematics."

Partial Bibliography

Alfred V. Aho, Monica S. Lam, Ravi Sethi, Jeffrey D. Ullman, *Compilers*, Addison Wesley, 2006.

Scott Ambler, "The Disciplined Agile Enterprise: Harmonizing Agile and Lean," www.youtube.com/watch?v=QyHWeiBIOoY/, 2016.

Jurgen Appelo, *Management 3.0*, Addison Wesley, 2011.

Samuel Arbesman, *The Half-Life of Facts*, Penguin, 2012.

Elan Ariel, "Memory and Decision Processes," Wharton School, May 14, 2014.

Thomas Bayes and Richard Price, "An Essay towards Solving a Problem in the Doctrine of Chances," in *Philosophical Transactions*, volume 53, pages 370 to 418, 1763, Royal Society.

Kent Beck and Ward Cunningham, "Using Pattern Languages for Object-Oriented Program," OOPSLA, 1987.

Barry Boehm and Richard Turner, *Balancing Agility and Discipline*, Addison Wesley, 2003.

Frederick P. Brooks, Jr., *The Mythical Man-Month, Anniversary Edition*, Addison Wesley, 1995.

Brene Brown, *Daring Greatly*, Avery, 2013.

Philip B. Crosby, *Quality is Free*, Mentor, 1979.

Ole-Johan Dahl, Edsger Dijkstra, and Tony Hoare, *Structured Programming*, Academic Press, 1972.

Edgar G. Daylight, *The Dawn of Software Engineering*, Lonely Scholar, 2012.

Richard De Millo, Richard Lipton, and Alan Perlis published "Social Processes and Proofs of Theorems and Programs," in *CACM*, volume 22, issue 5, pages 271 to 280, ACM, 1979.

Peter J. Denning and Craig H. Martell, *Great Principles of Computing*, MIT, 2015.

Edsger W. Dijkstra, *A Discipline of Programming*, Prentice Hall, 1976.

Carol Dweck, *Mindset*, Ballantine, 2007.

Sandra Eibenberger, Stefan Gerlich, Markus Arndt, Marcel Mayor, and Jens Tüxen, "Matter-Wave Interference with Particles Selected from a Molecular Library with Masses Exceeding 10000 AMU," *Physical Chemistry Chemical Physics*, volume 15, issue 35, pages 14696 to 14700.

Anders Ericson and Robert Pool, *Peak*, Eamon Dolan, 2016.

George Fairbanks, *Just Enough Software Architecture*, Marshall and Brainerd, 2010.

James Fetzer: "Program Verification: the Very Idea," *CACM*, volume 31, issue 9, pages 1048 to 1063, ACM, September 1988.

Susan Fowler, *Why Motivation Doesn't Work*, Berrett-Koehler, 2014.

Eric Gamma, Richard Helm, Ralph Johnson, John Vlissides, *Design Patterns*, Addison Wesley, 1994.

Malcolm Gladwell, *David and Goliath*, Little Brown, 2013.

Mark Haddon, *The Curious Incident of the Dog in the Night-time*, Vintage, 2004.

David J. Hand, *The Improbability Principle*, Scientific American, 2014.

Jamie Holmes, *Nonsense*, Crown, 2015.

Thomas P. Hughes, *Rescuing Prometheus*, Vintage, 1998.

Matthew Hutson, *The 7 Laws of Magical Thinking*, Plume, 2012.

Daniel Jackson and Mandana Vaziri, "Finding Bugs with a Constraint Solver," ISSTA, pages 14-25, 2000.

Daniel Jackson and Mandana Vaziri, "Checking Properties of Heap-Manipulating Procedures with a Constraint Solver," TACAS 2003.

Donald E. Knuth, *The Art of Computer Programming*, Addison Wesley, 2011.

Donald E. Knuth, *Fascicle 6: Satisfiability*, Addison Wesley, 2015.

Craig Larman and Bas Vodde, *Scaling Lean and Agile Development*, Addison Wesley, 2009.

Jacques Laskar and Mickaël Gastineau, "Existence of Collisional Trajectories of Mercury, Mars, and Venus with the Earth," in *Nature* 489, pages 817 to 819, June 11, 2009.

Nathan Leites and Charles Wolf, Jr., *Rebellion and Authority*, Rand, 1970.

Stanislaw Lem, *The Cyberiad*, Penguin, 1974.

Michael Lewis, *Undoing Project*, Norton, 2016.

Benoit B. Mandelbrot, *The Fractal Geometry of Nature*, 1983, Freeman.

Abraham H. Maslow, *A Theory of Human Motivation*, Martino Publishing, 2013.

Sharon Bertsch McGrayne, *The Theory that Would Not Die*, Yale, 2011.

Bertrand Meyer, *Agile!*, Springer, 2014.

Susan Neiman, *Why Grow Up?*, Farrar, Straus, Giroux, 2014.

Yuki Noguchi, "Autism Can Be an Asset in the Workplace," on NPR All Things Considered, May 18, 2016.

James B. Orlin, "Max Flows in *O(nm)* Time, or Better," STOC, 2013.

Leon Osterweil, "Processes are Software, Too," ICSE 1987.

Daniel H. Pink, *Drive*, Riverhead, 2009.

Michael Puett and Christine Gross-Loh, *The Path*, Simon and Schuster, 2016.

L.B.S. Raccoon, "The Chaos Model and the Chaos Life Cycle," in *Software Engineering Notes*, volume 20, issue 1, pages 55 to 66, ACM Press, January 1995.

L.B.S. Raccoon, "The Chaos Strategy," in *Software Engineering Notes*, volume 20, issue 5, pages 40 to 47, ACM Press, December 1995.

Brian Randell, keynote at ICSE 2018.

Hanna Rosin and Duncan Watts, "Radio: The Pattern Problem," on NPR Invisibilia, 46:42, March 13, 2018. (**verify**)

Winston W. Royce, "Managing the Development of Large Software Systems," in *Proceedings of IEEE WESCON*, pages 328 to 338, August 1970.

Mary Shaw, keynote at ICSE 2016.

Nate Silver, *The Signal and the Noise*, 2012, Penguin.

Herbert A. Simon, *The Sciences of the Artificial*, MIT Press, 1996.

Edward Slingerland, *Trying Not to Try*, Broadway, 2015.

Brian Cantwell Smith, *On the Origin of Objects*, MIT Press, 1996.

SWEBOK V3, https://www.computer.org/web/swebok/v3/.

Hirotaka Takeuchi and Ikujiro Nonaka, "New New Project Development Game," *Harvard Business Review*, January 1986.

Matti Tedre, *The Science of Computing*, Taylor and Francis, 2015.

Shankar Vedantam, "Predictably Unpredictable: Why We Don't Act Like We Should," on NPR Hidden Brain, October 23, 2017.

Shankar Vedantam, "The Trick to Surviving a High-Stakes High-Pressure Job? Try a Checklist," on NPR Hidden Brain, October 30, 2017.

Shankar Vedantam and Daniel Kahneman, "Daniel Kahneman on Misery, Memory, and our Understanding of the Mind," on NPR Hidden Brain, March 12, 2018.

Shankar Vedantam and Richard Thaler, "Predictably Unpredictable: Why we Don't Act Like We Should," on NPR Hidden Brain, October 23, 2017.

David Weinberger, *Too Big to Know*, Basic, 2011.

Virginia Vassilevska Williams, "Multiplying Matrices in $O(n^{2.373})$ Time," 2014.

Niklaus Wirth, *Algorithms + Data Structures = Programs*, Prentice Hall, 1976.

Niklaus Wirth, "Modula-2 and Oberon," in HOPL 3, 2005.

"The Algorithmic View of the Universe," in *Alan Turing Centennial Conference*, June 15 to 16, 2012.

8
Five Tides

Subtle changes can be hard to see on small scales. The long history of programming enables us to zoom out to reveal some of those changes. The Machine, Language, Waterfall, and Agile tides express some of the key paradigms or zeitgeists of programming over the past 70 years.

We originally wrote this chapter to explain why Waterfall processes came and went and why Agile processes are here, for now – in other words why Agile superseded Waterfall. Our main answer is that each captures a zeitgeist and that the transition from Waterfall to Agile corresponds to the shift from obsessing over determinism to tolerating emergence.

In the first two sections, we present a Stream and Tide model of the history of programming. And in the third section, we explain why everyone should be wary of this account.

Tides Express Periods of Stability

In figure 1, we depict the rises and falls of five tides of programming. Strictly speaking, the Machine and Language tides precede software engineering. However, they strongly influenced everything that followed and contemporary software engineers still respond to their legacies.

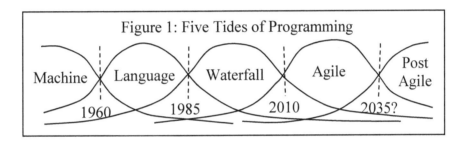

Machine

The Machine tide concerned the creation and evolution of modern electronic hardware, which at the time got all of the attention. Matti Tedre notes that the first two decades were about "mastering the machine." (Tedre, 126) In 1946, the first electronic computer combined both electronic and mechanical elements. By 1959, computers (like the IBM 7090) were fully transistorized and, by 1961, computers (like the IBM 7030 Stretch) had modern CPU architectures with speculative execution. The ENIAC and Stretch computers bracketed this tide.

Origins: In 1645, Blaise Pascal unveiled a working calculator called Pascaline. In 1833, Charles Babbage began working on the Analytical Engine, which he never completed. Mechanical calculators were built by Yazu Ryoichi in 1902, Kawaguchi Ichitaro in 1905, and Ohmoto Tarajiro in 1923. Konrad Zuse built a mechanical computer between 1935 and 1938. In 1944, the electromechanical Mark 1 became operational. And in 1946, ENIAC, the first electronic computer, became operational.

Separation of Hardware and Software: The Mark 1 was programmable with punch tape, but the distinction between hardware and software was murky because switches still needed to be flipped and cables still needed to be patched. (Evans, pages 32 to 33) ENIAC was programmed using switches, cables, and digit trays. The full separation of hardware from software only occurred with the ARC2 and SSEM computers in 1948. The word "software" wasn't even coined until halfway through this tide, perhaps by Paul Niquette or Richard R. Carhart in 1953.

Availability: Throughout the Machine tide, hardware became more widely available. Matti Tedre notes that the U.S. had a handful of computers in 1950, about 240 computers in 1955, and about 5,400 computers in 1960. (Tedre, page 106) It took into the late 1950s and early '60s for powerful computers to get into the hands of lots of programmers. Only then could software thrive.

Reliability: Matti Tedre notes that from 1945 to 1955, "it took heroic efforts to get computers to work at all." (Tedre, page 105) Throughout this tide, reliability improved so that users could focus on what the machines did rather than on the machines themselves.

Memory Size: The first computer memories were tiny and therefore programs were tiny. As computer memories grew, programs grew. Throughout this tide, computer memories roughly doubled in size every year, as shown in table 1. Memory sizes plateaued at 2k to 4k words through the mid-1950s and computers remained little more than oversized calculators. (Tedre, page 73) As core memories became available in the late-1950s, memory sizes surged forward again, finally making complex software possible.

Table 1: Memory Sizes			
Operational	**Machine**	**Length**	**Width**
1946	ENIAC	0 words	0 bits
1948	SSEM	32 words	32 bits
1949	EDSAC	256 words	18 bits
	BINAC	512 words	31 bits
	EDVAC	1k words	44 bits
1951	UNIVAC	1000 words	sign + 11 digits
1953	IBM 701	2k words	36 bits
	MIT Whirlwind	2k words	16 bits
1954	IBM 650	4k words	10 digits
	IBM 704	4k words	36 bits
1957	Electologica X1	32k words	27 bits
1958	RCA 501	64k words	32 bits
1958	AN/FSQ-7 (SAGE)	$4 \times 64k$ words	32 bits

Note that we omit most cryptography computers from this list. Also note that memories were often upgraded in the field, so they may have been larger in practice.

Women

Before hardware computers, humans carried out all computations by hand or with help from mechanical calculators. Starting in the late 1800s, these humans were called "computers." In the U.S. in the early 1900s, women came to do most of this work. In the U.S. during World War 2, thousands of women worked as computers using mechanical calculators. (Shetterly, pages 82 and 86) Computing was so much a woman's job that, mathematicians rated the first machines in terms of "girl-years" or "kilo-girls." (Evans, page 11)

After World War 2, the "girls" went from rivals of hardware to keepers of hardware. (Evans, page 25) Sadie Plant noted that women built, programmed, and operated the early hardware computers. (Evans, page 80) Women soldered and wired the components together. (Evans, page 41 to 42) Lady Ada Lovelace programmed Babbage's Analytical engine. Grace Hopper programmed the Mark 1. Kathleen Antonelli, Jean Bartik, Betty Holberton, Marlyn Meltzer, Frances Spence, and Ruth Teitelbaum programmed ENIAC. ENIAC even looked like a telephone switchboard. In 1947, NACA Langley got a Bell-Labs electronic calculator and put Sara Bullock in charge. (Shetterly, pages 137 to 138) EMCC hired some of these women to work on the BINAC and Univac computers. (Evans, page 56)

Economics: Organizations have always cared about labor costs. Some hardware computers, like Mark 1, were programmed and operated mainly by men. But, by 1954, labor costs exceeded computer costs. (Tedre, page 115) Since women in the U.S. were treated as sub-professional clerical workers and were paid half to two-thirds as much as men, women took over most hardware operation and programming.

Murky Goals: Compared with the difficult and glamorous hardware, everything else was supposed to be easy. (Hughes, page 55) However, during the 1940s and '50s, it was unclear what anyone should actually do. The women at EMCC performed a murky combination of operation, programming, and technical support. Programming wasn't separate from operation, so women could do it. (Evans, page 52) Betty Jean Jennings noted that if managers had known how complex programming would become, they might not have given it to women. (Evans, page 52)

Female computers always worked with hardware computers. Margot Lee Shetterly notes that female computers oversaw the hardware computations and double-checked the results. (Shetterly, page

138) Claire Evans notes "It seems only natural that human computers should train their own replacements." (Evans, page 42)

Thomas Hughes even argued that engineers "demeaned programming" by using women. (Hughes, page 55) We doubt that engineers actually gave programming that much thought. Claire Evans wrote "Women did the jobs nobody thought were important, until they were." (Evans, page 4) Peter Wegner noted that programmers were unimportant. (Tedre, page 105)

Matti Tedre notes that women became the real masters of programming. (Tedre, page 107) Most likely, women invented assemblers, libraries, code generators, and linkers and loaders. If Betty Holberton was not the actual first to write an assembler and assembler code (C-10 for BINAC) and to write program generators (sort-merge), then she was certainly among the first. (Evans, page 59) Grace Hopper wrote the first linker-loader (the A0 compiler) in 1951 and many more compilers that followed. (Evans, page 67) These women innovated out of sheer intellect, pragmatic necessity, and historical opportunity.

From Machine to Language – 1960

We put the transition from the Machine tide to the Language tide at about 1960, though we could also believe that it occurred in 1958 to match the emergence of high-level languages or in 1962 or '63.

After the Availability of Large, Reliable Computers: The rise of the Language tide could only occur after large computers became reliable and available. It took powerful processors and large memories to build and run sophisticated programs and compilers.

After the Awareness of Software: The rise of the Language tide could only occur after the awareness of both the importance of and the difficulties of developing software. A body of experiences, both good and bad, was essential for progress.

After the Fein Report: The rise of the Language tide should occur after the Fein report in 1959. (Tedre, page 43) Louis Fein argued that universities should focus on theory, rather than on technology. Peter Wegner noted that "it took until the 1960s before the emphasis [in computing education] had shifted [from hardware] to theory and mathematics." (Tedre, page 105)

After High-Level Programming Languages: The rise of the Language tide must occur after the creation of effective programming languages. The first four high-level languages (Fortran, Lisp, Algol, and Cobol) became operational between 1957 and '60 and they mark an important shift in emphasis from controlling machines to writing programs, perhaps the most important tipping point or paradigm shift ever in software.

Language

The Language tide concerns the creation and evolution of modern programming languages. Throughout this tide, languages evolved rapidly at both the statement and encapsulation levels. Compilers and optimizers improved correspondingly. The military languages Cobol and Ada and the academic languages Algol and Eiffel bracketed this tide.

Origins: Corrado Böhm wrote the first language compiler and Grace Hopper wrote the first linker and loader (the A-0 compiler) in 1951. The first conference on programming languages was held in 1954. (Daylight, page 22) John Backus developed the first Fortran compiler from 1954 to 1957. John McCarthy developed the first Lisp interpreter from 1956 to 1958. Algol was standardized in 1958 and 1960. The first Cobol and Algol compilers became available in 1960.

Statements: In 1958, Fortran II had *goto* and *for* statements. In 1960, Algol had *if* and *for* statements. PL/I provided a *do while* loop in 1966. Corrado Böhm and Giuseppe Jacopini published the Structured Program theorem in 1966, which showed that all code can be written using only *if* and *while* statements. Edsger Dijkstra published the essay "Go To Considered Harmful" in 1968. Algol 68 provided a clean *while* loop. Pascal and C, which had modern *if, while,* and *for* statements, were developed in 1969.

Encapsulation: Functions were provided by Fortran II in 1958 and recursive functions were provided by Algol in 1960. Modules were provided by C in 1969 and Modula in 1975. Objects were provided by Simula in 1967, Smalltalk in 1971, C++ in 1979, and Eiffel in 1985. The core of Eiffel is remarkably modern, presaging Java, Go, and other contemporary languages.

Structured Programming: The concept of structured programming was developed around 1969. Ole-Johan Dahl, Edsger Dijkstra, and Tony Hoare published their classic book *Structured Programming* in 1972. Structured programming promoted good abstractions rather than anti-goto. (Tedre, page 127)

Throughout the Language tide, hardware was still more important than software. Fred Brooks noted that even in the mid- and late 1960s, operating systems (like OS/360) were deemed much less important than computer hardware (like S/360). IBM could always sell the hardware, but often gave the software away. (Brooks, *Design of Design*, page 336)

Ad-Hoc, Artisan Practices

Matti Tedre states that software development during the 1950s was "anarchistic, free-wheeling, shoot from the hip." (Tedre, page 43) Hughes notes that, in the late 1950s and early 1960s, Lincoln engineers were surprised that the software for SAGE took as much effort as the hardware. (Hughes, pages 55 to 58) (Ceruzzi, page 56) Of course the ENIAC "girls" knew that programming was hard more than a decade earlier. (Tedre, pages 61 and 105) Throughout the Language tide, software was created by artisans applying what little they knew as best they could, learning as they went.

Emerging Professions

Throughout the Language tide, practice and theory improved steadily and computing slowly evolved into a coherent set of professions. The first volume of Donald Knuth's *The Art of Computer Programming* came out the same year as the first NATO conference on software engineering, which is probably more than mere coincidence.

Software Engineering: During this tide, people were mostly "programming" and only slowly becoming aware of the need for "engineering." Margaret Hamilton began discussing "software engineering" in 1963. (Hamilton) NATO sponsored the first conferences on software engineering in 1968 and 1969. Brian Randell argued that everyone used the concept of software engineering to justify whatever it was they were already doing, often with little justification. (Tedre, pages 121 to 122) So, the NATO conferences didn't change anything directly, though surely they stimulated progress. Royce published his classic essay on improving the Waterfall a year later in 1970.

Computer Science: During the 1950s, education was informal, independent, and apprentice-like. (Tedre, page 44) In 1959, about 150 colleges and universities in the U.S. offered computing courses, which largely focused on the hardware technology. (Tedre, page 41) The emphasis in education slowly shifted to software. The first computer-science departments were established at Cambridge in the U.K. in 1953 and at Purdue in the U.S. in 1962. Edsger Dijkstra began teaching programming at Eindhoven in 1962. Education in software improved rapidly after that. Throughout this tide, theory made huge leaps forward in algorithms, computability theory, and complexity theory.

From Female Computers to Female Programmers

The early 1960s "signaled the beginning of the end of computing as women's work." The early 1960s was the dividing line between women as computers and machines as computers. At NACA Langley instead of farming tasks out to "girls," Dorothy Vaughan sent them to the IBM 704. (Shetterly, page 205)

Women transitioned from computers to programmers from the mid-1950s through the early 1960s. (Shetterly, pages 144 to 145) At Langley, Dorothy Vaughan enrolled in programming classes in late-'50s and became a programmer around 1960. (Shetterly, pages 139 and 205) Mary Jackson took Fortran classes in the 1960s. (Shetterly, page 254) Melba Ray managed and Dorothy Hoover programmed the IBM 7090 in the early 1960s. (Shetterly, page 218)

Of course, many non-computer women were also recruited into programming. Throughout the 1960s, women comprised 30% to 50% of all programmers and they earned about 2/3 of what male programmers earned. (Evans, pages 76 and 77) Nyota Uhura from *Star Trek* and Gwen DeMarco from *Galaxy Quest* are pop-culture symbols of the many women who worked directly with hardware.

Male Programmers

Margot Lee Shetterly notes that around 1960, computing began to get increasing numbers of men. (Shetterly, page 205) As everyone began to understand that programming was a new profession, distinct from operation and customer support, men started taking over and women were increasingly segregated into Cobol or support roles. It seems likely that SDC hired mostly men to program SAGE. These men may also have been encouraged by the macho culture of the U.S. military, which sponsored many software projects of the era.

Engineering: Claire Evans claims that software engineering kicked women out of programming. "The more the discipline professionalized, the more it grew implicitly masculine." (Evans, page 78) At most companies, problems with pay discrimination and inadequate childcare actually drove women away, but software engineering and certifications signaled to women that they were no longer welcome. (Evans, pages 77 to 78) Many women programmers were self-taught and had family obligations, which made certifications difficult to obtain. Programming would become engineering, "rather than a rogue, wild-blooming field roamed by fiercely independent, self-directed misfits and women." (Evans, page 77)

Europe: One can also think of software engineering as the "Europeanization" of programming. European computers seem to have been programmed mostly by men. The NATO conferences were held in Europe to emphasize the ideals of men and no women were invited. (Evans, page 77) The new generation of male programmers in the U.S. imported Edsgar Dijkstra and Tony Hoare from Europe as professional role models to sidestep the influences of Betty Holberton and Grace Hopper. The strong personalities and rigorous ideals of men counterpointed the pragmatism of the women of the previous tide.

Crisis: The software crisis coincided with the long, slow decline of women in senior programming positions. The term "software crisis" was coined at the first NATO conference on software engineering and it fizzled out soon after the women had left.

Men benefitted economically from kicking women out, but the profession of software engineering probably did not. Sociology research shows clearly that diversity has many benefits for creativity and for understanding diverse groups of users. Yet software engineers deliberately chose homogeneity in the sixties and they still do in the teens. Women won't return to programming for many decades, if they ever do. The few high-profile women in the profession (like Grace Hopper, Margaret Hamilton, and Mary Shaw) obscured the fact that almost all other women left.

From Language to Waterfall – 1985

We lump the transition from the Language tide to the Waterfall tide at about 1985. David Grier also puts the rise of software maturity in 1985. (Grier) We observed that many software-development organizations started using Waterfall-inspired processes in earnest in the mid-1980s.

After Networks and Personal Computers: The Waterfall tide got rolling with the era of personal computers and networks (ethernets). The costs of hardware continued to plummet, while costs of software improved only slowly and so the costs of software became increasingly obvious. The transition from the Language tide to the Waterfall tide encompassed the shift from big hardware to big software.

After Empirical: The rise of the Waterfall tide occurred after the rise of experimental and empirical research in computer science. The NSF sponsored a workshop about "rejuvenating experimental computer science" in 1978 and the Feldman report about it appeared in 1979. (Tedre, pages 176 and 184) The "Discipline in Crisis" report by Peter Denning, AKA the "Snowbird Report" arguing that CS needed more empirical research, also appeared in 1979. (Tedre, page 185) Both reports implicitly advocated for statistical determinism in computing.

After TQM: The rise of the Waterfall tide occurred at about when Total Quality Management (TQM) became a world-wide fad in the mid-1980s. The economic rise of Japan was an obsession with U.S. business and government leaders. The TQM movement was inspired by the broadcast of "If Japan Can... Why Can't We?" in 1980. (NBC News) The book *Quality is Free* by Philip Crosby appeared in 1979, which inspired both Capers Jones and Watts Humphrey to apply statistical quality control to software.

Before CMM: The rise of the Waterfall tide most likely occurred before 1986 or 1988, when the CMM was first presented to the world.

Waterfall

The Waterfall tide concerns the creation and evolution of software factories. Everyone strove to develop software systematically in order to improve productivity and quality. The Factory model combined planning with defined processes and metrics to organize and control the hodge-podge of increasingly well-developed tools and practices.

The Waterfall tide reflected a combination of the frustrations (or desperations) centered around the increasingly large and complicated software projects and the hopes (or naivetés) centered around the rapidly improving tools and practices of the time. Big-business and big-government resorted to the authoritarian measures of defined processes and metrics in an attempt to force improvements. Advocates of factories (like Watts Humphrey and Capers Jones) promised simple, deterministic, reductionistic solutions.

Origins: Managers since the 1950s and '60s have complained about programmers. Programming occurred any which way. (Tedre, page 126) Programming was a "smorgasbord of sloppy practices."

(Tedre, page 126) Programming had an aura of mystique and was a free-wheeling black art. (Tedre, pages 106 and 108) In 1968, Dick Brandon described average programmers as excessively independent, mildly paranoid, egocentric, neurotic, schizophrenic, ruggedly individualistic, and non-conformist. (Tedre, page 109) Programmers are unmanageable – actors and artists are easier to manage. (Tedre, page 116) Matti Tedre notes that in the late 1960s, everyone was disappointed with the computing age. (Tedre, page 114) These complaints inspired the processes and metrics of the Waterfall era.

The Grass is Greener: Many people seemed to suffer from a "grass is greener" syndrome when comparing software to hardware. In "No Silver Bullet," Fred Brooks explained why the goal of a tenfold improvement in software productivity over 10 years to match similar improvements in hardware performance could never be met. More powerful hardware is a completely different kind of problem than more powerful software. Note also that CPUs have not improved noticeably since the late oughts and the shoe is now on the other foot.

Origins: The origins of Waterfall processes go way back. Matti Tedre notes that process models for programming started in the 1950s. (Tedre, page 121) Factory metaphors were discussed by Robert Bemer at the first NATO conference and by Winston Royce two years later. (Bemer) (Royce)

Capability and Quality: Waterfall corresponds to both capability and quality: the whole family of process and meta-process standards that include CMM, CMMI, TQM, Six Sigma, ISO 15504 (SPICE), ISO 9001, IEEE 12207, and DOD 2167. Capability seems more of a government concept. Quality seems more of an industry concept.

Written Knowledge: In 1987, Leon Osterweil argued that processes are software and Kent Beck and Ward Cunningham described software patterns. (Osterweil) (Beck and Cunningham) Both approaches treat programming skills as documentable, teachable, and testable knowledge.

Empirical and Experimental: The Waterfall tide emerged at about the same time as experimental and empirical research in computer science. In the 1980s and '90s, controlled experiments gained footing. (Tedre, page 185) Empirical validation in papers rose from 64% in 1985 to 81% in 1995. (Tedre, page 180) In the 1990s, empirical software engineering and meta-analysis became fashionable. (Tedre, pages 131 and 177) The maturity of algorithms in the 1980s led to approximation and empirical work that shed light on heuristics and practical implementations. The *Journal of Experimental Algorithms* began publishing in 1996. The use of empirical within research corresponds to the increasing use of metrics within industry. All empirical research and metrics attempt to predict the future based on statistical models of the past.

Determinism: We believe that the Waterfall era culminated 500 years of idealizing determinism as suggested by clockwork mechanics and spurred on again by computers and statistics. From 1968 to 2010 (the heyday of software engineering) and especially from the late 1980s to the late 1990s (the heyday of the SEI), managers wanted projects to be under control; they wanted programs to run close to the machine; they wanted programmers to be rational and behavioral; they wanted processes to be Waterfall and Factory(like ISO 9001, SPICE, and CMM); and they wanted certifications (like CSDP and PSEM) to reveal the characters of workers. CMM crested the wave of determinism that was nudged forward by computers and statistics.

The good-intention and anything-goes processes from the 1950s and '60s were the only alternatives worth considering, so the deterministic ideals of the Waterfall era made perfect sense at the time. Almost everyone in the 1980s would have created something similar to the CMM. Into the early 1990s, our (the authors') own efforts at understanding software development were also factory-like.

From Waterfall to Agile – 2010

We lump the transition from the Waterfall tide to the Agile tide at about 2010, though it could also have occurred earlier, say in 2005.

After the Agile Manifesto: The transition should occur after the 2001 Snowbird conference that wrote the Agile Manifesto.

Before the End of CMMI: The transition should occur before 2013 when the SEI half-heartedly dumped the CMMI. Many people and organizations still cling to deterministic Waterfall ideals. For example, the SEI still sponsors the CMMI Institute, PSP certifications, and an industry award that honors Watts Humphrey.

Agile

The Agile tide concerns the acceptance of unknowns and changes in software projects.

Proto-Agile Origins: Margaret Hamilton and her colleagues did iterative development at the system level in the 1960s. (Hamilton) The first proto-Agile processes were proposed in the 1970s and '80s. Peter Checkland proposed the Soft System Methodology (SSM) in the 1970s, which was flexible and lightweight. Rapid Application Development (RAD), which emphasized the use of Fourth-Generation Languages (4GLs) emerged in the 1980s. Its main innovations were to be small and fast, but it was still Waterfall in spirit and it had yet to consider and adopt many of the issues that have come to define Agile, such as accepting that users don't know exactly what they want and respecting the psychological and sociological needs of programmers. The emphases on traditional planning and motivation explain why we see SSM and RAD as not quite Agile. Yet, SSM, RAD, and other processes laid the groundwork for the true Agile processes that followed.

True-Agile Origins: True-Agile processes emerged in the mid-1990s. Dynamic Systems Development Method (DSDM), which began in the late 1980s as a refinement of RAD, was presented in 1994. Scrum and Extreme Programming were presented in 1995. Lean was presented in 2003. These processes provide frequent opportunities to change the goals of projects as new bits of information arise.

During the Agile tide, almost everyone accepted that factories just don't work very well because software projects change continually and going with the flow is often the best that anyone can do. Project managers and developers increasingly accept that project goals are murky and unbounded, requirements have never been precise, programmers are not robots, and on and on. Agile is a collection of pragmatic practices for coping with changes, errors, and unknowns that work well with today's CRM, cloud, mobile, and web projects. For example from psychological and sociological points of view, pair programming makes the work less lonely, it shares knowledge and skills about how to program well, and it ensures that all code gets reviewed at least once.

Metrics Waned: We realize now that metrics frequently reveal little that people don't already know. In "Measuring Software Productivity," Steve McConnell points out that managers already know which developers are most productive without metrics. In "Lies, Damn Lies, and Software Analytics," Margaret-Anne Storey points out that developers already know which modules of code need work without metrics. Metrics per se do not make significant differences in either productivity or quality. Metrics usually just put concrete numbers on otherwise known information. We learned once again that metrics often undermine productivity and quality because they increase gamification and other problems. (Muller)

However today, many companies seem to be pushing a new wave of statistical determinism based on big data. While we expect them to deduce many useful facts, they won't ever deduce everything that people want to know. Nate Silver argues that big data makes false positives worse. (Silver, page 253)

Emergence: We believe that the Agile era is a pragmatic response to accepting emergence as suggested by quantum mechanics. Since 2010, most software engineers have accepted that at least some parts of projects defy prediction and that some amount of emergence is inevitable. Programs like Microsoft Office, Google search, and Facebook run close to users and evolve continually and unpredictably. And managers at all levels of organizations increasingly aspire to enlightened practices.

Today, Agile presents an effective alternative to Waterfall. Agile could not have emerged back in the 1970s or '80s because the world did not work that way. The ideals of determinism and planning were still too strong, drowning out all other approaches. On the other hand if anyone were to recreate the CMM or CMMI today, they would create something completely different, something a lot more Agile. They could not do otherwise because emergence and irrationality can no longer be denied. For example in the book *Integrating CMMI and Agile Development*, Paul McMahon advocates a bottom-up approach to processes to help developers demonstrate what they do for their managers. (McMahon, page 23) Further, his entire book shows how to make CMMI more effective by adopting a variety of Agile techniques. Barry Boehm and Richard Turner make similar points. (Boehm and Turner)

From Agile to Post-Agile – 2035?

Continuing change in software engineering is inevitable. Based on the sequence of tides, we speculate that, sometime around 2035 or perhaps 2030, Agile will be eclipsed. The Post-Agile tide is a placeholder to remind us not to get attached to current perspectives.

Many people are already working to go beyond Agile. Discussions about "Post-Modern" software stem from 1998, "Wagilefall" stem from around 2006, and "Agilefall" stem from around 2010. The Scaled-

Agile processes SAFE, LESS, and DAD all stem from around 2005 to 2010. Bertrand Meyer offers many criticisms of existing practices in his book *Agile!* Searching for "agile is bad" on the web leads to many additional criticisms. To us, all of these proposals seem like fine tuning. We haven't seen any coherent visions that seem likely to drive a tidal change or paradigm shift, though we could be wrong. Yet, we suspect that today someone is already working on whatever the core of this tide will turn out to be.

Based on the ideas expressed in this book, our main prediction is that many more projects in the future will resemble CRM projects. That prediction hardly takes a leap, since many corporate and government systems have had large CRM components for decades. We expect that everyone will have more realistic expectations about unknowns, that more sponsoring organizations will fulfill their Bride-of-Agile obligations, that more project teams will combine deterministic and emergent practices, and that psychology and sociology will become more prominent. Note that ICSE 2018 had an entire track devoted to psychology and sociology.

We also expect that artificial intelligence will be used more prominently; that software engineers from across Asia will make many prominent contributions; and that all programs and databases will be defined as historical repositories. Since code repositories, database logs, and blockchain already exist, that hardly makes a leap. But those changes are mostly ignored explored in this book, so we will not comment further.

Streams Express Continuity

Streams link the techniques and goals that have always been important and will always remain so, even though each stream emphasizes different concepts in different times and the relative importance of each stream ebbs and flows. For example, there have always been and there will always be programs, tools and practices, project management, and factories. People have always striven to and will always strive to improve productivity and quality and to deliver more value to users.

Techniques

Programs: There will always be simple, computer-oriented programs and there are many niches where deterministic realities will endure, for example, in embedded programs and device drivers. Today, programmers write GPU code to drive graphics-hardware pipelines efficiently. Similarly, there have always been user interactions and user-oriented programs. Even the earliest programs needed some way to get results out to operators and users. GUIs will only get more sophisticated. Increasingly, everyone realizes that embedded systems work on behalf of people to extend the capabilities of people.

Tools and Practices: There have always been software tools and practices, and we expect that they will continue evolving and improving forever. Tools and practices began improving around 1950, with the first libraries, assemblers, linkers, loaders, and editors. They have improved steadily if in fits and starts ever since. Everyone has always been and will always be expected to use the latest tools and practices consistently and well.

Factories: There have always been and there will always be software factories. The factory metaphor lies at the heart of TQM, CMM, and ISO 9001. Today, both consulting companies and vendors (like Microsoft and Google) resemble factories, having pipeline stages like sales and marketing, development, and support. Yet, the factory metaphor that separates the analysis, development, and testing phases peaked in the 1990s and seems to be fading. Michael Cusumano wrote a treatise on the factory concept in 1989. (Cusumano)

Metrics: Metrics have always been with us. Grace Hopper used metrics to judge her A-0 compiler in 1952 (Tedre, pages 107 to 108). Interest in metrics peaked in the 1990s and 2000s. Jerry Muller documents many problems with metrics. (Muller) Though we hope that the hype is over, metrics will always remain a tool in the kit for managing software projects.

Project Management: There has always been and will always be project management, though the style has been slowly evolving from authoritarian to enlightened.

Certifications: Certifications for programmers existed in the early 1960s. (Tedre, page 121) Since then, college degrees for computer science and software engineering have been created as well as industry certifications (like Microsoft MCP and Salesforce) and professional certifications (like CSDP and PSEM).

Goals

Sponsoring Organizations: Over time, different people with different goals became involved with software. Sponsoring organizations shifted from military agencies in the 1950s to government and commercial work in the 1970s. By 2017, one-quarter of the world population carried a smartphone.

Client Relationships: Ideal programmers match the client and the clients have steadily evolved. In the 1940s and '50s, mathematicians and physicists, who had traditionally worked with female computers, felt comfortable working with female operators and programmers. In the 1960s and '70s, white male business managers and white male aerospace engineers (SAGE) wanted to work with white male programmers. Since the 1990s, web designers and social media companies have worked with people of all races and nationalities and increasingly work with programmers from around the world.

Productivity and Quality: Productivity and quality have always been important to users and project managers, and they always will be. Since hardware costs continue to plummet and hardware reliabilities continue to rise, software productivity and quality matter more now than ever. As the relative costs and values of machine-time, developer-time, and user-time have changed, everyone has prioritized different kinds of code, which drove a lot of the evolution of programs, technologies, and practices.

Value: Creating value for users has always been important and it always will be. In the 1940s and '50s, computers cranked out ballistic and trigonometry tables because it was more cost-effective and error-free than using the manual techniques of the time. Because the cost of hardware continues to plummet, providing software value to users matters more today than ever.

Directness: Originally, code was machine-oriented. Assembly and JCL were very specific with many, many details, but code has been steadily abstracting away from machines. During the Waterfall era, factories tended to emphasize productivity and quality, which are abstract concepts. In other words, the work that was being done was often indirect to the results that users could see. Agile emphasizes concrete value to users, who want to be able to see and understand the efforts that analysts and programmers are making and the features that they are delivering as directly as possible. Of course, nobody can control how visible or understandable any given feature or task is.

Labor Shortage: "In the late 1950s and early '60s, there was talk about a programming labor shortage." (Tedre, page 118) Boehm and Turner also refer to a shortage of skilled labor in the 2000s. (Boehm and Turner, page 12) Note that this same labor shortage also occurs in most other skilled professions, like medicine. Rural hospitals throughout the U.S. and the whole world are perennially understaffed. Managers will always find it easier to whine that they cannot hire the skilled programmers that they want than to fight the economic forces that cause the problem.

Pushing Limits: Projects will always push limits. Most projects push the limits of what analysts, programmers, and testers can do using contemporary tools and practices because easier projects would have already been solved using the simpler tools and practices of prior years.

Beware

Most of what passes for history in computing feels like mythology. Readers should be skeptical of all histories and especially of histories by raccoons and dogs. In our defense, a short chapter cannot possibly describe everything that happened over the last 70 years in software engineering. We only scratch the surface. We oversimplify because SE is such a huge field and so much has been forgotten. We caricaturize distinctions in order to clarify our ideas. Yet, we do hope to raise some points that merit attention.

The Historical-Determinism Problem

One premise of this chapter is that the times really do influence events, which is known as "historical determinism." But, everyone should beware of historical determinism because people's choices and actions also affect outcomes.

Much has been written about the dangers of historical or creeping determinism. "Those who write about events almost invariably give the outcome the appearance of inevitability, [which] is achieved by suppressing some facts at the expense of others." (Hallinan, page 64) "Our impulse to deny the unpredictability of the future favors neatening the past into a tidy narrative" (Holmes, page 226)

Psychologists note that people can rationalize anything. They also note that anchoring overvalues recent information, so recent history may be overvalued.

One problem with this chapter is that people really do make choices and their actions really do have tangible consequences. The advocates of Capability (like Watts Humphrey) and Quality (like Capers Jones) could have made other choices. But, the new ideas of emergent reality and irrational humanism had yet to become prominent enough to make such choices obvious or easy.

Historical determinism gives the folks at the SEI and the ESI (Technalia) an out, a chance to claim that history made them do what they did, that it isn't their fault that the CMM and SPICE were so wrong. The alternative is to believe that they naively or maliciously chose to ignore history and repeat the failures of the past, that they deliberately reapplied the ideas of Taylorism that had been discredited 50 years earlier and repeatedly since then. One could even argue that the Waterfall tide attempted to stave off the looming era of emergence and humanism.

Yet, we also believe that the CMM and SPICE were necessary experiments that reflected the choices of individuals who were in tune with the overwhelming spirits of their times. Almost everyone seemed surprised that 500 years of progress toward a deterministic universe and rational, behavioral people came to an end when Agile emerged.

The Constructivist-Epistemology Problem

Philosophers note that Scientific Realism does not explain revolutionary change, such as the transitions between the tides. If current scientific theories are actually true, then there really should be no more revolutionary changes. All changes should be minor refinements, such as slightly-more-precise measurements. However on occasion, new data appears as "black swans" that undermines existing theories and provokes revolutions. (Wikipedia, "Scientific Realism")

Physics: Relativity and quantum mechanics arose from the need to reconcile new observations and data, specifically the Michelson-Morely and Double-Slit experiments. In one sense, relativity and quantum mechanics are incremental changes because they only appear with huge objects (like stars) or small objects (like photons) that nobody can experience directly, while everyday objects (like baseballs and cars) still move according to Newtonian mechanics. In another sense, relativity and quantum mechanics are revolutionary changes because nothing in them could be predicted by anything from Newtonian mechanics.

Software Engineering: During all tides, everyone strives to improve productivity and quality, though the emphases differ.

The Waterfall tide was not a refinement of the Language tide. The issues and ideals of the Waterfall tide came from emphasizing processes and quality and were unrelated to improving languages. In one sense the Waterfall tide incrementally improved on the Language tide because everyone continues using programming languages. In another sense, the Waterfall tide was revolutionary because processes and testing have nothing to do with programming languages.

The Agile tide was not a refinement of the Waterfall tide. The issues and ideals of the Agile tide came from coping with change (the unpredictable and unknown parts of projects) and were not about processes or quality (the predictable and known parts of projects). In one sense, Agile is an incremental refinement of Waterfall because everyone still strives to plan projects whenever they can. In another sense, Agile is a revolutionary change from Waterfall because it acknowledges and tolerates unknowns and uncertainties, which Waterfalls and Factories could never do.

The Feedback Problem

More than 70 years of computing has profoundly affected our perceptions of reality and of people, which in turn affects computing again. Feedback loops muddy the future.

In the 1950s, '60s, and '70s, computers made "thought" increasingly predictable, inexpensive, and error-free. The brain was interpreted as a biological computer. In the 1960s and 70s, computers on TV and in movies were omniscient and people deferred to them. The movie *2001* from 1968 broached the question of whether computers could possibly lie. (Kubrick) Today, software enables social media and fosters the spread of fake news. Post-truth and anti-science flourish through software.

In the late 1970s and early '80s as personal computers began reaching the masses, people began prying into and unleashing whole new Pandora's Boxes of complexity and uncertainty. Computers and graphics played key roles in bringing fractals and Bayesian statistics to society. The limits of computers began to be appreciated.

Only computers could reliably demonstrate chaos and complexity. Herbert Simon noted that computers made chaos appreciable in the 1970s and 1980s. (Simon, page 177) Before computers, chaotic behaviors were often treated as errors in hand calculations or as messes to be avoided. In turn, complexity theory and Bayesian statistics have affected both computing and society.

Practices

Some practices have come full circle from the earliest days.

Artisans: Matti Tedre noted that in the 1950s software was a craft that required artistic talent. (Tedre, page 43) Will Tracz noted that Agile processes have returned to artisanship. Denning and Martell recently wrote "programmers are artisans in using tools." (Denning and Martell, page 87)

Shareware: Tedre noted that in early 1950s, hardware was sold but software was free. SHARE freely exchanged programs and vendors supplied other programs free. (Tedre, page 113) Today, open-source software plays an increasingly large role in sharing software-engineering knowledge.

The Lost-History Problem

Before 1960: Before about 1960, hardware got all of the attention and most software of that era has been lost or forgotten. For example, almost all of the information available about SAGE describes the size of the hardware: that it weighed 250 tons, that it had 60k vacuum tubes, and that it was the largest computer ever built. We know nothing about its software or how it was created, except that around 1959, 800 programmers worked at System Development Corporation (SDC), about half of the programmers in the U.S. (Tedre, page 43) Same with ENIAC and Univac.

Practitioners: Most histories of computing reflect the science rather than the practice. Research was published in the scientific record and got preserved while practice was generally forgotten. We know almost nothing about who the programmers were and what they actually did on the job during the first two tides. We mean real day-in-the-life biographies, not the silly fictions by Boehm and Turner. (Boehm and Turner) Unfortunately, this chapter also relies primarily on scientific sources.

Women: The active participation and intellectual contributions of women were often forgotten. Margot Lee Shetterly argued that their goal wasn't to stand out for their differences but to fit in because of their talent. They were just doing their jobs and many espoused excellence in their work. They did want the recognition and salary associated with titles like Mathematician and Engineer, though they rarely asked for such promotions. (Shetterly, page 251) At the beginning of the next tide, Margaret Hamilton asked for recognition for her work in software engineering and received it. (Hamilton)

Outside of the U.S.: This chapter focusses mainly on programmers in the U.S. Computers were also built and operated around the world. We know very little about the programmers of those machines.

In this chapter, we triangulate a handful of facts about the 1940s and '50s and then speculate. We would like to know a lot more about the first decades of programming, but most of that knowledge may already be lost to time. We hope that others with better access to historical and geographical information will delve deeper.

Notes

Stream and Tide Model

This chapter adapts the Stream and Tide model from the essay "Fifty Years of Progress in Software Engineering." (Raccoon) According to that model, the many changes from different streams that occur are tightly bound together. If any change occurred alone, which we suspect happens frequently, nobody would notice.

The transitions between tides are slow and incremental, each taking at least a decade. It takes time and context for new ideas to become appreciated and for old ideas to lose favor. The transitions or tipping points or paradigm shifts between these tides did not appear on any particular day. Others can reasonably argue that these shifts occurred years earlier or later, which is why we explain our choices.

The major ideas in the profession take a long time to develop and appreciate. However, some ideas do develop quickly. For example, structured programming went from the theorem to the Pascal and C languages in just 3 years.

Avoiding Predictions

In this book, we mostly make observations about the past and we mostly try to avoid predicting the future. We do of course make a few predictions, though most are totally obvious. Even so, we don't expect all of our predictions to come true because we cannot predict the future any better than anyone else. Our predictions about the future in the essay "Fifty Years of Progress in Software Engineering" also turned out badly. (Raccoon)

Even so, the spirit of Agile software engineering is embodied in books like Jurgen Appelo's *Management 3.0*, Mark Burgess's *In Search of Certainty*, and Jay Xiong's *New Software Engineering Paradigm Based on Complexity Science*.

Acknowledgements

We want to thank our friends and colleagues for sharing their ideas and examples. The organization of this material is ours, but many of the examples and details were suggested by others. We especially want to thank Anthony J. Giancola and Suzanne Sluizer.

We want to thank Matti Tedre for the book *The Science of Computing*, which provided a trove of examples and references. It enabled us to develop this chapter and we use it as the history of record. Edgar Daylight's books were also helpful.

We want to thank Claire Evans and Margot Lee Shetterly for shedding light on programming during the 1940s and '50s. In the book *Broadband*, Claire Evans documents the accomplishments of many women. In the book *Hidden Figures*, Margot Lee Shetterly documents a few more glimpses into the world of women programmers and especially of African-American women programmers. Before reading their books, we knew almost nothing about programming during the 1940s and '50s.

Some recent talks provide more details on early software engineering, including the ACM webinar by Grady Booch and the ICSE 2018 keynotes by Fred Brooks, Margaret Hamilton, and Brian Randell. (https://learning.acm.org/webinars April 25, 2018) (https://www.icse2018.org/info/keynotes)

Partial Bibliography

Jurgen Appelo, *Management 3.0*, Addison Wesley, 2011.

Kent Beck and Ward Cunningham, "Using Pattern Languages for Object-Oriented Program," OOPSLA 1987.

R.W. Bemer, "Machine-Controlled Production Environment," in *Report on the NATO Conference on Software Engineering*, pages 94 to 95, October 7 to 11, 1968.

Barry Boehm and Richard Turner, *Balancing Agility and Discipline*, Addison Wesley, 2003.

Frederick P. Brooks, Jr., *The Design of Design*, Addison Wesley, 2010.

Frederick P. Brooks, Jr., *The Mythical Man-Month, Anniversary Edition*, Addison Wesley, 1995.

Frederick P. Brooks, Jr., "No Silver Bullet," in Brooks, *The Mythical Man-Month*, chapter 16.

Mark Burgess, *In Search of Certainty*, O'Reilly, 2015.

Paul E. Ceruzzi, *Computing: a Concise History*, MIT Press, 2012.

Philip B. Crosby, *Quality is Free*, Mentor, 1980.

Michael A. Cusumano, "The Factory Approach to Software Development: a Strategic Overview," MIT Sloan School of Management, October 1989.

Ole-Johan Dahl, Edsger Dijkstra, and Tony Hoare, *Structured Programming*, Academic Press, 1972.

Edgar G. Daylight, *The Dawn of Software Engineering*, Lonely Scholar, 2012.

Peter J. Denning and Craig H. Martell, *Great Principles of Computing*, MIT, 2015.

Claire L. Evans, *Broadband*, Penguin, 2018.

David Alan Grier, "Software Engineering: History," in *Encyclopedia of Software Engineering*, www.tandfencys.com/ese/Entry.pdf, 2010.

Joseph T. Hallinan, *Why We Make Mistakes*, Broadway, 2010.

Margaret Hamilton, keynote at ICSE 2018.

Jamie Holmes, *Nonsense*, Crown, 2015.

Thomas P. Hughes, *Rescuing Prometheus*, Vintage, 1998.

Donald E. Knuth, *The Art of Computer Programming*, Addison Wesley, 2011.

Stanley Kubrick, *2001*, Warner Brothers, 1968.

Steve McConnell, "Measuring Software Productivity," ACM Webinar, January 11, 2016.

Paul E. McMahon, *Integrating CMMI and Agile Development*, Addison Wesley, 2010.

Bertrand Meyer, *Agile!*, Springer, 2014.

Jerry Z. Muller, *The Tyranny of Metrics*, Princeton University Press, 2018.

NBC News, "If Japan Can… Why Can't We?" NBC News, June 24, 1980.

Leon Osterweil, "Processes are Software, Too," ICSE 1987.

L.B.S. Raccoon, "Fifty Years of Progress in Software Engineering," in *Software Engineering Notes*, volume 22, issue 1, pages 88-104, ACM Press, January 1997.

Winston W. Royce, "Managing the Development of Large Software Systems," in *Proceedings of IEEE WESCON*, pages 328 to 338, August 1970.

Margot Lee Shetterly, *Hidden Figures*, William Morrow, 2016.

Nate Silver, *The Signal and the Noise*, Penguin, 2012.

Herbert A. Simon, *The Sciences of the Artificial*, MIT Press, 1996.

Margaret-Anne Storey, "Lies, Damn Lies, and Software Analytics: Why Big Data Needs Thick Data." ACM Webinar, May 5, 2016.

Matti Tedre, *The Science of Computing*, Taylor and Francis, 2015.

Jay Xiong, *New Software Engineering Paradigm Based on Complexity Science*, Springer, 2011.

You Cannot Predict the Future

9
A Sunrise Primer

The Sunrise problem (as originally described by Richard Price and Pierre Simon Laplace) asks how one should convert analysis of the past into predictions about the future or, more specifically, how one should convert the number of past observations into certainties or probabilities about future observations.

In the chapter "Unknownness," we argued that big chunks of software projects are unknown, wrong, or destined to change. But, we didn't say how much of each project has problems or will change. In his FSE 2016 keynote, Daniel Jackson asked "when a proof checker reports 'no errors found yet,' how strong is the evidence?" and "how much more work should developers invest to get to any given degree of certainty?" (Jackson)

In this chapter, we use the Sunrise equations to quantify the amounts of unknowns, changes, and errors that one should expect to see and how one should expect those amounts to vary within projects over time. The Sunrise equations are of course spherical-cow models, yet we contend that all rational investments in software should respect the Sunrise equations.

First, we discuss the Sunrise problem and three solutions: the original equations that Richard Price and Pierre Simon Laplace developed as well as a new equation inspired by Benoit Mandelbrot. Then we discuss what those equations mean. We care more about the shapes of the equations and what they portend than about the specific numbers they generate. All solutions are asymptotic, so stopping early is always necessary, yet where to stop will always remain unclear. We link the Sunrise equations to classic rules of two, three, six, and twelve from analysis and programming. Finally, we note that problems are often worse than the equations predict and worse than anyone admits.

The Sunrise Problem

Techniques for reliably predicting the future remain elusive. The Sunrise equations were developed more than two centuries ago to quantify the limits of how much can be known about the next binary event in a series.

Predicting the Future, Based On the Past

The Sunrise problem stems from the ancient question: "What are the odds that the sun will rise tomorrow?" It has come to mean estimating the probability or certainty of future observations based on the number of past observations. Specifically, what are the odds that an event will occur again, given that it has occurred n times in a row?

Consider three events in a row. One may see the sun rise three days in a row, when it should rise every day. One may see a flipped coin land heads-up three times in a row, when it should be 50-50. One may see a noobie poker player win three hands in a row (with beginner's luck), when he should lose most hands for a long time to come. An event that occurs three times in a row could come from any of these scenarios. In each case, one suspects that the event will occur again, but some doubt should remain.

Consider thousands or millions of events in a row. The sun has risen every day for all of recorded history and it still rises. The Space Shuttle survived falling-foam problems for 18 years before exploding. The Fukushima nuclear reactors survived earthquakes and tsunamis for 40 years before melting down. In these cases, everyone agrees that events should occur again, but few guarantees exist.

All of these situations suffer from "hasty generalization," "the law of small numbers," or "the problem of induction." Three or one thousand or one million positive events could begin almost any kind of series because, mathematically speaking, all finite numbers are insignificant and every finite series begins an infinite number of longer series. Psychologists find that people are consistently more certain than they should be. Nate Silver notes that people often mistake luck for skill when sample sizes are small and are much more certain than they should be. (Silver, page 338) So, people need tools to rationally estimate the uncertainty of future events.

A Family of Equations

The Original, Exponential, Prician Equation

Richard Price's equation is $f(n) = 1-(2^n)^{-1}$. The probability that a binary event will happen n times is 2^{-n}. First, assume that an event either will or won't happen, in other words assume it is 50-50. Then apply Bayes' law recursively because each event that does occur cuts the probability that it won't occur again in half. Price's uncertainty about the next event diminishes exponentially. (Bayes and Price, pages 409 to 411)

We believe that Price's equation is too optimistic because it equates means and ends: the observations seen so far with the underlying phenomena or the probability of the series seen so far with the probability of the next event. Price effectively presumes that all samples are independent and accurate, that nothing will go awry, and that a new sample won't disturb the system, which are as optimistic as possible.

The Original, Linear, Laplacian Equation

Pierre Simon Laplace's equation is $f(n) = n\div(n+1) = 1-(n+1)^{-1}$. If an event has always occurred, there must be some probability that it won't occur, so Laplace added one failure to the set of observations seen so far, the smallest discrete unit. Laplace's uncertainty about the next event diminishes iteratively or linearly. (Jeffreys, page 94)

We believe that Laplace's equation is too pessimistic. The only way it could possibly add up is if the probability that the next event will succeed is always *0.0*, which is as pessimistic as possible. We believe that adding in any other fixed probability p, such as *0.5* or *0.1*, is too optimistic before p^{-1} samples and is too pessimistic after that. One could even argue that Laplace presumed that one of the samples seen so far was wrong or that Laplace fell for the Law of Averages or the Gambler's fallacy.

The New, Hyperbolic, Mandelbrotian Equation

Another way to view our criticisms of the original equations is that they bound the space of certainty. Price was as optimistic as possible and Laplace was as pessimistic as possible, so the truth must lie somewhere in between.

Fractal spaces lie between linear-iterative and exponential-recursive spaces. In his first published paper, Benoit Mandelbrot improved George Zipf's equation for word distribution $f(s) = As^{-a}$ by using the same trick that had been used to avoid the ultraviolet catastrophe of the Weierstrass function. Mandelbrot added a constant and a scale to get the equation $f(s) = A(1+Cs)^{-a}$, where a is slightly greater than *1*. (Mandelbrot, *Fractalist*, pages 151 to 155)

In the related equation $f(n) = 1-(1+n^c)^{-1}$, as long as the exponent c lies between *1.0* and about *1.6*, Mandelbrot's equation lies between Price's and Laplace's equations, or more specifically, $\forall n \geq 0$, *price(n)* $\geq$ *mandelbrot(n)* $\geq$ *laplace(n)*. The scaling factor 4/3 is one of Mandelbrot's favorites, for which $c = ln\ 4 \div ln\ 3 \approx 1.26186$. For small numbers of observations, say less than 128, Mandelbrot's 4/3 equation approximates the geometric mean of the Prician and Laplacian equations. Smaller exponents, such as $c = 1.05$, may also apply in many circumstances.

We graph these equations in figure 1 and list some values in table 1. Notice that in a *linear* sense, the greatest differences lie in the range of 2 to 32 observations. In a *geometric* sense, they diverge forever.

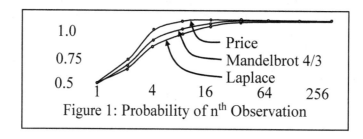

Figure 1: Probability of nth Observation

Table 1: The Probability of the nth Observation				
Prior Observations n	**Price** $1-(2^n)^{-1}$	**Mandelbrot 4/3** $1-(1+n^{1.26})^{-1}$	**Mandelbrot 1.05** $1-(1+n^{1.05})^{-1}$	**Laplace** $1-(1+n)^{-1}$
1	0.5000	0.5000	0.5000	0.5000
2	0.7500	0.7057	0.6743	0.6667
3	0.8750	0.8000	0.7602	0.7500
4	0.9375	0.8519	0.8109	0.8000
5	0.9688	0.8840	0.8442	0.8333
6	0.9844	0.9056	0.8678	0.8571
7	0.9922	0.9210	0.8852	0.8750
8	0.9961	0.9324	0.8988	0.8889
16	1.0000	0.9706	0.9484	0.9412
32	1.0000	0.9875	0.9744	0.9697
64	1.0000	0.9948	0.9875	0.9846
128	1.0000	0.9978	0.9939	0.9922
256	1.0000	0.9991	0.9970	0.9961

Notes

We cannot fault Price or Laplace for starting with simple equations because during their lifetimes, computations were done by hand. Furthermore, using hyperbolic equations to describe nature only began to be appreciated nearly 200 years after their equations were first published.

In *The Fractal Geometry of Nature*, Benoit Mandelbrot showed that many economic and management phenomena have hyperbolic shapes. In "Power Laws in Software," Panagiotis Louridas and colleagues showed that many software-engineering phenomena have hyperbolic shapes. So, the error rates for requirements and architectures might reasonably be described by hyperbolic equations.

To us, all of these equations seem off-by-one because the number of prior "observations" should start at zero. Saying that the table shows the nth "prediction" makes sense, but saying that it shows the nth "observation" is the historical terminology. Others (specifically programmers) have complained that the scaling constants to stretch the equations horizontally and vertically are implicit rather than explicit.

Correction Factors: Statisticians have developed a variety of correction factors to adjust probabilities in various ways. Friedrich Bessel used the inverse of Laplace's equation $n/(n-1)$ as a correction factor to adjust for the "degrees of freedom" in the data. The inverses of all of the Sunrise equations can act as variations on Bessel's correction factor. Each may also need an off by-one tweak.

Asymptotes

All of the Sunrise equations go to 1.0 asymptotically, meaning that attaining perfection would take forever. No program will ever become perfect. Hard work will eventually bring any app to within an epsilon of perfection for any epsilon that one might choose; but getting to epsilon will take a long time and a lot of effort, depending on the chosen epsilon; and analysts and programmers must stop at some point, which will leave varying amounts of potential error or change to fix later. Satisficing or stopping early is necessary; over-investing in short-term quality and ilities will waste resources; and good is the enemy of better. Because nobody can control how much is actually known about any given decision, there are no ideal times to stop, though some times may be better or worse than others.

The Sunrise Equations are Asymptotic

Iterative Narrowing Will Eventually Get Your Software Project to within an Epsilon of Perfection

To create a high-quality software program, incrementally improve it over a long time, repeatedly inspecting and testing it from independent points of view, polishing it, and narrowing the scope of change. At every step, reuse (or keep unchanged or don't break) whatever does work and change (or attempt to improve) whatever doesn't work.

Systematically polishing the code while narrowing the scope of change without adding new functionality will systematically reduce error and improve quality over time. The trick is to narrow the scope of change to identified problems at every step or release. Iterative narrowing will eventually bring any fixed program to within any chosen epsilon of perfection. If the scope of change widens by adding new features, then quality may also worsen.

Iterative narrowing applies to products as a series of upgrade projects or releases as well as within projects as a series of iterations. NASA projects often have long lead times, sometimes as much as ten years, which allow for many inspections and reinspections, many tests and retests, as well as the application of many analysis tools, and responses to fix any problems that are found.

Reusing (building on existing, established, known codes) is a key to high quality because everything that is not reused starts over from scratch, which directly increases the risk of error. Refining an existing app or prototype is often more productive than starting over because it saves all of the effort and risk involved with everything that was correct already, everything that remains the same. For this reason, we believe that reusability is the king of the ilities. All boilerplate and dead-certain tasks in a project come from the requirements and architectures that got reused in many projects. Note that we ignore software rot and presume that contexts remain unchanged.

Getting to Epsilon Can Take a Lot of Work

The first problem with asymptotes is that getting to within any particular epsilon of perfection can take a long time and a lot of sustained effort. In table 2, we turn the equations around and show the minimum number of observations needed to claim that any particular decision has any particular degree of perfection.

Observations for requirements include initial user requests and user responses to demos. Observations for architectures include programmer requests and uses of an API or function call within an existing code base.

To get to known (95%) correctness, if Mandelbrot's 4/3 equation were right, then 11 people would have to unanimously agree on every single observation, and if Mandelbrot's 1.05 equation were right, then 17 people would have to unanimously agree. To get to dead-certain (99%) correctness, one would need 39 and 80 unanimous observations, respectively. To get to one-in-ten-thousand correctness, one would need 1,479 and 6,449 unanimous observations, respectively. Developing ultra-high quality software can feel like running in quicksand because everything takes a lot more observations than anyone really wants to make.

Note that when we state that so many people must unanimously agree on every single observation, we mean with zero dissentions. That almost never happens since getting ten people to unanimously agree on anything is beyond rational hope. Also note that silently nodding one's head and voting with the majority does not equal agreement.

The best way to do a lot of work is to spread it out over a long period of time, so to maximize the quality within a project, take as much time and as many resources as one can afford. NASA has long lead times and massive resources to belabor projects: ten times as much effort per line of code, and maybe fifty times as much as most companies when everything is considered, such as their ability to expand scope.

Table 2: Number of Observations to Achieve a Given Certainty					
Segment	Certainty %	Price $1-(2^n)^{-1}$	Mandelbrot 4/3 $1-(1+n^{1.26})^{-1}$	Mandelbrot 1.05 $1-(1+n^{1.05})^{-1}$	Laplace $1-(1+n)^{-1}$
Unknown (Large)	50	1	1	1	1
Unknown (Small)	67	2	2	2	2
Semi-Known (Large)	69	2	2	3	3
Semi-Known (Small)	80	3	3	4	4
Known	95	5	11	17	19
Dead Certain	99	7	39	80	99
1 Error per 10,000	99.99	14	1,479	6,449	9,999
1 Error per 1,000,000	99.9999	20	56,871	517,947	999,999

An Epsilon of Error Will Always Remain

The second problem with asymptotes is that the probability of error will never get to zero – an epsilon of error will always remain. The Sunrise equations assign positive probabilities of error to the uses and reuses of requirements and codes, regardless of how old and stable they are or how much effort went into creating them. When contexts and goals are stable, then with hard work, apps will continually improve; yet apps will never become perfect, a la Zeno's paradox.

Low-Probability Issues Will Eventually Appear: As higher-probability errors are caught and fixed, lower-probability errors will start to appear, but there are probably many of them, so now and again something will go wrong. When problems do not occur appreciably, then they are lurking, stalking, preparing to pounce.

In *Wrong*, David Freedman argues that there can never be guarantees against unpleasant surprises. Just because someone got away with doing something in a given way for years or even decades, doesn't mean that they got it right or that everything will be fine tomorrow. (Freedman)

Space Shuttle Examples: The burnt O-rings on the Space Shuttle held for 24 flights (nearly 5 years), until one flight when they didn't. Damage from falling foam was tolerable for 112 flights (nearly 18 years), until one flight when it wasn't.

Fukushima Example: The Fukushima nuclear reactors worked for 40 years, surviving many earthquakes and tsunamis, until one particular earthquake and tsunami when the cores melted.

Software Examples: The SSL HeartBleed code appeared to work fine for two years, until the bug was revealed by inspection. The Java binary-search code seemed to work for 11 years with gazillions of calls, until the bug appeared in running apps. Slow resource leaks and low-probability synchronization problems may not appear until after long-running or heavy workloads.

Ongoing Bias: If someone failed to predict all of the errors in the first version of an app, there is no reason to believe that he or she could predict all of the errors in the nth version. Everyone who misunderstood the truth in previous releases probably harbors some form of bias and will continue to misunderstand the truth in similar ways.

The supply of software bugs is effectively infinite. The endless security patches to commercial software apps show that improving quality is a never-ending task. Note that formal methods and model-driven development cannot change this susceptibility to error because nothing can ever leap from inductive to deductive truth.

Stopping Early is Always Necessary

Decades ago, when working on Waterfall projects, our colleagues would usually finish a lot of what they had planned, useful prototypes, but bug fixes and enhancements always remained unfinished, and they would always ask for more time. Glen Self, an executive at EDS, complained repeatedly that "there's never enough time to do it right but always time to do it over." (personal communication) While we used to rankle at his observation, we have come to believe that it is both correct and necessary.

All Projects have Limited Budgets and Schedules

Time and resources are bounded by one's situations and opportunities. No project has the infinite time and resources needed to write perfect software or even the arbitrary time and resources needed to achieve arbitrary ends. Projects have only so many team members and so many hours to do useful work. So, all analysts and programmers will eventually run out of time and resources and be forced to ship code with whatever level of quality they have already produced.

In commercial software, windows of opportunity are limited. Most clients won't wait years for solutions – they want solutions, now. First movers often gain market advantages, so commercial companies must not wait longer to ship than their competitors.

The Space Shuttle had perhaps ten to fifty times the resources per line of code as any normal commercial project, the ability to expand scope to deal with problems, and near-complete control over what their trained, disciplined, cooperative astronauts would do. Yet even with all this largesse, the Space-Shuttle software had bugs. Even NASA could not afford to redesign the Space Shuttle after every failed launch and they eventually shut it down.

Normal analysts and programmers who work on normal projects that don't have such large budgets will most-likely make more mistakes. Many websites must deal with all of the old, incompatible browsers that Microsoft ever shipped (IE6 and IE8) and whatever crazy things that naïve or malicious users decide to do, and their budgets are often miniscule. Most software projects have resources that lie somewhere in between NASA and website projects.

Stopping Early is Always Necessary

The combination of limited resources with direct and opportunity costs in the presence of unknowns, changes, and errors implies that satisficing is necessary at every step of every project. Every step should make progress, but nobody can achieve perfection in a finite time, so every step must also deliberately achieve lower quality than is known to be possible. This does not mean that anyone should tolerate sloppy or lazy work, rather they should accept that there are limits to everyone's efforts and that software could always be better.

Brooks' Code Example: In chapter 15 of *Mythical Man-Month* from 1975, Fred Brooks wrote an example of good code that today seems seriously out-of-date. His code should have better names, less fussy comments, and proper unit tests. Should Fred Brooks have waited 30 more years before publishing to produce a better example? No. He wrote the best code that he could for his time and stopped early so that everyone else could benefit from his example in the interim. Kent Beck who wrote *Test-Driven Development*, Dustin Boswell and Trevor Foucher who wrote *The Art of Readable Code*, and Robert Martin who wrote *Clean Code* describe more contemporary coding practices. They cannot help but be aware of and build on Brooks' example. Today, everyone (including Brooks) would write a much better example because we have all learned a lot since then.

Animation: Brad Bird noted that scenes in animated movies "can always be better." (*The Incredibles* director's commentary, 1:12:10)

Opportunity Cost: In the presence of real costs and unknownness, everyone who over-invests in short-term quality or ilities will overpay and will then lack the resources to do other things later. The main reason why more does not get done is that people choose to do something else. To perfect one feature, other features must be ignored. To perfect one app, other apps must be ignored. Whenever analysts and programmers overdo one opportunity, they must neglect other opportunities, and they will pay for those missed opportunities, later, in other ways, which is called "opportunity cost." Note that people often later rue even their best choices.

Good is the Enemy of Better: The Sunrise equations help to explain why good is the enemy of better. Eventually, everyone will run out of time and resources and they will have to choose either to satisfice by accepting that what they have is good enough and moving on or to strive for perfection by finding more resources to continue working. They can only do one or the other, not both at the same time. Running out of resources forces the bifurcation of hard choices. Obsession (or genius) is a key to exceptional results because it overrides any willingness to satisfice, but it is also very expensive.

Nobody Can Control (or Even Know) What is Known

Of course, everyone should get as many observations (or specifically as many prior examples, inspections, and tests) as they can for each decision, but nobody can control how many times users request a given feature or how many times a body of code calls a given interface. In our experience, some problems are unique to each project. Even when many prior uses exist, analysts and programmers may not realize that they are present or, even if they do, bother to investigate them all before making decisions.

Nobody can know upfront how much of a project or task is unknown or wrong or destined to change without predicting the future. Nobody can know upfront which tasks will be high-risk because all such judgments are subject to error.

Function-Call Example: Decades ago, we noticed that when a function that one of us had written was called only once, the odds that it would be used again without change or refactoring were low. While we never did a formal study, 50% is in the ballpark. We noticed that when a function that we had written was called from two places, the odds of reuse without change improved significantly. We concluded that every function or method should be called more than once, whenever possible. Even so, most of our functions still get called just once.

When to Stop Always Remains Unclear

The need to stop early suggests that there must be some concept of *good enough for now* because otherwise nobody would ever finish working on anything. But, the Sunrise equations don't actually say what *good enough for now* means. Nobody can know how many steps to take in any given situation without knowing what will be gained by the additional steps, which cannot be known without predicting the future.

We believe that there are no perfect times to stop, even though there are often better and worse times. One good place to stop is just after fixing all important, known problems though, of course, one may misjudge what is important and nobody knows what unknown problems will arise. Another good place to stop is after investing a specific amount of effort as suggested by the rules of two, three, six, and twelve listed below.

Analysts and programmers have lots of practical experience with *good enough for now*. Software projects are full of arbitrary, short-term deadlines for tasks, iterations, and projects. We have seen many occasions when managers let their people "play" with difficult problems for days or weeks and then on a seemingly-random day demanded, "finish, now." Everyone ships what they have after running out of resources. These approaches to *good enough for now* are ad hoc and possibly even random, yet they embody reasonable heuristics.

Aware rather than Oblivious: Appreciating that all analysts and programmers must satisfice on every task may help to make the arbitrariness of these decisions a bit more overt and honest.

Caveat: Note that *good enough for now* differs completely from *good enough for later*. The Space Shuttle and Java binary search both worked fine for a while but not forever.

Good Enough For Now in Requirement and Software Engineering

How good should requirements and source codes be before moving on? When should one cut off near-term investments? How good is *good enough for now* or for one step forward in a project? Mike Hinchey noted that there will always be a tension between cost and reliability, though he didn't define the link. (Hinchey) Various rules of two, three, six, and twelve recommend investing corresponding amounts of effort. Empirically for most software projects, *good enough for now* means six to twelve observations for analysts and two to three observations for programmers.

The Spectrum of Number of Observations

The spectrum of the number of observations is vast. Each different number of observations embodies a different tradeoff of cost versus quality.

One Observation for Custom and Innovative Work

A lot of custom and demo software is based on one observation and gets developed just once.

Consulting: Consultants tailor a lot of software to individual clients and integrate seemingly random data sources in one-off projects. Consider writing a custom report for a VIP or piping yet another random feed into a database.

Innovation: True innovation means that there is no prior art. New software products have little prior information to base decisions on, except maybe (hopefully) one "visionary" opinion.

When one user asks for a new feature, based on the Mandelbrotian equations, the results are probably around 50% correct. The results of one-off decisions and tasks resemble pure luck.

Two Observations for Commercial Code

Reviews: We have seen many commercial projects require that all code be paired on or inspected at least once before commits.

Based on the Mandelbrotian equations, these commits are around 67% to 71% correct.

Three Observations for High-Quality Code

Refactoring: The number three looms large in the lore of refactoring. Martin Fowler quotes Don Roberts, writing, "The first time you do something, you just do it. The second time you do something similar, you wince at the duplication, but you do the duplicate thing anyway. The third time you do something similar, you refactor." (Fowler, page 58) It takes three observations to make good decisions about structuring code. If anyone could reliably design an architecture correctly the first time, they wouldn't need to refactor.

Reuse: The number three looms large in the lore of reuse. Will Tracz quotes Ted Biggerstaff, writing, "Before you can develop reusable software you need to have developed it three times." (Tracz, page 94) If anyone could predict how a chunk of code would be reused before then, they wouldn't need to keep redeveloping it.

Understanding: Bob Ballance stated that you understand a problem when you know three solutions to it as well as three reasons why each solution is wrong.

Reviews: In *Making Software*, Dewayne Perry describes a large, embedded project where all code was reviewed by at least three peers. (Oram and Wilson, page 455)

The Mandelbrotian equations imply that decisions based on three observations are probably around 76% to 80% correct. Decisions based on three observations are enough better than pure luck to allow developers to meaningfully proceed, but remain far from certain.

Six Observations for Commercial Analysis

Analysts have adopted various "rules of six" for requirements.

Interviews: Alan Cooper and colleagues encourage designers to interview four to six users for each role. (Cooper, Reimann, and Cronin, page 63)

Analysis: Karl Wiegers notes that large groups of analysts may be too unwieldy to make effective progress and in "Too Many Cooks" suggests that six may be a good upper limit on the size of a group. (Wiegers, page 119)

When six users or analysts ask for a new feature, like "I need auto-completion in field *f*," what does anyone really know? The Mandelbrot equations suggest that analyses based on six opinions are around 87% to 91% correct. These decisions are still semi-known and far from certain, yet everyone can proceed with a fair amount of confidence.

Twelve Observations for High-Quality Analysis

Analysis: We've heard that NASA projects often have teams of about twelve analysts. We have seen teams of about twelve analysts and programmers work on various healthcare projects.

Reviews: We have heard that a number of companies have architectural review boards with twelve or so members to verify conformance to standards. In *Making Software*, Perry noted that on his large, embedded project, architectural decisions were reviewed by teams of up to 15 peers. (Oram and Wilson, page 455)

If each requirement or architectural decision gets twelve observations, then Mandelbrot's equations suggest that around 92% to 95% of such decisions will endure. These decisions remain uncertain, yet analysts and programmers can proceed with a lot of confidence.

Twenty-Four or More Observations

We can imagine "rules of twenty-four." Analysis teams would have twenty-four or so members. Code would get inspected by twenty-four peers. If the Mandelbrot equations describe software, then such requirements and codes would be 96% to 98% correct.

Michael Lewis noted that (from a Frequentist point of view) it would take a sample size of 130 to get a 90% chance of generalizing to society or to the whole world. (Lewis, page 161)

Sweetspots and Tradeoffs

Sweetspots

The many rules of two, three, six, and twelve in analysis and design embody important heuristics that define *good enough for now* in the face of unknowns, uncertainties, and errors for most projects.

Newer or Less-Critical Work: By inspection, six observations for analysts and two observations for programmers is the heuristic sweet-spot of certainty for most requirements and source codes in younger and less-critical programs.

Maturer or More-Critical Work: By inspection, twelve observations for analysts and three observations for programmers is the heuristic sweet-spot of certainty for most requirements and source codes for maturer and more-critical programs.

Tradeoffs

Roughly speaking, doubling the cost halves the remaining error rate and vice versa. Getting fewer observations increases risk and reduces cost. Getting more observations increases cost and reduces risk. One can find incrementally better answers, only if one spends significantly more time and energy.

Larger numbers of observations can be effective when applications are more stable, when lots of stakeholders are well versed in the issues at hand, and when high-quality matters more. Getting more observations also provides more political cover when problems arise.

So, why not insist on 24 or 130 observations for every requirement and design decision? Because no organizations can afford to do so. Getting more observations becomes increasingly more expensive with diminishing benefits. Additionally, Fred Brooks noted that interactions grow with the square of the number of people in a group, which limits the effectiveness of large groups. (Brooks, chapter 2)

Projects that have the time and resources to get lots of real observations should go for it. But, in the meantime, progress on other features and programs will remain blocked. Six to twelve observations is the point of diminishing returns, even for NASA.

Diminishing Returns – Only Take One Step at a Time

Every task or iteration embodies one step forward in a project, at some scale. The Surise equations show how much quality can be achieved by each step, in general terms. Every step should only attempt one step's worth of effort and each step can only achieve one step's worth of results. Nobody can do more. Nobody can "eat an elephant" in (ummm) one requirement or "boil the ocean" in (ummm) one line of code.

Take Reasonable Steps Forward, but No More: For the sakes of productivity, efficiency, and consistency, one should take as many steps forward as one reasonably can afford, but do no more because additional steps become increasingly less effective. Due to diminishing returns, taking multiple steps leads to higher quality through disproportionately higher costs. Noticeable improvements may simply be too expensive.

Harder to Build Bigger Consensuses: Keith Sawyer notes that greater diversity tends to inspire greater creativity, as long as groups build effective consensuses. But, building consensuses is harder in larger groups. (Sawyer, pages 233 to 234) Whenever a group fails to build a consensus, then its diversity will be wasted, a la Wiegers's "Too Many Cooks." (Wiegers, page 119) Oversized groups will have more debaters and head-nodders, who will obstruct or mislead progress.

Over-Investing Wastes Resources: Everyone knows that greater efforts can produce better results. Analysts and programmers often aspire to higher standards of quality, which would surely be possible with more time and resources. But when returns diminish, then striving for additional quality will primarily waste resources.

The conflicts between the quality benefits of more steps and the productivity benefits of fewer steps suggest that everyone should start with modest number of steps and incrementally add effort, later.

When Multiple Observations Help

Note that multiple observations help most when the probability of getting each decision right is better than 50-50 but not by much. We believe that a lot of RE and SE decisions lie in these middle ranges. In table 3, the group success rates are the geometric means of the individual success rates.

When the odds of success are less than 50%, getting one observation is the best choice because adding more observations and voting will actually make decisions worse. When the odds of success are high, say more than 90%, then getting more inputs doesn't really help. So, teams and multiple observations help most when the odds of making a good choice are in the 55% to 85% range.

Table 3: Error Rates by Number of Observations and Probability of Correct Decision											
# Obs	0%	10%	20%	30%	40%	50%	60%	70%	80%	90%	100%
1	.000	.100	.200	.300	.400	.500	.600	.700	.800	.900	1.000
3	.000	.028	.104	.216	.352	.500	.648	.784	.896	.972	1.000
5	.000	.009	.058	.163	.317	.500	.683	.837	.942	.992	1.000
7	.000	.003	.033	.126	.290	.500	.710	.874	.967	.997	1.000
9	.000	.001	.020	.099	.267	.500	.733	.901	.980	.999	1.000
11	.000	.000	.012	.078	.247	.500	.753	.922	.988	1.000	1.000
13	.000	.000	.007	.062	.229	.500	.771	.938	.993	1.000	1.000

Worse than the Equations Predict – Worse than Anyone Admits

For many reasons, the error and reuse rates of all requirements and architectures are worse than the Sunrise equations predict. Behavioral economics, empirical software engineering research, and practical experience suggest that requirements and architectures are worse than anyone admits.

Lots of Software Decisions are Hard

Ambiguity: Everybody wants "easy to use," but that can mean opposite things for power users and noobies. Does it mean "fewer confusing details and fewer shortcuts" or "fewer steps and more shortcuts?" Does it mean "put together all of the controls that affect a decision," which can be overwhelming to noobies, or "put less-commonly-used controls into preferences or templates," which are harder to find and more annoying for power users. Or should it be configurable, which potentially adds detail for everyone? Consider good error checking. Reconfirming every input with a popup dialog is annoying and leads to habituation errors. Reconfirming no inputs turns every action into a potential typo or clicko. Exactly where should one draw the line? And, what does one do to accommodate both power users and noobies? These questions have few easy answers and the odds that any specific choice is correct might be poor.

Irrationality and Inarticulation: As we point out in the chapter "Unknownness," users, analysts, and programmers are all irrational (or crazy). More often than anyone admits, users either do not know the truth or (when they do know) cannot articulate it. Psychological anchoring affects everyone. Perhaps recent water-cooler discussions with colleagues influenced user opinions. Perhaps designers asked leading questions. People make mistakes (such as misspeaking) when stressing, multitasking, or rushing. So, when interviewees or analysts are under stress from a boss or a spouse, their answers will be wronger. Near deadlines, decisions will be wronger. The "IKEA" and "NIH" effects occur when users argue for their own mediocre ideas, rather than the better ideas of their peers and rivals. (Ariely, IKEA effect, pages 83 to 106, NIH effect, pages 107 to 122) If users are 90% rational and accurate when expressing their own needs (which we believe is insanely optimistic), then the odds of error will move at least 10% closer to 50-50. The real odds are probably much worse.

Biased Sampling: Participants in the inquiry process may or may not represent the true user-base. Maybe the interviewees know exactly what they need. Maybe they could be spared from other tasks or have pull to get out of meetings. Maybe they are power users, who have very different needs than the true noobie user-base, or vice versa, and their opinions are biased inappropriately. As a rule, designers want to interview users with above-average expertise, who will probably better understand and articulate their needs, but this also makes them less representative. Analysts and programmers often make decisions based on their own opinions and experiences, even though they are not representative users, either.

Social and Political Behavior: Social and political behaviors can increase speculation by users and analysts. A user may want to please a colleague or manager by forwarding a suggestion that otherwise he considers unimportant. How many of your friends have ever asked you to "like" a cause or project that you know nothing about? A busy user may say (and believe), "so and so can speak for me," even though the proxy says all the wrong things. A designer may focus too narrowly on friends and favorite users and omit important functionality. A designer may try to please too many users and add in too much confusing flexibility. The politics that decides who participates in the requirement process may affect the outcome more than any individual.

Fatigue: Decision fatigue occurs whenever anyone makes many, many decisions and eventually get tired and starts saying "whatever." All decisions after that are effectively random.

Inconsistent Input: In many cases, analysts and programmers get bugbases full of complaints, but complaints are much less meaningful than deliberate decisions about what to do.

Inconsistent Coverage: Most software projects entail many, many decisions and no project ever gets three opinions for every single decision.

Newer Projects are Worse

Many requirements and architectures have gaping holes and do wrong things deliberately, in well-intended but naïve ways. One can implement awkward or useless features and clumsy architectures that have no coding bugs and one can write useful features that have significant bugs in corner cases. This resembles the difference between sample errors and model errors in statistics.

Dewayne Perry notes that source codes are not the biggest problems for successful projects, rather the requirements and architectures are. He discusses "the lack of precision and completeness in requirements and design documentation." (Oram and Wilson, page 462)

Requirements: In our experience, new requirements are horrible. They are continually revised in every project that we have ever seen. During development, almost all requirements must be clarified or explained and many get changed to fix ambiguities or omissions, though sometimes they are rewritten from scratch. Many calls to user help lines implicitly criticize clumsy GUIs and features, in other words, implicitly criticize the requirements.

Architectures: In our experience, new software architectures are horrible. Architectures are expected to endure, so architects must predict the future. As they endure, architectures accrete cruft and work less and less well and they can't be fixed due to the need for backward compatibility. All glue code, work-arounds, and versionings implicitly criticize architectures.

Larger Projects are Worse

As apps get larger, the odds that individual requirements or APIs are correct decrease.

Contextual Complexity: A feature in isolation may be easy to find and obvious to use. The same feature in the context of a complicated app can be hard to find and confusing to use just because there are so many other distracting details to wade through. Users cannot use features that they cannot find and figure out. Users struggling with a large, unfamiliar app may not know where to look for a particular feature and may give up. Names and labels are often confusing in large programs due to context.

Tech-support workers field many questions that are supposedly obvious in the GUI or in the manual. We know of cases where magazine reviewers claimed that important features were missing from major commercial apps, when the developers had spent a lot of time implementing those features, even doing usability studies. Presumably, the reviewers were savvy users who either did not find what they were looking for or did not appreciate what they did find.

Crosscutting Effects: When many analysts work together, some details will cross boundaries of responsibility. What seems like an unimportant detail to each may coalesce into an important requirement for all analysts together. For example, when each dialog is designed by a different person, the flow from one dialog to the next may be inconsistent. Error handling is also hard to do consistently. Aspects can capture small crosscutting requirements by combining them into fewer, larger issues, if analysts can perceive them as such. These issues are often handled by style guides or standards and are treated as errors when wrong, but we believe that they should be treated more positively as explicit aspects.

Architects deal with fewer irrational users directly, so their decisions may seem safer, but architects have their own problems. Architectural decisions are often expected to endure a long time and often affect many parts of an app, so architects must predict further into the future. The conventions and standards that architects use can interfere with effective decisions in novel situations. Also, expectations are higher and architects probably need stronger egos to survive, which likely increases overconfidence and stubbornness.

Worse than Anyone Admits

Disagreement: The Sunrise equations only apply when all users agree unanimously about decisions. When users disagree about decisions, then the odds that a decision is right quickly move toward 50-50. Consider two users who want better search and another user who would rather have better reports. Consider two architects who want to move apps to the cloud and browsers and another architect who wants to stay with client-server and classic GUIs.

Negotiating a unanimous decision may neither change the underlying opinions nor improve the odds of being right. People often merely hold their tongues and nod their heads silently in the presence of others with more authority. Users can disagree about the most important things (such as what an app should do) and agree about the most trivial things (such as using the corporate color scheme and logo). Just because the users appear to agree, doesn't mean they are right. Just because the users appear to disagree, doesn't mean that the issue is unimportant or that a good answer cannot be found. Agreement per se should not be used to make decisions or set priorities.

Uncertainty: Getting many inputs from many different users doesn't guarantee useful opinions or insights. Many users don't have an opinion and don't even want one because they are busy with their own problems. Sometimes, users want things that are impossible, for example when they want web pages to change the appearance of the browser icons in the task bar. Getting a large number of code reviews from peers doesn't guarantee that anyone will say anything useful. In all of these cases, people may agree that there is a problem but not how to solve it.

Ease: Alan Cooper and colleagues encourage analysts to strive for six opinions from real users. Getting more than one opinion from an analyst or programmer grounds the process in reality. Cooper and colleagues also state that during analysis, later interviews should fill in missing details, rather than reconfirm known information, which lowers the number of effective observations. They also throw away all but the top one or two resulting "personas," which lowers the number of effective observations, again. We will oversimplify Cooper's process and give them the benefit of the doubt and say that on average they base each design decision (or requirement) on two or three user observations. (Cooper, Reimann, and Cronin)

Omission: Like nulls in databases, omitted opinions in user surveys are tricky. An omission could mean anything from "I agree" (I believe that others have made my point) to "I abstain" (I don't have a useful opinion or it does not apply) to "unknown" (I forgot to state my opinion) to "I disagree" (I didn't mention it because I want something else entirely). Presuming that users who say nothing intend to abstain is absurd. Perhaps each omission should be treated as a 50-50, which will not change the decision but will lower the certainty.

Notes

Binary Events: The Sunrise problem describes the probabilities of binary events, like flipping coins. In software, whether a feature or function will have bugs and whether individual requirements or architecture decisions will remain unchanged are also binary events.

Unfair Comparisons 1: Comparing the Space Shuttle and the Fukushima reactors to the Java binary search is problematic, even though they all concern errors. There were significant differences in complexity, quality control, and consequences. Richard Feynman showed that known Space-Shuttle errors were left unfixed. We don't know whether the Fukushima operators ignored known problems. The binary-search bug was not left unfixed for long, but probably many other Java bugs were.

Unfair Comparisons 2: Comparing analysis and programming is unfair. Programmers have tools that analysts lack, like linters and type-checkers, that catch many errors.

Appropriate: One difficulty with applying the Sunrise problem to RE and SE is whether it is appropriate at all. In many situations, one knows a lot more about an event than the number of times it occurred in the past. For example, we know from other scientific models that in about four-billion years, the sun will explode and around that time the odds that the sun will rise will steadily decrease, until one day they will become zero. But for all of the Sunrise equations, the odds will steadily increase until the day the sun explodes. On the last day, the estimates given by all of the Sunrise equations will be horribly wrong.

Testing, budgeting, and scheduling have similar problems with predicting the future and can also use the Sunrise equations, though we leave the elaborations of those topics as exercises for readers.

We are unaware of any other descriptions of the hyperbolic solution to the Sunrise problem. We hope that astute readers will point out appropriate prior work.

Pronunciation: One drawback to the Mandelbrotian equation is that the pronunciation remains unclear. We fear that debates over whether "Mandelbrotian" rhymes with "oh-shun" or "oh-tee-an" could fracture civil society in SE. We also fear that some may stubbornly cling to the wrong answer. We will.

The Sunrise equations are used in the next chapter "Polish versus Rot."

Laplace used the term "Rule of Succession" instead of the term "Sunrise Problem."

Another Laplacian Equation: Another Laplacian equation, $(x' + 1) \div (n + 2)$, adds one success and one failure to each set of observations. It moves the estimate toward 50-50 rather than toward zero.

Other Rules of Three: For many years, we (the authors) have tried to find three examples of each point in our essays. It takes three licks to get to the center of a Tootsie Pop.

The Sunrise problem puts numbers on the "sampling problem."

Frequentists tend to believe that low-probability events (like winning the lottery or unknown bugs) don't occur. The Sunrise equations are Bayesian because low-probability events will occur eventually.

Bibliography

Dan Ariely, *The Upside of Irrationality*, Harper, 2010.

Thomas Bayes and Richard Price, "An Essay towards Solving a Problem in the Doctrine of Chances," in *Philosophical Transactions*, volume 53, pages 370 to 418, Royal Society, 1763.

Kent Beck, *Test-Driven Development*, Addison Wesley, 2002.

Brad Bird, *The Incredibles*, Pixar, 2004.

Dustin Boswell and Trevor Foucher, *The Art of Readable Code*, O'Reilly, 2011.

Frederick P. Brooks Jr., *The Mythical Man-Month. Anniversary Edition*, Addison Wesley, 1995.

Alan Cooper, Robert Reimann, David Cronin, *About Face 3: the Essentials of Interaction Design*, Wiley, 2007.

Martin Fowler, *Refactoring: Improving the Design of Existing Code*, Addison Wesley, 1999.

David H. Freedman, *Wrong*, Little Brown, 2010.

Mike Hinchey, "Evolving Critical Systems," ACM Webinar, August 2, 2016.

Daniel Jackson, keynote at FSE 2016.

Richard Jeffreys, *Subjective Probability: The Real Thing*, Cambridge, 2004.

Michael Lewis, *Undoing Project*, Norton, 2016.

Panagiotis Louridas, Diomidis Spinellis, and Vasileios Vlachos, "Power Laws of Software," in *TOSEM*, volume 18, issue 1, article 1, ACM, September 2008.

Benoit B. Mandelbrot, *The Fractal Geometry of Nature*, Freeman, 1983.

Benoit B. Mandelbrot, *The Fractalist: Memoirs of a Scientific Maverick*, Pantheon, 2012.

Robert C. Martin, *Clean Code*, Prentice Hall, 2008.

Dewayne Perry, "Where Do Software Flaws Come From?," in Andy Oram and Greg Wilson (editors), *Making Software*, pages 453 to 494, O'Reilly, 2011.

R. Keith Sawyer, *Explaining Creativity*, Oxford, 2012.

Nate Silver, *The Signal and the Noise*, Penguin, 2012.

Will Tracz, *Confessions of a Used Software Salesman: Institutionalizing Reuse*, Addison Wesley, 1995.

Karl E. Wiegers, *Software Requirements 2*, Microsoft Press, 2003.

10
Polish versus Rot

During development, quality primarily improves via polish or multiple app refinement. After development ends, quality primarily worsens via rot or multiple context change. We strive to organize and clarify a variety of well-known details about polish and rot – that they affect all programs and standards; that all programs and standards have bounded lifespans; and that analysts, programmers, and testers can only affect quality in limited and specific ways.

Polish and rot correspond to the two forms of emergence – change that occurs inside and outside of projects. All development and refactoring happens because of context change. Technical debt is the choice of when and how to respond. Traditionally, technical debt corresponds to deferring polish but another form also corresponds to deferring rot.

First, we list many examples of app refinements and context changes in order to provide an empirical foundation for this chapter. Then, we contrast polish with rot to reveal aspects of their natures. Then, we delve into the mechanisms for increasing polish and deferring rot to clarify the economic tradeoffs of technical debt. Finally, we combine polish and rot to define a wave-shaped upper bound on software quality.

Examples

Listing many real-world examples of app refinement and context change grounds this chapter in "empirical" data.

Examples of App Refinements

The mechanisms of app refinement include multiple analyses, developments, refactorings, inspections, and tests, both within and across projects. They also include training, prior experience, pairings, and checklists.

Serial App Refinement within Projects

Royce Waterfall Example: In his classic paper on the Waterfall, Winston Royce recommended developing software three times within each project – first as a paper design with 50 times more detail than for a comparable hardware system, then as a quarter-scale prototype, and finally as a full-scale system. Each stage informs the rest of the project. (Royce, pages 332 to 334)

Debugging Example: Debugging usually proceeds via serial app refinement. Developers try one potential solution after the next, hopefully the most cost effective or highest odds of success first, until they fix the bug.

Testing Example: Testing usually proceeds via serial app refinement. First, developers write some unit tests and then run some manual tests on features in isolation as they write code. Then, testers consistently retest each feature in the context of the whole program. And finally, users do alpha and beta testing of the whole program in the context of the real world.

Parallel App Refinements across Projects

Software engineers develop many programs in parallel, independent projects and then the winners become standards.

Program Examples: In hot markets, many companies develop programs in parallel and only the most competitive survive. In the 1960s and '70s, many companies wrote database and accounting programs for mainframes, and Oracle won. In the 1980s and '90s, many companies wrote word processors and spreadsheets for PCs, and Microsoft Office won. In the 2000s and '10s, many companies wrote communication and game programs for mobile phones, and Snapchat and Pokémon Go are doing well, even though the race continues.

Library Examples: Developers often implement algorithms and protocols a variety of times and then committees select the best ones and add them into each standard library, for example the Java and .Net libraries.

Standard Examples: Standard organizations, like the Internet Engineering Task Force (IETF), Institute of Electrical and Electronics Engineers (IEEE), and Object Management Group (OMG), bring people from a variety of project-sponsoring organizations (companies, government agencies, and open-source projects) together to work in parallel on each revision of each network and communication standard. Large working groups bring ten, twenty, or more organizations together. The participants in each working group collectively revise their standards until they become effective.

NIST Examples: When the US National Institute of Standards and Technology (NIST) created the Advanced Encryption Standard (AES), they considered 15 different algorithms and selected Rijndael. When NIST created the Secure Hash Algorithm 3 (SHA3), they considered 51 different algorithms and selected Keccak.

Serial App Refinements across Projects

Stepping close to look at individual programs and standards shows that sponsoring organizations refine them through long series of projects over decades. At each step, analysts and developers attempt to keep whatever works and to improve whatever doesn't.

Program Examples: All enduring programs evolve through a long series of projects. Microsoft Windows has evolved through many major versions: $1.0 \rightarrow 2.0 \rightarrow 3.0 \rightarrow 3.1 \rightarrow NT \rightarrow 95 \rightarrow 98 \rightarrow ME \rightarrow XP \rightarrow Vista \rightarrow 7 \rightarrow 8 \rightarrow 8.1 \rightarrow 10$. Microsoft Office for Windows has evolved through many major versions: $1.0 \rightarrow 1.5 \rightarrow 1.6 \rightarrow 3.0 \rightarrow 4.0 \rightarrow 95 \rightarrow 97 \rightarrow 2000 \rightarrow XP \rightarrow 2003 \rightarrow 2007 \rightarrow 2010 \rightarrow 2013 \rightarrow 2016$.

Standard Examples: Fortran has evolved through many standards: $I \rightarrow II \rightarrow III \rightarrow IV \rightarrow 66 \rightarrow 77 \rightarrow 90 \rightarrow 95 \rightarrow 2003 \rightarrow 2008 \rightarrow 2015$. Secure-communication protocols have evolved through many standards: $SSL1 \rightarrow SSL2 \rightarrow TLS1.0 \rightarrow TLS1.1 \rightarrow TLS1.2$. Secure-hashing algorithms have evolved through many standards: $SHA0 \rightarrow SHA1 \rightarrow SHA2 \rightarrow SHA3$.

Both Parallel and Serial App Refinements across Projects

Stepping back to look at programs and standards in their contexts shows that rich ecosystems encourage improvement. Programs and standards improve both in serial and in parallel at the same time – improving on themselves as appropriate as well as adopting the best ideas vetted in rival products.

Program Examples: Operating systems inhabit a rich ecosystem that includes Windows, MacOS, Linux, iOS, and Android. Consider that Microsoft changed Windows 10 to use the app-store distribution model pioneered by iOS and Android. Games and utilities also inhabit rich ecosystems.

Standard Examples: Programming languages inhabit a rich ecosystem that includes Assembler, C, C#, Fortran, Go, Haskell, Java, Lisp, Perl, Prolog, and Python, all of which evolve in their own ways. Encryption algorithms inhabit a rich ecosystem that includes the Blowfish, DES, RC, and Rijndael families.

Examples of Context Changes

The mechanisms of context change include growing data, evolving expectations and usages, as well as evolving hardware and software platforms. Note that arbitrary limits exacerbate data growth problems and that platform changes encompass reusing and porting code. (Wikipedia, "Software Rot")

Mechanisms of Context Change

Data Growth: Perhaps the most classic example of software rot is data growth. As organizations accrue data and as databases get larger, access tends to slow down, search results tend to become overwhelming, users tend to run into arbitrary limits, and programs tend to become less usable.

Expectation Change: Users change their expectations as they get training and experience and learn to appreciate other sophisticated software. According to Sluizer's principle, whenever users interact with software, their expectations change, even if the requirements are otherwise perfect. (Sluizer) • Expectation change occurs both throughout projects and after releases. Users incrementally reveal their expectations as they slowly figure out what they want by discovering the possibilities, changing their minds, and demanding better features and more finesse. Evolving user expectations mean that nobody can describe programs once-and-for-all. We believe that expectation change actually causes most software rot.

Usage Change: Programs and source codes often get used differently than originally intended or tested. • For example, many Customer Relationship Managers (CRMs) delete records that are closed. But CRM agents may want to reactivate those records later without losing information, so they use tricks like adding "XXX" into the name or adding a "deleted" field to mark deletion, rather than actually closing the records. Such conventions complicate queries. Whenever CRM agents think of new bits of information to gather, they store them as text in existing note fields, which complicates queries. Ideally, those bits of information would reside in separate typed fields. • For another example, when users invoke features in different orders than testers, they may reveal previously undetected bugs and limitations. Architectural rot and code smells also occur when code gets used differently than programmers originally intended. (Le, Carrillo, Capilla, Medvidovic)

Hardware-Platform Change: Hardware platforms have evolved from mainframes to mobile phones and most have died. The programs written for the Mark 1, Zuse, Eniac, Univac, CDC 6600, System 360, Cray 1, Vax, Altair 8800, and Apple II all died long ago. Their contexts have vanished. Adventure for the PDP-10 died. WordPerfect and Lotus 123 for MSDOS died. A few programs might have survived since the 1950s or 1980s unchanged, but we don't know what they are, except maybe missile controllers. We expect that within fifty years, Wintel PCs and ARM mobile phones will also have died, possibly replaced by something based on pure graphics processors.

Software-Platform Change: Operating systems have evolved from monitors to CP/M to Windows 10. Programming systems have evolved from switch and patch-cord panels to Assembler to Java 10. Databases, user interfaces, communication protocols, and libraries have also evolved dramatically. With HTML and Javascript, web browsers now act as freestanding software platforms that evolve in their own ways.

Arbitrary Limits Exacerbate Data Growth Problems

Programming has always involved a lot of working around arbitrary limits. As computers get more powerful and as memories get larger, arbitrary limits become less of a problem, but they never go away. Arbitrary limits arise from the difficulty of predicting the future and the real costs of unused hardware and software today.

Maximum Array Size: On Wintel PCs, the maximum array size grew from 64 kB per array on the 8086 and Win16 runtime, to 2gB for all data on the 80386 and Win32 runtime, to 2gB per array on the Pentium and Win64 runtime. Java arrays currently max out at about 2g elements. As data grows and programs run into those limits, developers write workarounds. As computers get larger and those limits evaporate, developers remove the workarounds.

IPv4 and IPv6: IPv4 used 32-bit network addresses in 1981 when the Arpanet only connected mainframe and mini computers at government research laboratories, ten years before home PCs could connect. Using 32 bits was huge at the time, but Bertrand Meyer recently complained about the shortsightedness of 32 bits. (Meyer, page 60) IPv6 used 128-bit network addresses in 1998 after PCs started connecting to the Internet and before the Internet of Things (IOT) became a thing. Using 128 bits was huge at the time, but we expect that someday, maybe in century or so, someone will criticize IPv6 for the same reason, the shortsightedness of 128 bits. Network addresses could have started with 256 or 1024 bits, but that would have cost more in the short-term.

Governor Limits: Today, Salesforce programmers wrangle with bulkification and governor limits, like the maximum number of queries and callouts allowed per webpage and the maximum number of records returned per query. These limits ensure that users won't have to wait long for webpages to load, but can cause problems for many otherwise reasonable programs.

Platform Change Encompasses Reusing and Porting Code

Developers usually focus on making their software work in the target environment and they rarely worry much about how software could fail if ported to or reused in different contexts, which would occur in some arbitrary and unknown future. The following examples resemble installing a program on a faster computer linked to a bigger network and just presuming that everything will continue working fine.

Therac-25 Example: The Therac software worked fine on one platform that had hardware interlocks (safety features), but killed people when the company ported it to a different platform that lacked the hardware interlocks. Looked at one way, the software relied on the hardware. Looked at another way, the hardware masked potential bugs in the software. The context change revealed the discrepancies between how the software did work and how it supposedly worked.

Ariane-5 Example: The Ariane 5 contained software written for the Ariane 4, which wasn't even really used. The software worked just fine in the Ariane 4, but failed during the first launch of the Ariane 5, causing the rocket to explode. The context had changed. Using Ada may have increased the delusion that the Ariane-4 software would work without change in the Ariane-5.

Telnet and FTP Examples: Telnet and FTP have remained essentially the same for fifty years, but their contexts have changed dramatically. • Telnet and FTP originally ran on the Arpanet. In the 1960s and '70s, the Arpanet needed little security. Only trusted researchers could access the privileged terminals. Anyone who misbehaved, could have their physical access revoked. The Arpanet primarily exchanged documentation about science and technology projects, so most everyone could see and access the shared information anyways. PCs didn't exist, so nobody could hack into the network. The new network technology meant that obfuscation still worked. In that original context and for those original purposes, protocols like Telnet, FTP, and later RSH worked well. • Today, Telnet and FTP run on the public Internet. Anyone can get a PC and watch packets go past on the local network or send packets to and receive packets from almost any IP address. People now use the Internet to access information that truly should remain private, such as financial, medical, and voting records. Malicious behavior provokes few penalties, unless someone gets carried away. Telnet and FTP still work on the Internet, but everyone should avoid using them because they still transmit account names, passwords, and data in the clear.

Encryption Examples: DES, SSL2, and SHA1 embodied the best cryptography of their times. Eventually, powerful computers made the small keys of DES easy to crack. SSL2 and SHA1 have also been deprecated as better cryptography theory and more powerful computers loom ominously. Note that these encryption standards remain the same as they ever were, only the contexts have changed.

Polish Versus Rot

Polish and rot mirror each other in many ways, as shown in table 1. Contrasting them helps to reveal their natures.

Table 1: Polish versus Rot		
Issues	**Polish**	**Rot**
Definitions	Multiple Positive App Refinements	Multiple Negative Context Changes
Timeframes	Before Release	After Release
Natures of State	Finite and Known	Infinite and Unknown
Natures of Change	Enumerated, Explicit, and Visible	Infinite, Implicit, and Invisible
Agents of Change	Project Team Members	Other People in Society
Testability	Positive Past Properties Are	Negative Future Properties Aren't
Equations	Sunrise	Decay
Technical Debt	Deferring Polish	Deferring Rot

Definitions

Multiple Positive App Refinements: Multiple positive app refinements tend to improve quality. First drafts of programs and standards usually start out wonky and need many revisions to get good just like all other forms of writing, including technical essays and poetry. In general, higher-quality programs and standards emerge from lots of polish.

Multiple Negative Context Changes: Multiple negative context changes tend to worsen quality. But, programs and standards don't spontaneously change for the worse on their own because bugs don't spontaneously multiply and algorithms don't spontaneously switch to worse versions. On rare occasions, bits in memory or on disk do spontaneously degrade, but restarts or reinstalls can fix those problems. The real sources of rot come from outside the program or standard and include changes in user expectations and usages as well as changes in hardware and software platforms. All context changes reveal that the foundations below programs and standards really are shifting sand.

Emergence Spectrum

App Refinement: Polish includes the whole spectrum of single, dual, and multiple positive app refinements. Polish usually emerges slowly through many positive app refinements, though the spectrum also includes single app refinements or doing things once. Individual app refinements rarely make much of a difference on their own because they provide the fewest opportunities for improvement. Note that most programs have many features that need separate polish.

Context Change: Rot includes the whole spectrum of single, dual, and multiple negative context changes. Rot usually emerges slowly through many negative context changes, though the spectrum also includes single context changes. Individual context changes rarely make much of a difference on their own, though some (like the Y2K and Y2K38 date rollovers and the DYN and WannaCry malware attacks) provoke catastrophes.

Cut Both Ways

Not all app refinements benefit programs and standards. Not all context changes damage programs and standards. Most of each actually improve quality, benefiting users, programs, and standards alike, even though some of each do worsen quality. So, both app refinements and context changes cut both ways.

App Refinement: App refinements usually improve quality. As analysts, developers, and testers work on programs and standards, refining them through multiple analyses, designs, codings, inspections, and tests, whether in series or in parallel, quality tends to improve. App refinements sometimes worsen quality, which is called "code entropy." Adding bugs during app refinement occurs routinely, but in our experience occurs much less often than quality improves. When programmers fail to clean up after changes or fail to refactor, the structure of the code can degrade making future changes harder.

Context Change: Context changes usually improve quality, helping users, programs, and standards alike. Context changes include computers getting faster and memories getting larger as well as operating systems and libraries adding features, improving security, and fixing bugs. In general, everyone should want contexts to improve because they should want to gain the benefits of the upgraded platforms. Context changes sometimes worsen quality. The term "software rot" applies whenever context changes cause problems for users, programs, or standards, such as data growth, expectation change, and platform obsolescence.

Examples: In general, more powerful computers make programs run better, but not always. For example, powerful computers both strengthen and weaken cryptography. As embedded devices get faster processors and better sensors, users expect embedded programs to do more useful work, and they tend to become disappointed when programs remain unchanged.

Timeframes

The time of discovery and fix can affect whether requirement problems and coding bugs seem more like polish or more like rot. Usually, quality peaks just as development finishes, at release.

Before Release: Quality primarily improves during development. In general, before the release of a program or standard, analysts fix requirement problems and developers fix coding bugs as they are found. In general, everyone interprets those fixes as polish.

After Release: Quality primarily worsens after development ends. In general, after the release of a program or standard, rot will reveal any remaining requirement problems and coding bugs. In general, these problems will remain unfixed and will accumulate until the next upgrade.

Rot Actually Occurs All the Time: Context changes actually occur both before and after release or, in other words, rot also occurs throughout development. For example, users often change their minds about goals during projects, we know of projects that competitors rendered obsolete before release, and architectural rot can occur as long as developers change code. Yet, as long as a project continues, analysts, developers, and testers can potentially counteract rot.

Natures of State

Finite and Known: Users, analysts, and developers can only describe and implement finite and known properties. Requirement and specification documents explicitly describe the desired finite and known features of each program and standard.

Infinite and Unknown: Everyone struggles to describe the enormous, complicated, and continually evolving contexts because they lack the time and energy to understand everything about their hardware and software platforms. Even though in theory, platforms are finite and known, in practice, they are so large that they are effectively infinite and much remains unknown to each analyst and developer. Nobody has the time to describe or implement infinite properties. Nobody knows how to describe or implement unknown properties.

Platform Examples: The enormous platforms provided by Windows and Linux and the enormous libraries available for Java and .Net are overwhelming. Requirement documents almost never describe the platforms below programs except in the most general terms, for example, "the program shall run on Androids and iPhones."

Great Oral Tradition Example: Analysts and developers have enormous bodies of conventions, expectations, knowledge, and experiences that remain undocumented. Creating effective architectures and pleasing UIs still requires a lot of murky intuition and aesthetic judgement. Decades ago, IBMers referred to this body of knowledge as the "Great Oral Tradition" and it continues getting larger for everyone today.

Natures of Change

Enumerated, Explicit, and Visible: Users and analysts tend to explicitly enumerate the desired changes of each project in requirement documents. In general, everyone can explicitly see and count the changes that users have requested. • Changes to programs (specifically features) must be visible and explicit because users cannot use and testers cannot test what they cannot see.

Infinite, Implicit, and Invisible: Infinitely many potential context changes could occur, so nobody can describe everything that must remain unchanged for a program or standard to remain vital. Most potential changes have low probability and should go unmentioned even though they could conceivably occur. Nobody can analyze the risks of an infinite number of context changes, either. • Many context changes easily elude detection. For example, users can easily see when a UI becomes unfashionable, but they cannot see when a security system becomes unsafe.

Security Examples: The context stabilities needed for AES and SHA3 to remain vital include that computers won't get more powerful faster than current growth curves estimate, that quantum computing won't become practical any time soon, that nobody will find low-degree polynomial algorithms for NP-complete problems, that no new theory will break AES or SHA3 directly, that AES and SHA3 won't fall out of fashion in favor of different technologies, that new hacking techniques won't expose hardware and software platforms in ways that render AES and SHA3 moot, that clairvoyance won't become common, and that extraterrestrial aliens won't invade. Note that improved theories and computers have already undermined many security standards.

Agents of Change

Project Team Members: Project team members exert a good deal of control over programs and standards because they can take deliberate actions to make programs and standards behave in specific ways. Users and analysts can indirectly modify programs and standards by changing the requirements. Developers can directly modify programs and standards by changing the source code. People in computer science, requirements engineering, and software engineering study how to take control of and thereby improve programs and standards through explicit actions during projects.

Other People in Society: Almost nobody has control over the contexts of programs and standards because other people in society cause most context changes. The causes of rot remain beyond the control of anyone on project teams. • Some context changes occur predictably, in general if not in specific. Intel, ARM, Nvidia, and AMD continually tinker with their CPUs and graphics processors, occasionally adding instructions and cores. Microsoft, Apple, Android, and Linux make major upgrades to their operating systems every few years. Standard organizations upgrade programming languages and protocols every 5 to 15 years. • Other changes defy prediction. Nobody predicted that the U.S. National Security Agency would give tools to hackers to create WannaCry. Nobody predicted that cryptographers would find weaknesses in Diffie-Helman and SHA1. Users continually change their expectations and usages and, in general, nobody can predict what users will want next.

The fact that different agents-of-change control polish and rot helps to explain why solving the polish problem cannot solve the rot problem. Users, analysts, and developers can only add more polish, which affects only half of how quality changes. Until someone learns to predict the future changes in expectations, usages, and platforms, they will never solve rot. Specification languages and model-driven development will not solve rot, either.

Testability

Positive Past Program Changes Can Be Tested: In general, test plans work well for the specific, positive properties of programs. For example, one can test that records get inserted, updated, and fetched in a database. Note that testing focusses on properties that already exist in working programs from the known and finite past.

Negative Future Context Changes Cannot Be Tested: In general, test plans do not work for the negative properties of contexts. No plan can test that a context has not changed in an unexpected way. No plan can test that future context changes won't reveal any bugs. No plan can test whether security algorithms (like AES and SHA3) remain secure. No plan can test that FTP remains fit for some purpose. No plan can truly test ilities (like the portability or reusability of a program) without knowing the specific contexts that will arise. No plan can test whether users did or didn't change their minds about what they want, though of course they eventually will. • Note that context test plans would ideally detect the changes that will occur in any of the infinite possible futures shortly before they materialize. Detecting that a platform will change many years ahead does not help because obviously many things will change by then.

Edsger Dijkstra knew about the limits of testing 50 years ago when he wrote, "testing shows the presence, but not the absence of bugs." We would add another caveat about contexts, "testing shows the presence of bugs in programs, but neither the absence of bugs in programs nor anything about context changes." (Dijkstra, page 16)

Thoroughly retesting each program in context before delivery is a best practice. But, nobody can afford to retest programs every day as contexts incrementally evolve.

Equations

We offer the Sunrise and Decay equations as the key patterns for how quality changes over time as shown in table 2 and figure 1. Note that each equation expresses a different rate of diminishing returns and that the Sunrise and Decay equations mirror each other.

Sunrise

The Sunrise equations describe the shapes of polish, showing how quality improves over time. Small statistical samples can capture the underlying truth with luck, or get it totally wrong without luck, or anything in between. The Sunrise equations show how to understand the quality of small statistical samples or equivalently the incremental benefits of each additional sample or equivalently how many samples are needed to achieve any desired degree of certainty.

Feature Example: When one user asks for feature x, he or she could agree with all other users, but analysts have no guarantees that the next user won't contradict the first by having a different and better idea. When three users ask for feature x, analysts have more certainty, but still not a lot. For example, analysts may have asked three users in the support department, but may not have asked anyone in quality control, accounting, or management – users who wield far more clout in the organization. Analysts may not even think to ask those other users. Analysts must necessarily start discovery with small samples, but small samples invariably lead to at least some mistakes, like wrong or missing requirements. Asking everyone takes a long time and costs a lot for large user-bases.

Decay

The Decay equations describe the shapes of rot, showing how quality worsens over time. These equations model atomic decay in physics and fund payouts in economics.

Fractal Example: One could also think of Decay in terms of the function $f(n) = (1-\varepsilon)^n$. Robert May's logistic map, Benoit Mandelbrot's set, and Edward Lorenz's attractor all have some initial values that have predictable outcomes and other initial values that have unpredictable outcomes, but telling them apart can be tricky. In the unpredictable cases, the discrepancy between initial estimates and final outcomes will become clear at some scale of n where $\forall x{\leq}n \rightarrow f(x){\geq}c$ and $\forall x{>}n \rightarrow f(x){<}c$. For large error rates, $\varepsilon \approx 2^{-6}$, discrepancies will show up quickly. For tiny error rates, $\varepsilon \approx 2^{-\text{gazillion}}$, discrepancies will show up only

121

after a long, long time. For zero error rates, $\varepsilon = 0$, discrepancies will never appear. The certainty c indicates the desired probability of success or level of quality, for example 0.99, 0.9, or 0.5.

Table 2: Sunrise and Decay Equations		
Names	**Formulas**	**Notes**
Prician Sunrise	$1-(2^n)^{-1}$	independent and serial evidence
Mandelbrotian Sunrise	$1-(1+n^c)^{-1}$	mixed serial and parallel evidence
Laplacian Sunrise	$1-(1+n)^{-1}$	interdependent or parallel evidence
Exponential Decay	$(2^{dn})^{-1}$	opposite of Prician Sunrise – atomic decay
Mandelbrotian Decay	$(1+dn^c)^{-1}$	opposite of Mandelbrotian Sunrise
Hyperbolic Decay	$(1+dn)^{-1}$	opposite of Laplacian Sunrise

Technical Debt

Deferring Polish: The classic concept of technical debt is stopping investment in polish early or cutting off development effort before release. This concept is often thought of as inadequate development, maintenance, or refactoring and is well-understood, based on the Managing Technical Debt workshops.

Deferring Rot: Another concept of technical debt is deferring or ignoring rot. Keeping older programs alive means that they become less useful and risks accrue over time, whether anyone is aware or not. This concept has received scant attention.

Root Causes: The root causes of both forms of technical debt are context changes, which nobody on project teams can control. They appear in the guise of the costs of polish and the changes that evoke surprise. Surprises arise from the inability to predict the future.

Making Choices: Accruing technical debt means choosing to delay investing resources or to avoid responding to (or coping with) context changes. Both forms of technical debt defer development or maintenance by trading lower short-term cost for greater long-term risk.

Balancing Forms of Debt: In one important sense, technical debt is the opposite of resource debt. Anyone who could borrow resources (time and money) to invest in development or maintenance could reduce their technical debt. Balancing resource debt against technical debt is a reasonable strategy for choosing how much technical debt to accrue.

The Tradeoffs of Increasing Polish

Increasing polish improves quality by fighting mistakes upfront during development. The mechanisms for increasing polish create and extend opportunities to find better solutions to the problems at hand, however they cannot necessarily catch all mistakes. These mechanisms embody complex economic tradeoffs because their benefits and detriments mirror each other as shown in table 3.

Table 3: The Tradeoffs of Increasing Polish		
Mechanisms	**Benefits**	**Detriments**
Practice	Proficiency and Fewer Mistakes	Redundancy and Waste
Time	Polish	Delay
Diversity	Better Solutions	Feature Creep
Competition	Creativity and Productivity	Exposes Private Information
Surprise	Learning	Remediation
Economic Tradeoffs	Lower Risks after Release	Greater Costs before Release

Practice

Proficiency and Fewer Mistakes: Dual and multiple development increase practice and reduce mistakes as in "practice makes perfect." Strong analysts, developers, and testers have practiced skills and decisions many times. High-quality programs and standards follow from a lot of practice in the form of multiple analyses, developments, inspections, and tests, whether in the current or previous projects.

Redundancy and Waste: Each additional implementation beyond the first takes additional work, which can seem redundant or even wasteful, especially as returns appear to diminish.

Time

Polish: More implementations usually take longer to finish. The implementation that takes the longest tends to extend the deadline for everyone else, giving them more opportunities to think things through and to polish their results.

Delay: Multiple development takes more time than single development, occasionally a lot more time, which slows down projects and results.

Diversity

Better Solutions: Diversity helps to find better solutions. Different analysts and developers using different approaches in different contexts often produce different results, doing different things well and different things poorly. Hopefully, each poor idea in one implementation will overlap an excellent idea in another. The greater the diversity, the greater the likelihood that one project or another will implement each feature well.

Feature Creep: The final versions of programs and standards based on multiple app refinements tend to contain more of the cool features from the union of all implementations. Because diversity tends to generate more cool ideas, programs and standards tend to ratchet or accrete features and flexibilities.

Competition

Creativity and Productivity: Healthy competition can increase both creativity and productivity. Many people struggle to find the problems within their own work and input from outsiders can provoke constructive conflict, which can help to avoid settling for flawed results or groupthink. (Grant, pages 184 to 185) In organizations working on standards (like the IETF, IEEE, and OMG), competing companies, government agencies, and open-source organizations collaborate with each other. Motivated partly by competitive spirit, participants strive to find problems in each other's work as well as strive to avoid screwing up and looking bad compared to rivals.

Exposes Private Information: Collaboration requires the sharing of information, so organizations cannot keep everything secret.

Surprise

Learning: Ideally, multiple development evokes the surprises that drive learning as opposed to the proverbial insanity of rote repetition. Hopefully through comparison, participants will discern the differences and then figure out which ideas and implementations work better than others.

Remediation: Whenever someone else's code surprises a developer, he or she must often remediate his or her own code, which takes additional time and effort. Ignorance is bliss because it takes less time and effort in the short-run.

Economic Tradeoffs

Lower Risks after Release: Increasing polish lowers long-term risks. Increasing polish will most-likely give programs and standards higher quality as perceived by users and possibly even longer lifespans.

Greater Costs before Release: Increasing polish or doing more work upfront raises short-term costs.

The Tradeoffs of Deferring Rot

Deferring rot improves quality by fighting context change after the release of a program or standard. The mechanisms for deferring rot can extend the lifespans of programs and standards, however they cannot necessarily avert any given expectation change or malware attack. These mechanisms embody complex economic tradeoffs because their benefits and detriments mirror each other as shown in table 4.

Table 4: The Tradeoffs of Deferring Rot		
Mechanisms	**Benefits**	**Detriments**
Stabilize Platforms	Keep Legacy Systems Unchanged	Forego Platform Changes, Clutter
Restrict Platforms	Hide Problems	Forego Context Expansions
Stabilize Subsystems	Factor Out Volatility	Distortion
Economic Tradeoffs 1	Lower Short-Term Costs and Risks	Greater Long-Term Costs and Risks
Economic Tradeoffs 2	Greater Short-Term Productivity	Lower Long-Term Productivity
Economic Tradeoffs 3	Economy of Scale	Stuck in the Past, Delusion

Stabilize Platforms

Keep Legacy Systems Unchanged: Stable platforms enable legacy systems to endure longer without change. Techniques for keeping hardware and software platforms stable include stubbornly never changing them, maintaining backward compatibility, and emulation or virtual machines. Changing and sunsetting old platforms force bifurcation because everyone who has legacy systems on those platforms must either port them to another (possibly upgraded) platform or watch them die. Note that stabilization requires maturity because immature platforms change routinely.

Forego Platform Changes: When platforms remain stable, users and developers must forego the benefits of changes, such as the increased power and energy-efficiency of newer processors as well as the bug fixes, security fixes, and new functionalities of newer operating systems and libraries. Whenever developers cannot use upgraded platforms, they may need to duplicate the upgraded features and bug fixes themselves.

Clutter: Stable platforms often succumb to clutter. Marie Kondo argues that slogging through clutter in the real world wastes time and energy. (Kondo) Decluttering by removing old programs saves time and energy in the virtual world, too. Users can voluntarily get rid of old programs and vendors can voluntarily get rid of old platforms. Like a dust mop, sunsetting an old platform sweeps away many old, unsafe, incompatible, undesirable, unfashionable programs at once. Charging annual fees to keep apps alive in stores also encourages decluttering.

Embedded-System and Cloud-Server Examples: Embedded systems seem most amenable to stable platforms. For example, embedded devices in electricity meters can remain in place for twenty years or more. Even so, many embedded devices now have the ability to remotely upgrade the software. Cloud servers that communicate solely via web-APIs can also remain stable for decades.

Restrict Platforms

Hide Problems: Platform restrictions enable developers to hide some kinds of security problems. For example, one could physically separate the network so that programs that have weak security can endure longer without change.

Forego Context Expansions: Platform restrictions make context expansions riskier. Context restrictions also prohibit legitimately accessing the device or program from centralized service centers on the Internet.

Protocol Examples: Restricting devices to communicate through serial ports or private networks enables Telnet, FTP, SSL2, and SHA1 to continue running safely, but those contexts should expand only with great caution. Changing from physically-isolated networks to virtual-private networks may seem innocuous, but it increases risk. Adding any new device into a restricted network also increases risk.

Stabilize Subsystems

Factor Out Volatility: UIs tend to have much greater volatility than backends. Factoring UIs out to isolate or absorb change can enable backends to remain stable longer. UI developers can even run interference to work around some issues that would otherwise force backends to change.

Distortion: Factoring increases distortion. Using Corba or web-APIs complicates and distorts communication more than using native function calls. When designers guess wrong about what will remain stable, or get unlucky, they may still have to change the backend anyways or, even worse, have to change both the UI and the backend. When backends remain stable, changes to UIs become increasingly awkward

124

as backends become increasingly out of date. Factoring a program into pieces can also cost a lot in its own right.

Economic Tradeoffs 1

Lower Short-Term Costs and Risks: Deferring rot lowers short-term maintenance costs in terms of money to pay for upgrades and new programs. Upgrading legacy systems can require substantial resources, which often belong to "someone else." Recreating lost source codes tends to require tremendous resources. Deferring rot also lowers short-term risks. In general, legacy systems that worked fine yesterday will also work fine today. All changes that update or replace legacy systems today increase the short-term odds of breaking something.

Organizations don't want to upgrade platforms because recertifying all of the apps that they support tends to be painful. When upgrading operating systems, some computers may be out for service and miss the upgrade, causing additional problems. Many people resent upgrades because, without retraining, their skills can become out-of-date or obsolete.

Greater Long-Term Costs and Risks: Deferring rot increases long-term costs. No longer having to support legacy systems frees up resources to work on more-contemporary, more-relevant systems, which should foster better software sooner. Deferring rot also increases long-term risks. The risks that someone will misuse each legacy system only increase over time, for example due to outdated security. As long as Telnet and FTP exist, even if only to communicate with legacy systems connected directly to a server via a private network, someone will eventually say, aware of the risks or not, "we can use FTP to transfer these top-secret files." The longer a system remains stable, the more likely someone with vital knowledge about it will leave.

Economic Tradeoffs 2

Greater Short-Term Productivity: Deferring rot avoids the disruptions that lower short-term productivity. Users don't have to learn new or upgraded software. Admins don't have to install new or upgraded software. Developers don't have to develop or maintain software. Nobody will disrupt their learning curves. Organizations can apply all of those resources (that time and energy) to other problems.

Lower Long-Term Productivity: Deferring rot delays the benefits of better software for longer. Users can be trained to use older, less-fashionable, lower-quality software, but they will remain more disappointed and less productive for longer.

Economic Tradeoffs 3

Economy of Scale: One well-established principle of economics states that expanding the scale of the economy lowers costs. Platform standards extend the base of transferable skills and programs across more projects, people, and organizations.

Stuck in the Past: Keeping legacy systems alive denies the benefits of moving on to use better and more contemporary programs and standards. It enables stakeholders to remain stuck in the past.

Delusion: Platform standards allow and even encourage people to believe that they can prevent all rot. In our experience, those who obsess over platform standards tend to deny all other changes as well. After all, people standardize platforms specifically to avert change. But, platform standards cannot affect any other aspects of contexts, such as user expectations, user interfaces, and cryptography, which will all continue evolving beyond the influence of any platform standard.

Everyone struggles with these economic tradeoffs.

DOD-Standard Examples: The DOD routinely tries to control the contexts of their programs. DOD platform standards include the 1750a processor, the Cobol and Ada programming languages, and the Popcorn Linux operating system. These standards change rarely and to improve software projects must increasingly switch to other platforms that change more often.

Commercial-Standard Examples: Microsoft (.Net), Oracle (Java), and Apple (Swift) provide "standard" development platforms to the world, which change routinely. All major operating systems provide their own standards for functionality and look and feel.

The Wave-Shaped Upper Bound on Quality

Combining the Sunrise and Decay equations together defines a wave-shaped upper bound on the quality of software, as shown in figure 1. The wave could appear as a triangle if plotted on a log-log graph, as shown in the inset. The horizontal axis represents time with an unstated scale and the vertical axis represents the level of quality or probability of success, ranging from 0 to 1. The light curve shows quality as seen by analysts, developers, and testers and the bold curve shows quality as seen by users, who only receive the improvements after the release.

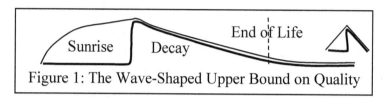

Figure 1: The Wave-Shaped Upper Bound on Quality

Always Imperfect

According to the Sunrise and Decay equations, human-produced programs and standards can never become perfect.

Polish and Imperfection: No finite amount of analysis, programming, and testing can guarantee finding all bugs before the release of a program or standard. No matter when anyone cuts off effort to perfect a chunk of code and moves on, he or she must rationalize that all remaining problems in that chunk of code will remain unimportant or unlikely. But, nobody can ever know for sure. Only by committing unbounded or infinite resources to polishing code can anyone guarantee perfection. Obsessing over perfection (or undetected errors) will prevent analysts, programmers, and testers from ever moving on to do new work. In other words, obsessing over perfection will prevent all further progress on everything else.

Rot and Imperfection: Continuing to use a program or standard means presuming that the context has remained stable and that all negative context changes so far have remained unimportant or unlikely. But, nobody can ever know for sure. Even for embedded systems, manufacturers will eventually upgrade the hardware, developers will eventually upgrade the software, cryptographers will eventually deprecate the protocols, and users will eventually want different features. Only by stopping the rest of the world from changing can anyone truly stabilize the context and avert all rot.

Bounded Lifespans – Evolve or Die

Doomed: Rot kills all programs and standards over the long-term. Programs rarely endure unchanged for more than a few years and we don't know of any that have endured for decades, except maybe military software. For every program and standard that we have considered, we can easily imagine a platform or user-expectation change that will render it moot. Of course, nothing else in the real world endures forever, either.

Ephemeral: All programs and standards live in the present and must eventually either evolve or die. The dashed vertical line in figure 1 represents the end of the useful life of each program and standard. At best, sponsoring organizations develop programs and standards for the near future. Nobody can make their products endure for arbitrary lifespans and, in particular, nobody can make them endure forever.

Commercial Examples: In June 2017, Apple dropped support for 32-bit apps from iOS 11, and the older, less-popular apps that didn't get maintained simply vanished. In 2018, Microsoft continues trying to drop support for Windows 7.

Write-Once-Run-Forever is Impossible

Some people claim to have devised ways to write programs once that will run forever. Such claims are delusional because all polish (all software projects) comes to an end, but rot never ceases. Writing a program once means that nothing will ever improve after release via polish, yet the program will continually undergo context change.

Formal Methodists: In the 1970s, Edsgar Dijkstra and Tony Hoare interpreted programs as algorithms, inspiring generations of researchers to support formal methods and their legacy continues today. Algorithms and abstract data types formalize mathematical concepts. Specifications and models formalize murkier user concepts. While specifications and models may remain correct forever, they will not remain useful forever. Even math and algorithms rot because as more new math gets created, older math gets lost in the noise.

Managers: Managers want simplicity and continuity. Some managers have argued that they could develop computer systems that would remain stable for years. But, data will continue to accrete and expectations will continue to change forever.

Java: Java claims to be write once and run everywhere. The statements and classes within Java may remain stable but the contexts around Java will continue to evolve forever. Java user interfaces have already changed from AWT to Swing to JavaFX to Android and they will continue to evolve. Secure network protocols will continue to evolve. So, no versions of Java libraries can endure forever.

The End is Rarely Obvious until after It Passes

In general, predicting the end of a life (the vertical dashed line in figure 1) ahead of time remains impossible. In physics, everyone can know the distribution of the decay of atoms, but nobody can predict when any specific atom will decay, until it does. In software, everyone can know the distribution of the decay of programs and standards, but nobody can predict when any specific program or standard will decay, until it does. The rare situations where someone can predict the end of life include date-based rollovers (like Y2K and Y2K38) and platform sunsets (like Windows-XP and 32-bit apps on iOS 11).

Smooth and Long-Tailed: The Decay equations have no obvious indicators where risk flips from good to bad. Ideally, everyone would stop using programs and standards before the probability of error crosses some threshold, say 90%, 50%, or 10%, depending on their risk tolerance. Statisticians can calibrate the Decay equations to reveal those threshold crossings. But, those equations cannot reveal what everyone really wants to know – specifically when each program or standard will decay or when the next crisis will occur.

The proverbial frog should hop out of the pot before it boils. Someone should shut the barn door before the proverbial horses escape. Someone should maintain and upgrade each program and standard before the next crisis occurs. The slow and steady decline of rot enables laggards to continue using old programs and standards far beyond when they should, rationalizing the whole time that everything remains fine so far.

Maintenance is the Ongoing Wrangle between Polish and Rot

As programs and standards succumb to rot, as their contexts change, project teams need to respond appropriately by adding polish so that programs and standards can adapt, remain relevant, and endure. Programs need continual redevelopment as data grows and as user expectations and usages evolve. Source codes need continual refactoring, recompiling, and relinking as hardware and software platforms evolve.

A series of maintenance projects can extend the lifespans of programs and standards as shown in figure 2. The light curves show quality as seen by analysts, developers, and testers. The bold curve shows quality as seen by users, who only receive the improvements after releases. After maintenance stops, programs and standards slowly fall out of use and fade away.

All projects are finite prefixes of an infinite series of projects. Microsoft Office and Facebook will only get bigger for a long time to come. When they stop evolving, other apps will replace them.

Fads: Finite lifespans can make programs and standards seem faddish and some have argued that software fads are bad. However, fads show the flow of time. Slowly evolving GUI styles and features are markers for the age and functionality of programs. These markers provide valuable information to users for setting reasonable expectations about how programs should work. As expectations evolve, old software inevitably becomes less useful and updating programs to make them appear contemporary shows ongoing maintenance.

Figure 2: The Quality of a Series of Projects

Notes

Inspirations: This chapter was partly inspired by Peter Neumann's "Risks" column and by a paper by Dalal and Chhillar in *Software Engineering Notes* as well as by the "List of Software Bugs" page on Wikipedia. (Neumann) (Dalal and Chhillar) (Wikipedia, "List of Software Bugs") Those sources enumerate many problems and failures in software. This paper was also partly inspired by Malcolm Gladwell's discussions of inverted-U curves and "no unmitigated good." (Gladwell, pages 52 to 62)

Follow Up: This chapter follows up on the essay "The Uncertainty Principle in Software Engineering" and the chapter "Unknownness" by providing a shape to the uncertainties and unknowns described. (Ziv, Richardson, and Klosch)

Applies to Both Programs and Standards: The observations in this chapter apply to the qualities of both programs and technical standards or informal specifications, but not to the qualities of algorithms, which can be proven correct. We mostly avoid discussing formal specifications and models, though they are doomed as well.

Processes: Processes in organizations for programming and support also undergo polish and rot.

The Word "Rot": The term "software rot" historically referred to software entropy. In the literature, "software entropy" seems to equal "sloppy maintenance" or "inadequate refactoring" but those concepts have nothing to do with context change, which is the root cause of the problem. Perhaps we should use a different word than "rot" in this chapter to avoid confusion, but we don't know of a better word.

The Word "Hyperbolic": The Hyperbolic decay equation has a problematic name because both Mandelbrotian equations also have hyperbolic shapes.

No matter where anyone stops development, he or she accrues technical debt.

Acknowledgements

We want to thank to our friends and colleagues for discussing these ideas and suggesting many improvements to this chapter.

Bibliography

Sandeep Dalal and Rajender Singh Chhillar, "Empirical Study of Root Cause Analysis of Software Failure," in *Software Engineering Notes*, volume 38, issue 4, July 2013.

Edsger Dijkstra, in *Software Engineering Techniques: Report on a Conference Sponsored by the NATO Science Committee*, October 27-31, 1969.

Malcolm Gladwell, *David and Goliath*, Little Brown, 2015.

Adam Grant, *Originals*, Penguin, 2016.

Marie Kondo, *The Life-Changing Magic of Tidying Up*, Ten Speed, 2014.

Bertrand Meyer, *Agile!*, Springer, 2014.

Duc Minh Le, Carlos Carrillo, Rafael Capilla, and Nenad Medvidovic, "Relating Architectural Decay and Sustainability of Software Systems," in WICSA and CompArch 2016.

Peter Neumann, "Risks," ongoing column in *Software Engineering Notes*, ACM, also catless.ncl.ac.uk/Risks/.

Winston W. Royce, "Managing the Development of Large Software Systems," in *Proceedings of IEEE WESCON*, pages 328 to 338, August 1970.

Suzanne Sluizer, private communication, 2017.

Wikipedia, "List of Software Bugs," en.wikipedia.org/wiki/List_of_software_bugs, June 20, 2017.

Wikipedia, "Software Rot," en.wikipedia.org/wiki/Software_rot, August 13, 2017.

Hadar Ziv, Debra J. Richardson, and Rene Klosch, "The Uncertainty Principle in Software Engineering," ICSE 1997.

11
A Subjective Search Primer

"The cause is hidden, but the result is known." – Ovid
"Error is the path of truth." – Hans Reichenbach

Subjective search combines Subjective probability and Bayes' law to find hidden causes when all that can be seen are the effects. It uses multiple observations and deductions to choose the best among a set of models. Selection search chooses among a fixed set of models and Evolution search chooses among a changing set of models. Subjective search provides a foundation for Agile and Bride-of-Agile practices that could be called Subjective software engineering.

Basics

Drawing Warm Water Example

Consider drawing warm water to wash your hands, as shown in figure 1. Nobody ever knows exactly where to turn the handles of a faucet to get the desired temperature of water, so everyone uses a familiar search process. They, first, guess where to turn the handles and, then, repeatedly test the temperature and adjust the handles accordingly. Finally, when the water feels close enough to the desired temperature, they stop and wash.

Everyone uses interpolation to estimate which direction and how far to turn each handle. When the water feels too cold, they increase the hot water and/or decrease the cold water, and vice versa. When the temperature feels much too hot or much too cold, they turn the handles a lot. When the temperature feels close to what they want, they turn the handles a little.

This iterative process of testing and adjusting using interpolation is the essence of Subjective search. Each adjustment of the handles is one application of Bayes' law. This process enables everyone to draw whatever temperature water they prefer.

Some hidden causes are so simple and intuitive that people search for and find them without even realizing. Young children draw warm water by themselves all the time. The cause is the position of the handles and the effect is the temperature and flow of the water. Other hidden causes take a lot of disciplined, hard work. Writing software is truly difficult. The cause is the source code and the effect is the behavior of the program.

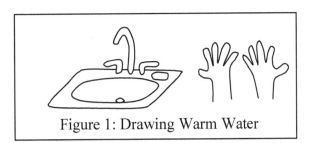

Figure 1: Drawing Warm Water

Subjectivity

The Word "Subjective"

The many different meanings of the word "subjective" can cause confusion. In this chapter, we use the word "subjective" to mean two specific things: observer-based and opinion-based. We use the words "observer" or "opinion" to mean one or the other and we use the word "subjective" to mean both.

Observer-Based: Subjective probabilities are assessments from the point of view of a specific observer, as opposed to assessments derived from the external world, independent of observers. Note that observer-based knowledge can be completely objective and that observers usually agree with objective knowledge.

Opinion-Based: Subjective probabilities can be based on personal opinions and arbitrary rules. Deductions are completely objective when all of the evidence is objective. Deductions are subjective when any of the evidence is based on personal opinions or arbitrary rules.

In general, the word "Bayesian" means the same thing as the word "Subjective" and the word "Frequentist" means the opposite.

Metaphors for Personal Opinions

Richard Jeffreys wrote, "The most important questions in the theory of probability concern ways and means of constructing reasonably satisfactory probability assignments." "Your subjective probability is not fetched out of the sky on a whim." (Jeffreys, page 76) Think drawing warm water.

Bet: Some people think of opinion-based probabilities as bets. Émile Borel concluded that individuals can quantify their degree of belief with a bet. The amount he or she is willing to wager shows how much he or she believes. (McGrayne, page 51) Nate Silver argue that an observer's prior should equal the odds that he or she is willing to bet. (Silver, page 256)

Measure of Belief or Ignorance: Other people think of opinion-based probabilities as measures of certainty or lack thereof. Sharon Bertsch McGrayne wrote that Subjective probability is "a measure of informed belief." (McGrayne, page 11) David Hand wrote that Subjective probability is a measure of ignorance. (Hand, pages 59 to 60)

Placeholder: Yet other people think of opinion-based probabilities as placeholders for objective knowledge. Richard Jeffreys wrote, "'The chance of H' is a placeholder for as-yet-unknown information." (Jeffreys, page 21)

Subjective Deduction

Absolute probabilities and Bayes' law enable one-step deductions.

Absolute Probabilities

Binary Events

Absolute probabilities concern the odds of individual binary events, such as whether a flipped coin will land heads-up and whether a new species will be found within a given area. In software, binary events include whether users will be satisfied with a given dialog (as described by a requirement document or implemented by a body of code) or whether a bug lurks within a specific requirement or function.

Meanings of Absolute Probabilities

Observers can use three kinds of evidence as absolute probabilities.

Objective Samples: An observer can use objective facts when he or she has enough objective samples. Probabilities like *0.7*, *0.5*, and *0.01* mean that the observer has seen binary events occur at those specific rates.

Personal Opinions: Richard Jeffreys noted that a lot of problems are "not about statistics, but about judgments." (Jeffreys, page 4) An observer can use personal opinions when he or she can make educated guesses. • "Probability is a measure of how much information an observer has about the physical world." (Stone, page 124) The probability *0.5* means that the observer is completely unsure whether a belief is true. Probabilities like *0.7*, *0.9*, and *0.99* express varying degrees of certainty that a belief is true. Probabilities like *0.3*, *0.1*, and *0.01* express varying degrees of certainty that a belief is false.

Arbitrary Rules: An observer can use arbitrary rules when he or she knows nothing, such as presuming that for events with *n* outcomes the odds for each outcome are *1/n*. The probability *0.5* means that the observer knows nothing about the odds of a binary event. Also note that statisticians often use the arbitrary numbers *0.95* to represent *true* and *0.05* to represent *false*.

Bottle Cap Example

Consider estimating the odds that a flipped bottle cap will land heads up.

Objective Samples: An observer might actually flip a bottle cap 100 times and see that it lands heads-up 16 times, and so he or she might initially guess that the odds are 16-84.

Personal Opinions: An observer who has never flipped a bottle cap yet knows a little physics might guess that the odds lie somewhere between 50-50 and say 10-90, and so he or she might initially guess that the odds are 30-70.

Arbitrary Rules: An observer who has never seen a bottle cap before and has no idea what will happen might initially guess that the odds are 50-50.

Empirical Bayes Means as Objective as Possible and as Subjective as Necessary

Naturally, everyone should use the best evidence that they can get to guide decisions. They should use objective information whenever possible. Then, they can use effective opinions to fill in gaps. Then as a last resort, they can use arbitrary rules to fill in gaps. When people run out of objective information, they can, should, must fill in with personal opinions and arbitrary rules because there is nothing else to use. Always using the best evidence that one can get is called "Empirical Bayes."

Bayes' Law

"In decision making, it is deliberation, not observation, that changes your probabilities." (Jeffreys, page 103) Bayes' law is the equation that shows how to incrementally improve an assessment that a belief is true based on new evidence.

Bayes Law: $P(b|e) = [P(e|b) \div P(e)] \times P(b)$

In this equation, b is a belief, e is new evidence, $P(b)$ is the observer's initial assessment (probability) that belief b is true, $P(b|e)$ is the observer's updated assessment (probability) that belief b is true given the new evidence e, and $P(e|b) \div P(e)$ is an update function that uses interpolation. Probabilities before the computation, like $P(b)$, are called "priors." Probabilities after the computation, like $P(b|e)$, are called "posteriors." Update functions are called "likelihoods."

Interpolation

The update function shows how much to change the assessment $P(b)$, based on how close the evidence e comes to what the observer expected.

Knows Little: When the observer knows little about the probabilities of either e or $e|b$, then he or she learns little. In symbols, when the observer knows little, then $P(e|b) \approx 0.5$ and $P(e) \approx 0.5$ and so the update function $P(e|b) \div P(e) \approx 1.0$ and nothing will change, $P(b|e) \approx P(b)$. This happens when the observer sees a truly new phenomenon and has no idea what to think about it.

Learns Little: When the probability of the evidence e is the same whether or not an observer believes b, then he or she learns little. In symbols, when the observer learns little, then $P(e|b) \approx P(e)$ and so the update function $P(e|b) \div P(e) \approx 1.0$ and nothing will change, $P(b|e) \approx P(b)$. This happens when the observer repeats an experiment and learns nothing. This happens when the observer moves the handles on the sink, but the temperature of the water still feels the same.

Learns a Lot: On the other hand, when the observer knows something about the probabilities $P(e|b)$ and $P(e)$ and they differ from each other, then he or she will learn a lot. The difference reveals both a potential error and an opportunity for learning.

One-Step Deduction

Bayes' law shows how to reassess the odds of a specific belief given new evidence using one deduction. Before electronic computers, when computations were made by hand, one deduction is all anyone ever wanted to do. Many books and essays about Bayesian statistics emphasize one-step deductions.

Beach Example

At one beach, 10% of kids are visitors; 90% of kids are locals; all visitors swim; 60% of locals swim; and 40% of locals surf. You just saw a kid swim. What are the odds that the kid is a local?

First, we need to know the odds that any kid swims, which is the weighted average that visitors and locals each swim. *P(swim) = P(swim | visitor) × P(visitor) + P(swim | local) × P(local) = 1.0 × 0.1 + 0.6 × 0.9 = 0.64.*

Then, Bayes' law can answer the question directly, going from *P(local)* to *P(local | swim)*. *P(local | swim) = [P(swim | local) ÷ P(swim)] P(local) = [0.6 ÷ 0.64] × 0.9 ≈ 0.84.*

The exact answers to problems like this can be computed in one deduction. The odds in this example are completely objective.

Subjective Search

Relative probabilities and sequential analysis enable Selection and Evolution search.

Relative Probabilities

N-Ary Events

Relative probabilities contrast the odds of multiple models within a set. A coin could be represented by two models: heads and tails. A die could be represented by six models: one for each face. When choosing which tasks to implement in the next iteration, each task could be represented by its own priority. When implementing a feature or fixing a bug, each possible set of code changes could be represented by its own model.

Meanings of Relative Probabilities

When comparing *n* models, the probability *1/n* means that all outcomes are known to be equally likely, that they are believed to be equally likely, or that nothing is known about them. For example, the odds that each face of a fair coin will appear is *1/2* and the odds that each face of a fair die will appear is *1/6*. The probabilities differ when one model is more likely than another. Note that the probabilities associated with each model can embody objective data, personal opinions, and arbitrary rules.

The probabilities of all models often sum to *1.0*, but they don't need to. Models can sum to any value as long as the observer updates the probabilities of all models consistently. For a fair die, an observer could assign each face a probability of *0.5*, which would sum to *3.0*. For a bottle cap, an observer could assign *P(heads) = 0.1* and *P(tails) = 0.3*, which would sum to *0.4*. When modeling task priorities, a backlog could have three tasks marked urgent or *0.99* and the sum of all priorities would be much larger than *1.0*. The probabilities of models need not even remain within the range of *0.0* to *1.0*.

Rounding errors and quirks in computations can easily cause the sum of all probabilities to drift above *1.0*. After every experiment, an observer could renormalize the probabilities so that they sum to *1.0* but that does not always make sense. For example when the probabilities represent priorities, renormalizing makes no sense. Absolute and relative probabilities should only be mixed with care. To convert relative probabilities to absolute probabilities, perhaps they should be renormalized so that the sum equals *1.0*. To convert the other way, perhaps they should be denormalized.

Always Choose the Best Model

As a rule when choosing among models, observers should always choose the one with the highest probability. Jerzy Neyman and Egon Pearson argued that "the only correct reason for rejecting a statistical hypothesis was to accept a more probable one." (McGrayne, page 49) For example, if an observer must choose among three options and he or she believes that the probabilities are *P(A) = 0.65*, *P(B) = 0.64*, *P(C) = 0.52*, then he or she should choose *A* because it is most likely right, if only by a little bit.

Murky Decisions: Observers often struggle to articulate and formalize everything that they know about their decisions. Observers may choose models with lower probabilities for intuitive reasons that are not expressed in the model and that they cannot otherwise articulate. For example, an observer could choose models *B* or *C* above for reasons that he or she cannot explain.

One well-known heuristic states that observers can be certain that one model is correct when it is three times more likely than all of the others, though many searches never achieve such certainty.

Sequential Analysis

Big endeavors are often carried out through a series of many small steps because people can only do a small amount of work at a time and because experiments often reveal only a small amount of information at a time. Many real-world Subjective-search problems require tens or hundreds or thousands of experiments to solve – or more. For these problems, Subjective deductions compute trends, rather than direct results, which is called "sequential analysis." Bayesian models resemble Infinite Impulse Response (IIR) filters. As observers gather more data and more becomes known, assessments should improve and the error should go toward zero.

Selection Search

Selection search is a statistical process for shopping or choosing among a relatively small and fixed set of models. After each experiment in a series, the observer improves the probability of each model. The results are probability distributions.

Hidden Billiard-Ball Example

For some problems, the models are essentially alike. In his original thought experiment, Thomas Bayes wanted to find the location of a hidden, randomly-placed billiard ball. (Bayes and Price) Bayes divided the billiard table into a fixed grid of n identical segments. Each grid segment is one model. Table 2 shows Bayes' process.

Priors

Arbitrary Rule: To start, Bayes presumed that the original ball had a $1/n$ probability of lying within each segment. In table 1, the observer divides the billiard table into 8 equal segments and initially guesses that the odds that the hidden ball lies within each segment are $1/8$.

Personal Opinion: If the observer had other beliefs, for example if the observer believed that the table were not level, he or she could have assigned different priors to each segment as appropriate.

Experiments

Then, Bayes performed a series of experiments to improve the estimate. During each experiment, Bayes rolled another billiard ball randomly onto the table and determined whether it stopped to the left or right of the hidden ball. After each experiment, he updated the probability that the hidden ball lies within each segment using his law, *P(in-this-segment | result) = [P(result | in-this-segment) ÷ P(result)] × P(in-this-segment)*. The values for *P(result | in-this-segment)* are shown in the last two rows in table 1 (presume the hidden ball lies in the middle of each segment); *P(result) = 0.5*; and *result* = either *left* or *right*. Note that ideally, *P(result) = ∑0≤s<8 P(s)×P(result | s)*.

After the first and second experiments, segment 5 does not look correct. After the third experiment, segment 5 could be correct. After 60 experiments, segment 5 stands out as obviously correct. Note that the priors use arbitrary rules and the experiments produce objective data. Also note that after the second experiment, the models do not sum to *1.0* and that the probabilities of some models exceed *1.0*.

Table 1: Hidden Billiard Ball Example								
Segment	0	1	2	3	4	5	6	7
Arbitrary Rule Prior	0.125	0.125	0.125	0.125	0.125	0.125	0.125	0.125
After 1 Left, 0 Right	0.016	0.047	0.078	0.109	0.141	0.172	0.203	0.234
After 1 Left, 1 Right	0.029	0.076	0.107	0.123	0.123	0.107	0.076	0.029
After 2 Left, 1 Right	0.003	0.029	0.067	0.107	0.138	0.148	0.124	0.055
After 3 Left, 1 Right	0.000	0.011	0.042	0.094	0.156	0.203	0.201	0.103
After 14 Left, 6 Right	0.000	0.000	0.001	0.039	0.292	0.643	0.311	0.003
After 29 Left, 11 Right	0.000	0.000	0.000	0.010	0.874	7.284	3.357	0.001
After 42 Left, 18 Right	0.000	0.000	0.000	0.004	1.590	17.04	1.929	0.000
P(left | in-this-segment)	1/16	3/16	5/16	7/16	9/16	11/16	13/16	15/16
P(right | in-this-segment)	15/16	13/16	11/16	9/16	7/16	5/16	3/16	1/16

Most-Important Task Example

For some problems, the models differ significantly. A backlog might contain five tasks – refactor a class, improve the performance of search, add a new dialog, change the query logic, and update the legal boilerplate. Keiko is asked to prioritize the tasks in the backlog because she only has time to implement one before the next release. Table 2 shows her process.

Priors

Arbitrary Rule: If Keiko knows little, for example if she is a new hire and has never met the client before, she could presume that all tasks are alike and initially give each task a priority of $1/n$ or 0.2.

Personal Opinion: If Keiko knows more, for example if she has worked with this client before, she could give each task a different priority based on her experiences. If Keiko believes that the client prefers "big and visible," she might assign the priors as follows: refactoring a class gets 0.1 because it is invisible, improving the search performance gets 0.2 because it makes no functional difference, adding a new dialog gets 0.3, changing the logic of a query gets 0.3, and updating the legal boilerplate gets 0.1 because most users don't care. In this case, Keiko has opinions.

Experiments

From there, Keiko can perform experiments by asking other stakeholders for their thoughts.

Tarik: Keiko talks with Tarik, the programmer who last maintained the program. Tarik notes that both the performance and dialog tasks need the refactoring task first. So, Keiko multiplies the priorities of the refactoring task by 3.0, to make it equal to the highest priority, and the performance and new-dialog tasks by 0.6.

Emily: Keiko talks with Emily, who worked on the first version of the program and who remarks that the client recently got sued. So, Keiko multiplies the priorities of the boilerplate task by 2.0 and all other tasks by 0.89.

Sanjay: Keiko talks with Sanjay, who works in the legal department and who says that the lawyers are still rewriting the fine print. Keiko should hold off on that for now but he really wants the new queries. So, Keiko multiplies the priorities of the boilerplate task by 0.75 and the query-logic task by 1.2.

Now, the query-logic task has the highest-priority, 0.32, though not by much. Keiko used opinion-based priors and three different opinion-based bits of evidence. If Keiko could have determined objective probabilities, she would have used them, but here she couldn't. Keiko used her best-guess numbers.

Note that polling can give similar answers to Subjective search. But, Subjective search also allows observers to value each bit of evidence differently, for example when the observer has more confidence in one stakeholder's opinion than another's or when the observer compensates for known biases. Also note that within the limits of rounding, the probabilities of all models sum to 1.0.

Table 2: Most Important Task Example					
Task	**Refactor**	**Performance**	**New Dialog**	**Query Logic**	**Boilerplate**
Personal Opinion Prior	0.10	0.20	0.30	0.30	0.10
After Keiko	0.30	0.12	0.18	0.30	0.10
After Tarik	0.27	0.11	0.16	0.27	0.20
After Emily	0.27	0.11	0.16	0.32	0.15

Evolution Search

One might aspire to consider and track all possible models, but that can become overwhelming. Tracking tens of models is easy, tracking hundreds of models is possible, yet tracking thousands of models is simply impossible. Nobody wants to feel overwhelmed. Nobody wants to waste their efforts by evaluating a lot of low-probability models. In particular, combinatorial problems have too many models for anyone to track them all explicitly.

Prototype Evolution: When too many possible models exist, observers commonly start with one working prototype and then incrementally improve it. When the observer realizes that the current prototype is not good enough, he or she looks for a better if previously-unconsidered prototype and swaps it for the current one. The observer considers and makes small changes incrementally, one at a time. At each step, he or she explores the "adjacent possible" and then continues using the best improvement. The results are exemplars in the neighborhood of local maxima or samples from probability distributions.

Evolution search is a statistical meta-process for designing or creating new models. Evolution search deals with problems in models by improving the probabilities of the models and then improving the models themselves. In artificial intelligence and numerical analysis, prototype evolution is called "hill climbing" and observers generally strive to make the biggest improvement possible at each step.

Dialog Design Example

Consider a dialog with some controls to select and modify information, and a table to display the results. If an analyst limits the models to whether to rename each control, then the number of models to consider is exponential in the number of controls. Since each control can change in many different ways (order, position, name, style, graphics, functionality, and so on) and since controls can be added and deleted, the number of potential changes to consider is very exponential. Humans cannot explicitly consider all possible changes to small dialogs, say 8 controls. Computers cannot explicitly consider all possible changes to medium-sized dialogs, say 16 controls.

Priors

The users start by making their best guesses for the initial requirements. The analysts and programmers start by implementing the core features that the users asked for. The resulting dialog is the working prototype.

Experiments

After each sprint, the analysts and programmers demo their current working prototype to a group of users for feedback. When the analysts and programmers worked hard and implemented all of the features that the users asked for, they will expect that the users are pleased.

The users may respond "that's cool." The more the users like the demo, the more the analysts and programmers will raise their estimate that the current prototype is good enough. At some point, the analysts and programmers will conclude that they are finished and will move on to implement the next feature.

The users may respond "that's lame." The more the users dislike the demo, the more the analysts and programmers will feel crushed. Then, they will look for a small set of improvements to make. Thousands of potential changes exist, as hinted at in table 3. All of them take work to implement and potentially add noise for users, so nobody should implement any of them without good reason. Before the demo, the analysts and programmers gave little thought to these other changes because they were considered either unnecessary or wrong.

The analysts and programmers continue this process until either the users become satisfied or the resources run out.

Table 3: Some of the Many Possible Changes to a Dialog	
Change	**Users May Ask –**
Auto-Complete	That the dialog automatically fills in some fields.
Pretty	That the dialog be "prettier."
Columns	To add columns to or remove columns from the table.
Filters and Sorts	For filters and sorts when queries return too many records.
Segmentation	To segment the data.
Social Media	For links to social media pages related to the results.
Edit Row	To edit individual records.
Edit Many Rows	To edit many records at the same time.
Permissions	For different users to access different records.
Drill Down	For links to drill down into any value in the table.
Provenance	To show the history of changes to any given record.
Custom Views	To allow each user to add or remove columns in their own views.
Bookmarks	For bookmarks that will return the exact same results in the future.
Export	To download the table in Excel format for analysis with other tools.
Email Results	To email the table to a client.
Representation	To display numbers as graphs and statuses as colors or icons.

When an Experiment Fails

In general, analysts and programmers use Evolution search intuitively without numbers. Here we assign arbitrary numbers to show how it works. Some analysts and programmers work on a new dialog. They finish all of the initially requested features and believe that their implementation will make the users happy, so before the demo *P(happy-with-dialog) = 0.95*.

When the analysts and programmers realize that the current dialog doesn't work well enough, they estimate how disappointed or annoyed the users are and adjust accordingly. For example, the users may demand auto-complete or that the dialog be prettier. Say that the analysts and programmers are only one-quarter as confident in the working prototype as before, so *P(happy-with-dialog | demo) = 0.25 × 0.95 ≈ 0.24*. It may take a while to fix the dialog and users might even learn to like it. Regardless, everyone expects the worst and so the analysts and programmers will find a new model that should work better and modify the dialog to match.

Auto-Complete: Say all of the users vote for adding auto-complete. Before the demo, the analysts and programmers had thought that auto-complete was unnecessary, so *P(happy-with-dialog-plus-auto-complete) = 0.05*. Say that after the demo, they are ten times surer of this theory than before, so *P(happy-with-dialog-plus-auto-complete | demo) = 10.0 × 0.05 = 0.50*. When users complain about one detail, they will often complain about other details later, but auto-complete heads in the right direction for now.

Pretty: Say two-thirds of the users vote for making the dialog prettier. Before the demo, the analysts and programmers had thought that pretty was unnecessary, so *P(happy-with-dialog-plus-pretty) = 0.05*. Say that after the demo they are 6.7 times surer of this theory than before, so *P(happy-with-dialog-plus-pretty | demo) = 6.7 × 0.05 ≈ 0.34*. Maybe they don't know how pretty to make the dialog. When the users want it a little prettier, the team might assign a programmer to add some clip art. When users want it a lot prettier, the team might hire a graphic designer.

After deliberation, the analysts and programmers are much surer of the dialog with auto-complete, *0.50*, than of the original dialog, *0.24*, or of the dialog with pretty, *0.34*. So, they will add auto-complete before the next demo.

Problems with Evolution Search

Experience has revealed a number of problems with Evolution search.

Local Maxima: At discontinuities, models cannot improve easily. When a prototype gets to a local maximum, it may take a radical change, such as a massive redesign of a GUI or refactor of an architecture to continue improving incrementally.

Plateaus: On plateaus, improvements are unclear. Plateaus occur when users don't know what they want and when programmers don't know how to reproduce a bug. All efforts may seem like aimless wandering.

Slow: Progress can be slower than anyone likes. Finding effective solutions can take many more rounds of refinement than desired.

Horizon Effect: The horizon effect means that people may not be able to predict how the results will turn out. Dramatic surprises can arise continually and annoyingly.

Focus on the Product: Chip Conley noted that design processes tend to focus on the product rather than on the customer – on the features of the program rather than on how to best help the client. This distinction relates to the difference between the bottom and middle levels of Maslow's hierarchy: the bottom levels concern the users' functional needs and the middle levels concern their emotional needs. (Conley, Part 3)

Strengths and Weaknesses

Subjective search is both tremendously useful and enormously problematic. The strengths include that it sheds light on the ways that brains work and that deviations explain many biases and errors in human reasoning. The weaknesses include that results can have significant errors and that many problems are not Bayesian.

Insights into How Brains Work

Expertise is Subjective: Observers always have opinions. All analysts and programmers bring their own knowledge, experiences, trainings, facts, hopes, fears, purposes, and delusions to every project that they work on. In crime shows, like *Bones* or *CSI*, characters occasionally argue that everyone should avoid preconceived notions about evidence. They are dead wrong.

People's immediate environments inundate them with so much information that they need models and expectations to filter most of it out and to help them make sense of the rest. Kathryn Schulz writes, "Perception is interpretation of sensation." (Schulz, page 56) David DiSalvo writes, "Preestablished schemata guide our attention to evaluate new information." (DiSalvo, page 51) Tom Kelley writes, "You have to interpret or intuit shades of meaning to divine underlying motivations or needs." (Kelley, page 39) Preconceived, subjective notions enable everyone to find, understand, and use information.

Only young children actually believe what they see and have few preconceived notions, which is called "naïve realism," but they are unaware of the dangers of street traffic and are easily distracted by toys and candy. One would never ask small children to evaluate crime evidence or to design sophisticated software. All expertise is based on preconceived notions and subjective points of view.

Gain and Loss are Asymmetric: Becoming more certain and becoming less certain are asymmetric. Psychologists have shown that people gain confidence much more slowly than they lose it. When an observer starts out certain, 0.95, and loses half his or her certainty, $0.5 \times 0.95 = 0.48$, the loss is significant. When an observer starts out skeptical, 0.05, and becomes twice as sure, $2.0 \times 0.05 = 0.10$, the gain is incremental. This difference may help to explain why people worry so much more about loss than about gain.

Insights into Human Bias and Error

Many deviations from Subjective search correspond to specific human biases and errors.

Deny Personal Bias: Nobody can avoid personal bias and those who don't acknowledge their biases will succumb. The only alternatives to acknowledging personal biases are wishful thinking and naïve hope. Unfortunately, everyone fools themselves. People believe that they know more than they actually do. People believe that they are more impartial than they actually are. (Hallinan, pages 69 to 70) Everyone has systemic biases, but those who are aware can try to compensate. Nate Silver notes that with Bayes, people must choose a prior, so they cannot pretend that they have no biases. Subjective priors acknowledge that people perceive reality through subjective mental filters. (Silver, page 451)

Prefer Optimism over Realism: When given options, many people will assign probabilities based on what they want to happen rather than on what they expect will happen. Unfortunately, few people can control their circumstances. Fred Brooks' "Calling the Shot" is a useful prior because people should clearly state what they want, but it is also problematic because it can set up unrealistic expectations. (Brooks, chapter 8) Projects always change in unexpected ways. People should deal with their actual situations rather then their preferred situations, even though hope springs eternal.

Prefer Changing Probabilities over Changing Models: People can refuse to improve their mental models and stubbornly only improve the probabilities of their existing models. This can be seen as the difference between Selection search and Evolution search. Cranky old men who argue "in my day, we listened to Elvis and the Beatles and we liked it – kids these days and their rap" remain stuck in the past. Anyone who insists on following a flawed plan remains stuck in the past.

Prefer Facts over Probabilities: People are not statisticians. Nobody cares about the probabilities of binary events. Nobody wants to evaluate the probabilities of many different decisions or plans. They really just want to make one effective decision or plan. So, humans often treat opinions and judgments as facts. (Freedman, page 22) They take the highest probability model as a guaranteed success. Consider a case where $P(A) = 0.6$ and $P(B) = 0.4$. Most people leap directly to "*A* is a sure thing." Everyone converts estimates into promises – they just do. Discoveries for requirements and architectures become facts rather than possibilities.

The Best Decisions can Still Be Very Wrong

Unfortunately, Subjective search won't give anyone the warm and fuzzy feeling of certainty. Subjective choices often contain errors and assuredly some of them will be wrong. The best Subjective decisions are not right but are less wrong and, unfortunately, can even be arbitrarily wrong.

Planning helps to answer questions like "given what we know and ignoring what we don't know, what is the best answer?" and "given the stated requirements and ignoring the requirements that are missing, misunderstood, or wrong, what is the best architecture?" But the answers may be neither very good nor good enough. Until all details become known, then at least some details will remain unknown and only heaven knows how much pain they will cause.

Flipping around the logic for why everyone should choose the highest-probability model shows why they should also beware that model. When choosing among options, where $P(A) = 0.65$, $P(B) = 0.64$, $P(C) = 0.52$, A is the best decision, though it remains far from certain. The observer also knows that there is a 0.35 chance that A is wrong. One could argue that 0.35 of A is wrong, although such an argument would be incorrect. Consider the "20 doors" metaphor from security: locking 19 out of 20 doors does not make a building 95% secure. Option A could be horrible.

Note that when predicting the future, all other decision processes can be horribly wrong as well.

Many Problems are Not Bayesian

In the broad spectrum of problems, some are Bayesian and others are not.

Some Problems are Bayesian

Some problems can easily be solved by Subjective search. Historically, Bayesian researchers emphasized one-step deductions and Selection search. Evolution search is a more recent technique adapted from computing.

Bernoulli: A lot of early research into Bayes (and specifically Bayes' original essay) focused on Bernoulli trials. Bernoulli trials are binary events where each sample is independent and has a fixed probability, such as when flipping coins, throwing dice, or rolling billiard balls.

Exchangeable and Partially-Exchangeable: More recently, Bayesian research has focused on "exchangeable" and "partially exchangeable" events. Jeffreys notes that events are exchangeable when only the ratio of true to false matters and not the order, such as when drawing colored balls from an urn. Bruno De Finetti linked exchangeable with Subjective search in 1931. Jeffreys explains, "Exchangeability undoes the dreaded 'combinatorial explosion.'" Partially-exchangeable events have Markov dependencies, such as in Markov Chain Monte Carlo techniques. (Jeffreys, pages 78, 80 to 81, and 94)

Smooth Combinatorial: Evolution search can solve a wide variety of combinatorial problems, specifically ones that have smooth gradients (where discontinuities are smaller than step sizes) and affordable paths (where the total steps fit within the budgets).

Other Problems are Not Bayesian

Unfortunately, other problems cannot be solved using Subjective search.

Undecidable: Gödel's Incompleteness theorem shows some strict limits to what can be known. Undecidable problems (such as the Halting Problem) cannot be solved by any means, in general.

Intractable: Answers to intractable problems (like satisfiability or factoring large numbers) are easy to verify even though they remain difficult to find. Exponential and super-exponential problems cannot be solved by any means in any reasonable amount of time.

Hyperbolic, Chaotic, Fractal: The Central Limit theorem assumes a "linear" distribution with smoothness so that interpolation works. However, fractal, power-law, chaotic, and Pareto properties can have jagged or infinite paths for which interpolation is impossible.

Nash Equilibria: Jeffreys states that Bayes does not help with Nash Equalibria (such as the Prisoner's Dilemma) where information outside of the system (such as how an opponent will behave) affects the answer. (Jeffreys, 112) Note that all programs can be interpreted as Nash equilibria in games between users and programmers.

Magical Unknowns: Some problems require magical knowledge, such as passwords or lottery numbers. Magical unknowns can only be solved by sharing or discovering otherwise secret or random information. One of the hardest bugs to solve that we know of involved realizing that an API for detaching processes from the UI existed and that it would help. It was buried deeply within MSDN and was stumbled over only by accident. Magical knowledge often creates job security for experts.

Unknown Unknowns: In many cases, users know neither what they want nor how to get it. We have seen both users and developers say "this doesn't seem right, but I don't know what to do about it" or

"I can't describe it, but I'll know it when I see it," also called "IKIWISI." When the effects are unknown, then the hidden causes are buried one layer deeper.

However, Subjective search can still help to solve or approximate many instances of these problems. For example, Alan Turing used Subjective search to guide code-breaking efforts, back when cryptography was still fairly weak. In Nash equilibria, Subjective search may not be able to create strategies, such as tit-for-tat, though Subjective search can often help to choose which known strategy to apply.

Subjective Software Engineering

Subjective search provides a solid foundation for Agile and Bride-of-Agile practices because it is incremental and tolerates uncertainty. Subjective search applies to everyone in requirement and software engineering, however we mostly leave the applications to architects, testers, and managers as exercises for readers.

Analysts and Programmers

Most analysts and programmers using Agile processes in real software projects do Subjective search anyways, if informally, ad-hocly, inconsistently, and with varying degrees of awareness. Clearly, analysts and programmers make informal decisions based on incomplete information all day long. We suspect that analysts and programmers have ignored Subjective search mainly because it is so obvious.

Analysts

Priors: First, analysts should presume that users know what they want. They should document what users say literally, even if as The Oatmeal complained they say they "want an edgy website that pops," which nobody knows how to make. Second, analysts should fill in as many of the remaining details as they can using their best guesses based on their training, experiences, opinions, hopes, desperations, delusions, and so on. Third, analysts should fill in as many of the remaining details as they can using the arbitrary rules defined by conventions and standards.

Experiments: Then, analysts should repeatedly run experiments, questioning everything (user, analyst, and programmer input alike) and adapt as they learn. They should repeatedly ask "what do users *really* need, as individuals and as groups?" They should repeatedly show users the requirement documents, paper mock ups, working prototypes, and other applications. During each demo, they should ask for feedback and watch how users respond, seeking out missing, wrong, and ambiguous requirements. Analysts should use the responses as new evidence to improve the requirements.

Programmers

Priors: First, programmers should start each project with either an existing code-base or an empty code-base.

Experiments: Then, programmers should repeatedly run experiments to implement features and fix bugs. They should make their best guesses to improve the source code, make that improvement, and then assess the results. A programmer might show the code to some colleagues for review or demo the prototype to some testers or users to see how they respond. When a code change implements a feature, fixes a bug, or cleans up the code well enough, the programmer should commit the results and move on to the next task. If not, the programmer should undo the change and try his or her next best guess. Some features and bugs have been seen thousands of times before and programmers know exactly what code to write. Some features and bugs are unique to their experience and programmers must track down the lines of code doggedly, using guesswork and trial and error. And some features and bugs are beyond their understanding (such as satisfiability or heisenbugs) and they must wait until someone provides more information.

Both Selection and Evolution Search

Everyone shifts back and forth flexibly between Selection and Evolution search.

Analysts: Analysts routinely use Selection search to prioritize the tasks within backlogs. Analysts also routinely use Evolution search to refine, split, merge, add, or delete individual tasks.

Programmers: Programmers primarily use Evolution search to create source codes. The number of possible source codes is exponential in the number of tokens, so nobody can keep track of all possible solutions to new features and bug fixes. Source codes are in general so large that developers can only make small changes to them at a time anyways. Programmers also use Selection search to fix bugs when multiple possibilities exist and they are uncertain about which ones will work. Programmers may also use Selection search to develop several different prototypes of a feature at the same time. They can use the single best prototype as the final version or they can merge the best elements of each into the final version.

Researchers

In "Learning through Application: the Maturing of the QIP in the SEL," Vic Basili writes like a Bayesian. "The insights gained from pre-experimental designs and quasi-experiments became critical and we combine them with what we learned from the controlled experiments and case studies." (Oram and Wilson, page 74) The Experience Factory "requires the use of insights and intelligent judgment based upon observation for the application of ideas, concepts, processes, etc." (Oram and Wilson, page 75) "Informal feedback also, and perhaps surprisingly, provided the major insights." (Oram and Wilson, page 68)

If Subjective search works for researchers at NASA, it should work for practicing analysts and programmers, too. Note that Basili's arguments that research judgments are Subjective totally contradict his Frequentist ideals for GQM. He can't have it both ways, but he could become an Empirical Bayesian.

Scientific Processes: Enrico Fermi and Richard Feynman showed that "Bayes' law lies at the heart of the scientific process. Leonard Savage wrote, "When they have little data, scientists disagree and are subjectivists; when they have piles of data, they agree and become objectivists." Dennis Lindley wrote, "That's the way science is done." (McGrayne, pages 102 to 103)

Subjective Search is the Only Solution

We believe that only the deliberate discovery and refinement processes guided by Subjective search lead to effective requirements and source codes. We do not know of any other effective approaches, all of the rhetoric about planning in architecture and project management notwithstanding. We believe that software that cannot be written using Subjective search cannot be written at all.

When objective information runs out, people must guess or make Subjective decisions. David Freedman wrote, "Look over the evidence, weigh the biases, consider the qualifications and limitations, and take your best shot at deciding. No expert could do better." (Freedman, page 267) Taking one's best guess and following up on it is not hacking – doing anything else is.

Culture Wars

Statisticians have engaged in deeply entrenched culture wars over the years.

Frequentist versus Bayesian Statistics

Statistics spans a vast spectrum. Table 4 contrasts the two extremes.

Table 4: Frequentist versus Bayesian Statistics		
Issues	**Frequentist**	**Bayesian**
Essence	Objective Measures of the World	Personal Opinions
Context	Lots of Data – the Past	Little Data – the Future
Basis for Comparison	Minimize Maximum Loss	Minimize Expected Loss
Software Examples	Algorithms	Programs

Essence

Here are three significant points on the spectrum of statistics.

Frequentist: "Probability is the proportion of times an event occurs in an infinitely long series of trials." "[It] is a property of the external world." (Hand, page 58) Frequentists believe that probabilities are objective measures of the world. They reject both observer-based and opinion-based probabilities.

Half-Bayesian: Half-Bayesians generally accept observer-based and reject opinion-based probabilities. Judea Pearl argued that Bayes' original thought-experiment to find the location of a hidden ball would satisfy most Frequentists and that most Bayesian literature concerns topics like influence graphs and causality with which Frequentists have little problem. (Pearl, "Half-Bayesian")

Bayesian: Bayesians generally accept both observer-based and opinion-based probabilities.

Context

Lots of Data – the Past: Frequentist statistics requires a lot of existing, objective data, which comes from the past. When insufficient data exists, Frequentists can only twiddle their thumbs.

Little Data – the Future: When little existing, objective data exists, especially when predicting the future, Bayesians make best-guess, subjective decisions and proceed.

Basis for Comparison

When lots of data exists, Bayesians and Frequentists usually agree with each other. However, Bayesians and Frequentists can also use the same data to make different decisions.

Minimize Maximum Loss: Frequentists generally compare models by minimizing maximum loss, known as Minimax. This makes sense when deciders get only one chance, such as when projects near deadlines and deciders only have resources for one attempt.

Minimize Expected Loss: Bayesians generally compare models by minimizing expected loss. This makes sense when deciders get many chances, such as when projects have distant deadlines and deciders have multiple opportunities to fix problems later.

Software Examples

Algorithms: Algorithms are objective properties of the universe that exist independently of observers. Algorithms for sort and Fourier transform were used centuries before electronic computers existed.

Programs: All requirements and lines of code are observer-based because only analysts and programmers write them down. The universe does not cause them – the universe would be equally happy with anything. All requirements and lines of code are properties or opinions of people because they contain elements of someone's belief that a given requirement describes or a given line of code implements what the user wants. Fifty years ago, nobody wanted any of the requirements or lines of code for Microsoft Office or Facebook. Fifty years from now, they may want something else entirely.

Culture Wars

"What's the collective noun for a group of statisticians? A quarrel." (McGrayne, page 51)

Statisticians have fought philosophical battles that would put Lilliputians to shame. Frequentists have many criticisms of Bayesians. Bayesians have just as many responses and counter-criticisms. Battles between Bayesians and Frequentists raged throughout the 1900s, though over the past few decades, they seem to have come to a truce. (Stone, pages 125 to 128)

Frequentist Criticisms of Bayes

Some statisticians (including Ronald Fisher who developed Frequentism) reject Subjective approaches outright or at least give subjectivity as wide a berth as possible. Other statisticians (including Pierre Simon Laplace and Judea Pearl) switched, at least in part, from Bayesianism to Frequentism for the following reasons and others. Other statisticians ambivalently state "Bayes rule is wrong … except for the fact that it works." (McGrayne, page 241) Or, they complain that the fundamental vulnerability of Bayes is that "its magical powers depend on the validity of its probabilistic inputs." (McGrayne, Page 105)

Personal Opinions are Not Objective: One definition of Empirical Bayes is "be as objective as you can be and as subjective as you must be." Personal opinions should be avoided.

Arbitrary Rules are Not Objective: Ronald Fisher argued "thinking that you don't know and thinking that the probabilities of all the possibilities are equal is not the same thing." (McGrayne, page 134) Arbitrary rules (like *1/n*) should be avoided.

Priors are Not Objective: Ronald Fisher argued that stating a prior contradicts objective science. (Silver, page 252)

Small Samples are Not Objective: In general, applying Bayes' law many times based on many experiments leads to more truth and applying Bayes' law fewer times based on fewer experiments leads to less truth. This implies that fewer experiments should be avoided. In the task-priority example above, Keiko ran three experiments, which is far too few for any meaningful Frequentist poll.

Not Used Much: A recent survey of working statisticians found that few of them actually use Subjective probability on the job. (We alas cannot refind the reference.) In the textbook *Doing Bayesian Data Analysis*, John Kruschke barely even mentions subjectivity. Empirically, many statisticians avoid subjectivity. If only ad-hoc-decision makers actually use subjectivity, then it isn't statistics.

Bayesian Responses and Counter-Criticisms

Bayesians generally agree that the criticisms above contain elements of truth but also argue that they miss the point. In addition, they argue that Frequentism has similar problems, or worse. They even argue that all Frequentist models are subjective and so Frequentist statistics is actually a special case of Bayesian statistics.

All Models use Implicit Priors: Bayesians believe that Frequentists implicitly use uniform priors (arbitrary rules like *1/n*) in all of their models, despite their denials.

Choices of Models are Subjective: Bayesians believe that Frequentism is not actually objective. (Silver, page 253) The choice of any Frequentist model lies outside of the data and is therefore a subjective decision. For example, suppose a Frequentist wants to describe a typical member of a set, such as the height or income of a group of people. He or she could use the mean, the median, the geometric mean, the harmonic mean, or many other models. The choice of model is subjective and can profoundly affect the results.

Sampling Errors versus Model Errors: Sampling errors are well-defined with Frequentist confidence intervals, but model errors can be far larger. (Silver, page 252) Subjective searches are the only techniques that encourage statisticians to routinely reconsider models, which Frequentists need never do.

Different Units: David Hand notes that subjective and objective probabilities use the same mathematics. (Hand, page 56) Utility, which is probability × value, also uses the same mathematics. Ian Hacking noted that the differences between the kinds of probability are like the differences between weight and mass, which most people cannot tell apart. (Hand, page 60) When the math is the same, units may not matter. Consider that scrambled eggs may combine 3 eggs, ¼ cup chopped onions, 2 grams salt, and ¼ ounce of butter, which all have different units.

Coping: Bayesians strive to wring as much information from each observation and deduction as possible, regardless of what the evidence is. Frequentists resemble snobby programmers who refuse to work on any project with less than perfect requirements.

Path Toward Truth: Bayesians argue that Subjective probabilities are not meaningless – they are steps on the path toward truth. Bayesians take personal opinions and small samples seriously because they are approximations of greater truths that can be used now. Sharon Bertsch McGrayne wrote "Probability is a measure of belief that can 'escape from repetition to uniqueness.'" (McGrayne, pages 233 to 234) In the task-priority example, Keiko needs a philosophy like Subjective search to take small samples seriously.

Design versus Statistics: All of these criticisms highlight a key difference between design and statistics. Designers have relatively small amounts of objective data and make lots of informal, ad-hoc, subjective decisions. Only those who have lots of concrete data and want more formal decisions bother to call in professional statisticians. As decision makers acquire more data, they drift toward Frequentism. But, those who make lots of informal decisions, such as how to prioritize features and how to write lines of code, don't bother with Frequentist statistics.

Odds and Ends

Tomes have been written about Bayesian statistics, but we will stop soon.

Notes

Inverse Deduction: The term "inverse deduction" is the historical term for "Subjective search." It refers to reasoning from effect to cause or transmuting unknown causes into known causes.

Richard Jeffreys notes that an observer can update the probability of a belief by either adding or multiplying a reasonable number. (Jeffreys, page 30)

Moving Targets: Claude Shannon noted that Bayes' law can follow a signal that changes. (McGrayne, pages 76 to 77) The probability of finding a bug in a function will change as the function is maintained and Subjective search will adapt. Users can change their minds about the goals (or requirements) of a project and Subjective search will adapt.

Informal Reasoning: Richard Jeffreys argues that Bayes provides a formal basis for informal reasoning. (Jeffreys, pages 43 to 44) Bayes merely formalizes what people do naturally anyways. Bayes is "a logic for reasoning about the broad spectrum of life that lies in the gray areas between absolute truth and total uncertainty." (McGrayne, page xi) "We can learn from missing and inadequate data, from approximations, and from ignorance." (McGrayne, page x)

Rationality: Bayes provides a formal basis for rationality. Leonard Savage argued that "rational people make subjective choices to minimize expected loss." (McGrayne, page 103) Or in positive terms, rational people should always maximize expected gain based on their best guesses. We don't know of any better way to make uncertain decisions. Unfortunately, psychologists have shown that people are not rational, so Savage's ideal can only partially work. Even so, rationality remains an important ideal.

Notation: Notations about probability tend to drive programmers crazy. Programmers tend to idealize strict functions and strong types. Unfortunately, "$P()$" is not a function, "$|$" is not an operator, and the types of the priors b and the posteriors $b|e$ may or may not be the same. These notations drive us (the authors) crazy, too.

History of Bayes

Subjective search has been used for eons in both statistics and computing.

History of Bayes in Probability

Jacob Bernoulli wrote about Subjective probability around 300 years ago. Thomas Bayes, Richard Price, and Pierre Simon Laplace addressed hidden causes and predicting the future, 200 to 270 years ago.

Bayes defined his law operationally, so nobody knows whether he actually would have accepted opinion-based evidence. In other words, nobody knows whether Thomas Bayes would have actually been a Bayesian. Pretty funny. Richard Price thought that Bayes' law was so powerful that it could prove the existence of God.

Pierre Simon Laplace wrote that Bayes is the "primary method for researching unknown or complicated causes." (McGrayne, page 31)

Bruno de Finetti, Dennis Lindley, and James Berger linked opinion-based decisions with Bayes, more than 50 years ago.

History of Bayes in Computing

Bayesian techniques have been used to make decisions in computing and related fields from the earliest days.

Alan Turing: During World War 2, Alan Turing used Bayesian techniques to decide which messages cryptanalysts should actually attempt to decipher on machines. He started by arbitrarily presuming that the odds that a particular setting would decrypt a message were 50-50, $p = 0.50$. Analysts then repeatedly gathered evidence to refine the estimate. For example, observing a certain pattern in a cipher text might suggest that a particular key would work, so the odds for that key would be scaled by an appropriate amount, such as *1.01* or *1.1*. Once the odds became 50 to 1, $p = 0.98$, cryptanalysts would attempt decryption using that particular key on an actual machine. Using logarithms simplified the calculations. This process reduced the thousands to billions of possible settings to as few as 18. (McGrayne, pages 66 to 67)

Claude Shannon: At the dawn of the computing era, Claude Shannon used Bayesian techniques to define both information theory and secrecy. "If the posterior is quite different from the prior, something has been learned, [otherwise] the information content is very low." (McGrayne, pages 76 to 77)

Judea Pearl: Judea Pearl applied Bayes to artificial intelligence in *Probabilistic Reasoning in Intelligent Systems*. (McGrayne, page 228) (Pearl)

Database Analysis: Many researchers and companies have applied Bayesian techniques to mining databases.

Image Processing: Markov Chain Monte Carlo techniques work well for image processing.

Acknowledgements

We want to thank Mina Yamashita, Anthony J. Giancola, Bear, and other colleagues for their support and tolerance of our obsessions. Joe Hill introduced us to Bayes and Empirical Bayes, decades ago. Through her book, *The Theory that Would Not Die*, Sharon Bertsch McGrayne reminded us of our long-standing interest in Bayes. The books by David Hand, Richard Jeffreys, and Nate Silver also helped a lot.

Bibliography

Thomas Bayes and Richard Price, "An Essay towards Solving a Problem in the Doctrine of Chances," in *Philosophical Transactions*, volume 53, pages 370 to 418, Royal Society, 1763.

Frederick P. Brooks, *The Mythical Man-Month*, Addison Wesley, 1995.

Chip Conley, *Peak*, Jossey-Bass, 2007.

David DiSalvo, *What Makes Your Brain Happy and Why You Should Do the Opposite*, Prometheus, 2011.

David H. Freedman, *Wrong: Why Experts Keep Failing Us – And How to Know When Not to Trust Them*, Little Brown, 2010.

Joseph T. Hallinan, *Why We Make Mistakes*, Broadway, 2010.

David J. Hand, *The Improbability Principle*, Scientific American, 2014.

Richard Jeffreys, *Subjective Probability: The Real Thing*, Cambridge, 2004.

Tom Kelley, *The Art of Innovation*, Doubleday, 2001.

Sharon Bertsch McGrayne, *The Theory that Would Not Die*, Yale, 2011.

The Oatmeal, *5 Very Good Reasons to Punch a Dolphin in the Mouth and Other Useful Guides*, Andrews McNeal, 2011.

Andy Oram and Greg Wilson, *Making Software: What Really Works, and Why We Believe It*, O'Reilly, 2011.

Judea Pearl, "Baysianism and Causality, or, Why I Am Only a Half-Bayesian," in *Foundations of Bayesianism*, volume 24, pages 19 to 36, Kluwer, 2001.

Judea Pearl, *Probabilistic Reasoning in Intelligent Systems*, Morgan Kaufmann, 1988.

Kathryn Schulz, *Being Wrong: Adventures in the Margin of Error*, Harper Collins, 2010.

Nate Silver, *The Signal and the Noise*, Penguin, 2012.

James V. Stone, *Bayes' Rule*, 2013.

12
The Best Laid Plans of Mice and Men

"Planning" is a murky, kitchen-sink term for activities as diverse as project management, estimation, budgeting, scheduling, requirements gathering, architecting, designing, feature selection, prioritizing, and commitment. This diversity of uses should suggest that planning is called on to do too much and cannot possibly work as well as one might want. Empirically, planning is hard to do well and is fraught with delusions and abuses. Daniel Kahneman defines the "planning fallacy" as the tendency of people and organizations to underestimate the difficulty of tasks.

In this chapter, we elaborate on the limits of planning. Planning does have value, but the downsides must also be kept in perspective. We are concerned with goal-oriented plans (such as implementing features and fixing bugs), rather than schedule-oriented plans (such as time boxes and iterations). We are concerned with tasks that are larger than some minimum size, say 40 man-hours, which in our experience is where plans start to go seriously awry.

In the first section, we argue that all plans are inherently flawed. Because of unknownness (uncertainty, change, error, irrationality, and so on), all plans start out flawed. Then psychologically and socially, people prefer bad plans, which makes everything worse. Then politically, gatekeepers distort reality, which makes everything worse, again.

In the second section, we argue that planning is bad for everyone. Plans are rationalizations or prayers, which foster and disguise wishful thinking. Loss matters more than gain, so planning transmogrifies all change into loss. Even though all plans are flawed and must change, everyone converts plans into predictions and estimates into promises; they just do. The need for both stability and change at the same time increases everyone's schizophrenia. Also, everyone uses plans as weapons, whenever it suits their purposes, which exacerbates conflicts between managers and developers.

In the third section, we argue that planning is useful and natural but hard to do well. Advantages to planning include that people do it naturally, it fosters useful progress for some tasks, and it adds important delay for other tasks. But, planning is not enough. The real problems for projects are setting expectations and driving progress, both of which planning actually does poorly. A reasonable goal for planning is to be less wrong. Unfortunately, nobody wants to be less wrong; everybody just wants to be right. Making plans without getting carried away is simply beyond human capacity.

All Plans Are Flawed

We explain the flaws of planning in three steps. First, because of unknownness, all plans and all estimates start out inherently flawed. Second, people prefer bad plans, so they make choices that make their plans worse. Third, people play politics, so they make choices that make their plans worse, again.

Much Remains Unknown, so All Plans Start Out Flawed

People are limited by their understandings. They cannot plan for what they do not know, beyond say adding contingency factors. In the chapter "Unknownness," we argued that many aspects of software projects are unknown, uncertain, erroneous, destined to change, volatile, irrational, or arbitrary. People know neither the true states of their projects nor what it will take to complete them. REs know neither exactly what users will need nor what the requirements will be, so they cannot accurately do discovery or write requirements. SEs know neither the existing code base nor what code they will write, so they cannot accurately plan architectures or estimate tasks.

Unknowns and errors occur in two ways: what you don't know (whether you are aware of it or not) and what you think you know, but you don't. Many classical planners presume that the future is predictable, that everyone is rational, that everything is known, and so on, which are obviously untrue. These planners can neither predict the future nor divine any other source of unknownness. It works the other way around: plans are dissolved by unknownness.

Everyone Prefers Bad Plans, which Makes Everything Worse

For psychological and social reasons, everyone (including users, analysts, developers, and managers) deliberately prefers bad plans, in spite of themselves, even when they have the best of intentions. George Akerlof notes that many people make bad short-term decisions about procrastination, debt, drinking, and dieting, even when they understand the long-term consequences. (Partnoy, page 155) Freedman notes that people deliberately seek bad advice. (Freedman, page 69) Gilbert writes that people accept bad advice and reject good advice. (Gilbert, pages 235+)

Preference for Resonant: David Freedman writes, "Good expert advice will be at odds with [what] draws us to it." (Freedman, 81) People prefer "resonant" advice, which echoes what they've believed all along. (Freedman, 83) Expert advice that sounds good is clear-cut, doubt-free, universal, upbeat, actionable, palatable, dramatic, tells stories, uses numbers, and applies retroactively. (Freedman, pages 75 to 80) Of course, resonance has nothing to do with the usefulness of the advice.

Preference for Simple: People prefer simple advice, even when they suspect it is wrong. (Freedman, pages 69 and 75) Nobody wants to hear a complicated plan because like a Rube Goldberg contraption, it will probably be complicated in all the wrong ways. Freedman notes, "Were there simple truths to be had, we would have [found] them long ago." (Freedman, page 81)

Complicated Advice is Bad, Too: Silver notes that complex models can be wrong, too. (Silver, page 225) Complicated models and plans are more realistic because real problems and real solutions tend to be complicated, but that does not mean they are complicated in the right ways. All models have limits and everyone is skeptical of complexity.

Preference for the Familiar and Near: Shelling writes that, "There is a tendency in our planning to confuse the unfamiliar with the improbable." (Silver, page 419) And conversely, people confuse the familiar with the probable. Kahneman notes that people often overrate the likelihood of events closer to us in time and space, which is called the "availability heuristic." (Silver, page 424) The military refers to this as "fighting the last war."

Focus Illusion: Joseph Hallinan writes that people are prone to exaggerate the importance of any single factor. (Hallinan, page 206) Freedman wrote that over 3,000 factors influence body weight, but experts will talk about the importance of individual factors (like blueberries or exercise) as if only one or two things mattered. (Freedman, page 81) A myriad factors influence every software project, but enthusiasts will argue that individual factors, like Haskell or quality or CMMI or TDD or Scrum or Cloud, are the keys to success. Focus causes people to not attempt anything beyond what they understand.

In "Quality Wars: Open Source Versus Proprietary Software," Diomidis Spinellis studied four operating systems (Solaris, Microsoft Research, Linux, and BSD) to compare open and closed-source projects. Spinellis concluded that while there were significant differences, all processes produced remarkably similar results. (Oram and Wilson, page 288)

Few factors make much difference in a complex project because any factor that one might emphasize matters only a little bit. Overdoing any one factor necessarily draws attention and effort away from other important factors. (Freedman, page 83)

On the other hand, it is impossible for anyone to consciously balance 3,000 factors to manage their weight. It is impossible for anyone to remember and act on every fact about their software projects and processes. Enthusiasts who draw attention to individual factors can help to systematically improve practice over time. Keystone habits (such as unit testing) can improve other habits as well. However, your keystone habit may not work for me, and in the scheme of things, it probably doesn't matter.

Restraint Bias: People are naturally optimistic. They think they can handle more than they can. (DiSalvo, page 118) They naturally make and commit to plans that are beyond their abilities without realizing it. Everyone underestimates the difficulty of what they are trying to do. (Watts, page 252) "Our beliefs tend to be simplistic and optimistic." (Freedman, page 81)

Projection Bias: Wanting or intending something is much easier than following through and doing it. People think they will use a gift card or stop smoking, but they won't. (Hallinan, pages 203 and 204) Wanting or intending to follow a perfect process to create a perfect app (or advising someone else to do so) is much easier than actually doing so.

Peer Pressure: People want to please; they want to be as "can do" as possible; they rarely discuss worst case scenarios, in part because there is tremendous social pressure to avoid such topics. Worst case scenarios may occasionally be realistic, but in industry, those who talk about the worst case are usually considered Eeyores and nobody loves an Eeyore. Cassandra wasn't any fun, either. Comments about worst cases are often interpreted by bosses, colleagues, and clients as statements that you are uncooperative and don't even want to try.

Brain scans show that succumbing to peer pressure to accept an obvious lie feels like perceiving the truth. It is not a conscious or rational decision; it is not deception; succumbing to peer pressure is the unconscious and psychological accepting of the social truth. Because of the social truth, everyone who warned about the dangers of banking deregulation in the late 1990s and the early 2000s was ignored, until the world economy crashed.

Rational Bias: Silver notes that it can be rational to be biased or even deliberately wrong about predictions. (Silver, pages 197 to 200) Apparently, the Weather Channel overstates the chance of rain when the probability is low, possibly to avoid being blamed for ruined picnics. (Silver, pages 135 to 136) Many project estimates are deliberately padded to provide a cushion for error, which is the same thing.

In securities, unknown analysts often make wild predictions, hoping for press, while reputable analysts make predictions that stay with the pack. (Silver, page 199) Young software engineers often make exaggerated claims to stand out or get attention. They are probably not even aware of their own exaggerations. (We were like that ourselves, once.) While such behavior may run counter to the ideals of professionalism, getting attention is a basic need that will never go away.

Gatekeepers Play Politics, which Makes Everything Worse, Again

Aristotle argued that "man is the political animal." We would add that planning is merely politics by other means. Planning is (at least in part) a tool for organizing people. Larger projects have more need to set expectations, commitments, and so on, so planning matters more. The planning community has long understood that politics screws up all planning. They even named some of the problems.

The Dark Side of Planning

The "dark side of planning" is a euphemism for the abuse of power by managers and gatekeepers. Planning is often a fig leaf for doing what the most authoritative person in the room wants. People often defer to status, to "the highest paid person's opinion," also known as the "HiPPO." (Sims, page 75) This becomes clear when projects get sidetracked or "captured" by managers who have more authority.

Managers have many ways to get what they want. When managers only respond to answers they like and ignore answers they dislike, it sends a message. Over time, managers teach their subordinates to spin the truth and subordinates figure out what their managers want to hear. This is insidious because even though the manager trained his people to distort the truth, he can always shrug and say, "I never told them to lie." Everyone tells others what they want to hear to some extent, but whim can drown out truth.

Whenever managers or executives negotiate with developers, power imbalances will undermine the truth. Whenever managers negotiate for faster or cheaper, they are implicitly telling developers to underestimate their next project. When executives or managers say, "I want an aggressive plan," they often mean or are interpreted to mean, "Lie to me." To keep in good graces, analysts and developers must tell their bosses what they want to hear.

Executives and managers know that pushing subordinates or laying down challenges can inspire great effort. It can also inspire people to say what others want to hear. Apple employees had long joked about Steve Jobs and his "reality distortion zone." Sometimes his challenges worked (the iPhone) and sometimes they didn't (the external antenna), but Jobs got the decisions he wanted.

The Authorization Imperative

The "authorization imperative" or "strategic misrepresentation" occurs when planners need permission before their projects may proceed.

Gatekeeping is a heuristic that ensures that plans meet minimum standards. But, mistakes and abuses happen. Some planners with important projects (who are bad at playing the game or do not get along with the gatekeeper) will consistently lose approval. Other planners with bad projects (who excel at gaming the system or are pals with the gatekeeper) will consistently win approval.

As part of doling out approval, gatekeepers often play games like "guess the right number." Managers cause problems when they pressure subordinates and planners to over-promise or underestimate to get approval.

Other gatekeepers instinctively respond to an estimate by haggling. "I think I can do this task in 20 hours." "Can you do it in 10?" "Well, I can try." Each person walks away with a different expectation. Hagglers may not realize that they adversely affect results because they think in terms of negotiation or optimization rather than miscommunication or abuse.

Power is Seductive

Gatekeeping can be a force for evil. Gatekeepers embody distrust, gamesmanship, power, control, authority, and the right to say, "No." While people are often skeptical of and frustrated by the game, gatekeepers force everyone to play. Managers and gatekeepers could reduce the politics in projects and organizations, but they won't because that would reduce their personal authority. After all, many managers clawed their way up the hierarchy specifically to wield that kind of power.

We are sure that most gatekeepers believe that they are beyond the petty abuses of power. We are also sure that all gatekeepers do it. Most people are deluded about how good they actually are. Professionals in golf, psychology, securities analysis, and medicine all believe that they are better than they are. (Hallinan, pages 169 to 171) Even the managers we most admire have abused their authority on occasion, usually in late afternoons when they were tired.

We are not arguing to eliminate managers or gatekeepers. Organizations need managers and gatekeepers because employees must do more than just whatever they feel like. However, we are arguing for an appreciation of the limits of power and the costs of the abuses of power. Though this initial subjective estimate needs further research and refinement, we estimate that half of all planning and estimation errors result from the biases and abuses of managers and gatekeepers.

When gatekeepers squelch all forward progress, companies need their cowboys or wild geese to actually get some useful work done, and organizations know it. Grace Hopper famously said, "It is easier to ask forgiveness than to ask for permission." Grace Hopper was a hardcore cowboy, a gatekeeper's worst nightmare, someone who could get something done when everyone else said, "No."

Planning Exacerbates Human Nature

Planning exacerbates many problems for people. Planning is a fig leaf that helps people to hide their rationalizations and wishful thinking. Planning increases the feeling that all change is loss, which increases stubbornness. Planning increases the need for both change and stability, at the same time, and this bifurcation increases schizophrenia. And, programmers and managers use plans as weapons, which can inflame their conflicts. Planning causes many more problems than anyone ever admits.

Plans Are Fig Leaves for Rationalization and Prayer

"Rationalization [is] the act of causing something to be or seem reasonable." (Gilbert, page 163) John Cacioppo and William Patrick write "We humans often use words and logic merely to rationalize our primitive emotions and prior expectations." (Cacioppo and Patrick, page 245) All rationales are sales pitches. Fred Brooks writes that design reports are rationalizations. (Brooks, *Design of Design*, page 157) The brain works very hard to rationalize. (Gilbert, page 192)

We believe that most software plans are primarily rationalizations for what the planners wanted to do anyways, rather than well-considered evaluations or comparisons of alternate solutions. For example, many designs are elaborate euphemisms for "I want to use technology *x*," where *x* is python, mobile, cloud, analytics, or the buzzword du jour. It is well known that people can rationalize anything, including war and environmental destruction, especially for their own short-term benefit, such as profit. Rationales must never be naively accepted as meaningful.

Illusion of Rationality: The "illusion of rationality" means taking an unproven model as reality, often a memo or a plan. Everyone uses this illusion instinctively every time he sets a coffee cup on a table or sits in a chair. The brain builds models that suggest that the tables and chairs are safe to use, based on minimal evidence, such as looking like a table or a chair at first glance. The brain creates illusions for larger plans, too. Robert McNamara believed that his high-level plans and systems analysis would win the Vietnam War. (Sims, page 25)

First, People Use Their Distorted Realities to Make Plans: Selection or attention or confirmation bias is the tendency for people to notice facts that support their biases and desires and to ignore facts that contradict them. Daniel Gilbert writes, "The eye [agrees] to look for what the brain wants." (Gilbert, page 183) People create plans that describe what they want to happen, more than what anyone should actually expect to happen.

Then, People Use Plans to Distort Their Realities: People use plans and estimates to distort their own perceptions. They look for what is in the plan and ignore what is actually happening. (DiSalvo, page 34) Planning narrows the scope of attention. People counting basketball passes will fail to notice someone in a gorilla suit wandering across the court.

One might think that planning would help people to distinguish between what they do and don't understand. But, planning also hides what people don't understand from themselves and from everyone else. Disguise happens because one shifts from arguing about what should be done, which is partly known, to arguing about what is in the plan, which may be fully known, regardless of whether the plan means anything useful. Plans are like Zaphod's sunglasses, which "at the first hint of trouble, they turn totally black and thus prevent you from seeing anything that might alarm you." In other words, like a good story, planning causes suspension of disbelief.

Plans are Self-Serving Prayers: Too often, saying or writing the correct words and repeating them convincingly to managers and clients matters more than actually expressing anything useful about the future. "With this sacrifice of our time and effort to make this plan, we beseech thee oh Lord, make the users happy, let the app will be delivered on time and budget, and no bugs. Amen." Like the lottery, plans enable people to delude themselves and believe that their hopes and desires will come true.

Loss Matters More than Gain, so Planning Makes All Change Feel Like Loss

Businesspeople talk about gain when they talk about maximizing profit or increasing market share. Engineers talk about gain when they talk about new features. Politicians and government workers often strive to minimize negative results to avoid angering voters. Safety and quality engineers strive to minimize loss. In general, users want both to maximize gain and to minimize loss. They want apps that have useful, new features as well as fewer bugs and lower cost.

Statisticians more or less define loss as negative gain ($loss \approx -gain$), and when using appropriate sigmoid and scaling factors, these two concepts seem mathematically fungible. However cognitively, people treat gain and loss very differently, even irreconcilably. Everyone undervalues gain and overvalues loss in at least three ways. Neutral terms don't exist, so we expect that gain and loss will never be reconciled.

Value: Losing $100 is about twice as painful as finding $100 is pleasurable. People are much more interested in avoiding a surcharge than in getting a discount, when the base price is the same. Users and product managers will value a feature differently, by two to one, depending on whether they presumed it would be there versus whether they presumed that they would have to pay extra to get it.

The difference between half full (positive) and half empty (negative) also shows up in perception mismatches between developers and clients. We have seen the following conversation endlessly repeated. "I just got feature x working. Let me show you." "But, that button is gray; it was supposed to be blue." "We'll fix that later." "But, gray means we cannot use it." "Why are you hung up on that? This is cool. It's what you asked for. You should be happy." "I don't care." Everyone interprets the same murky situations differently, even irreconcilably because of their differing perceptions of gain and loss. They simply do not understand each other. Whiny customers are not always right (and can be very annoying), but their perceptions are their perceptions. Also, developers cannot reliably inspect, test, or evaluate their own code because they cannot reconcile gain and loss within themselves.

Risk: Consider the following choices. You are a medical expert brought in to make a decision during a deadly viral epidemic. Would you rather "save 1/3 of the victims" or "take a 1 in 3 gamble that everyone will be saved." You are later brought in to make a decision during a deadly bacterial epidemic. Would you rather "let 2/3 of the victims die" or "take a 2 in 3 gamble that everyone will die." These two decisions are mathematically identical, but more than half of people answer differently. (DiSalvo, page 39) When people face loss, they prefer to take big risks to avoid the worst and will gamble to save everyone. When people face gains, they prefer to cling to sure gains and will prefer to guarantee saving the smaller number of people. (Hallinan, pages 94 to 95)

Software users and product managers perceive "getting some of what they want" and "giving up some of what they want" very differently, even when it is the same question. Your project is behind schedule. Would you rather "finish half of the remaining features" or would you rather "take a 50-50

149

gamble that you can finish all the features?" Would you rather "cancel half of the remaining features" or "take a 50-50 gamble that all remaining features will fail?" Most people will answer these questions differently, even though they are mathematically the same. How a question is framed can matter more than the question itself.

People Prefer to Err through Inaction: (Hallinan, page 53) Studies show that two-thirds of the time when test takers have doubts about an answer, changing it would improve their scores. Studies also show that test takers believe that changing a right answer into a wrong answer will feel twice as bad as changing a wrong answer into a right answer will feel good. Even though changing answers would probably improve their scores, few people actually do so because their fear of regret outweighs the anticipated reward of a better score. (Hallinan, page 52) Even when people are told to change, they don't. (Hallinan, page 52)

In software, changing requirements or architectures during development entails risk and people are often more comfortable allowing a poor decision to fail without making changes. Few people want the responsibility or regret if the changes go awry. In addition, students "remember sticking with the first answer as being a better strategy than it actually was." (Hallinan, page 55) Plans enable people to be even wronger because plans absolve them from the need to act responsibly as their circumstances change. On the other hand, Gilbert notes that people regret inaction more than action, after the fact. (Gilbert, page 197)

All Change is Loss: Whenever a developer realizes that a requirement or feature will be hard to deliver, or a developer finds a better solution, then he or she may offer to change the plan. But, unless the change provides at least twice the replacement value for the same cost, most people will perceive it as a loss or as an unwelcome risk. Tradeoffs that produce at least twice the value for the same cost probably don't exist because those sorts of tradeoffs were probably already in the original plan. So once a reasonable plan is set, all change is loss.

Everyone Clings to the Past, so All Planning Causes Schizophrenia

All Plans and Estimates Become Promises that Cannot Change: Everyone says things like planning is not to predict the future (Beck and Fowler, page 2) and "estimates are not commitments" (Beck and Fowler, page 58), but nobody means it. Everyone knows that they should treat plans and estimates with suspicion, but they cannot. Everyone, absolutely everyone, especially a power-that-be like a manager or client, converts plans into predictions and estimates into promises. They do so for well-known psychological reasons.

Anchoring: People cling to the first numbers they hear. Write down one irrelevant number, like a phone number or birth date. Then make an unrelated decision, like the price of a yard-sale item or the hours to complete a software task. The numbers will be correlated. (Hallinan, page 102) The first offer in a price negotiation determines the result. (Hallinan, page 107) Once a plan is suggested, everyone begins to treat it as a promise. Once an estimate is given, it becomes a commitment. Anchoring is universal and insidious. Gilbert notes that multitasking increases anchoring. (Gilbert, page 150)

Participation Attachment: People overvalue their own work. (Ariely, page 94) Daniel Ariely calls attachment the "IKEA" effect (Ariely, pages 83 to 106) and the "Not Invented Here" or "NIH" effect. (Ariely, pages 107 to 122) In the case of origami, amateurs valued their own work nearly as much as they valued the work of other professionals. (Ariely, page 94) Furthermore, "We mistakenly think that others love our work as much as we do." (Ariely, page 99) Things that are harder to attain, we buy into more. (Ariely, page 89) The more we participate in planning, and the harder the project, the more we will believe that our plan is good and believe that everyone else agrees.

Advertising Attachment: When people see an ad, they imagine themselves driving that car or eating that cereal. They slowly attach themselves to the product. Advertising proves that people attach easily. So, the more often managers repeat the plan and explain how everyone will benefit, the more everyone will buy into it, regardless of its merits.

Sunk Cost: Planning is a sunk cost and people have a hard time walking away from sunk costs. The cost of planning is not insignificant, but is rarely much of a problem. Yet, people who make or pay for plans will be loath to let them go. (Schulz, page 194)

Plans Enable Everyone to Cling to the Past: People love consistency and certainty. (Freedman, pages 68+) (DiSalvo, page 17) So, once people make a decision, they often simply refuse change. The problem is that planning gives everyone concrete visions from the past to cling to. When a plan exists, explicit action is required to make changes. If people didn't have a plan, they would have nothing to get hung up on that prevented change.

Schizophrenia: Planning leads to a bifurcation of reality. People need to believe in the plan or else they will not commit to it. But, plans are invariably flawed and must evolve. So, plans must both change and remain the same, at the same time, which is impossible and causes duress for everyone. In other words, planning causes schizophrenia.

Conflicts between the need for change and the need for stability are universal to the human condition. Everybody wants both. In most societies, the political spectrum splits fairly evenly between liberals who want change and conservatives who want stability. Even small groups, such as the eight participants in Biosphere 2, split into two factions, one group arguing for change and the other for stability.

A Weapon that Escalates Conflict

There are always power imbalances between managers and developers, so there will always be conflicts. Everyone uses plans as weapons, in their own ways, whenever it suits their purposes.

A Stick to Hit With

Beck and Fowler write "Plans can be used as a stick to beat people with." (Beck and Fowler, page 2) Too often, managers use planning as a weapon to justify micromanagement, rather than as a pragmatic tool for getting better day-to-day results. When a manager deems that a plan is inadequate or that the plan is not being followed well enough, he may feel justified in stopping by your desk every hour or two to check up on things, to nag, to harass, to intimidate. There are better ways to handle these problems, but weak managers instinctively lash out.

Exaggerating Power Imbalances: Plans exaggerate power imbalances in hierarchies. Developers become more accountable for lower-level processes and decisions and lose authority, while managers sidestep accountability and gain authority. By passing off responsibility, managers gain political position. They just adore plans.

Laying Blame: Planning helps managers to scapegoat programmers. When people look for the source of errors, they look down at the last person to blame. (Hallinan, page 191) At the demise of one dot-com, the CEO gave a speech where he complained, "The software engineers failed to implement my vision." This was after they added video ads to the site. Executives were proud of the increased revenue per ad, but the slow and annoying videos drove users away. The CEO and sales team didn't have to reconsider any of their own decisions because they already knew who to blame.

A Shield to Hide Behind

Beck and Fowler also write that planning is an illusion to conceal trouble. (Beck and Fowler, page 2) When your boss stops by your desk every hour for a status update and you are stressing out, what do you do? You say, "I have a plan and I am following the plan," even when you are lost at sea. Getting your boss out of your office, right now, matters most of all. You also want your manager to grow up, even though you know that will never happen. After he leaves, you can return to posting on Facebook or polishing your resume. Managers do this to their bosses, too, arguing that they have a plan and are following it.

Dodging Blame: Following the plan often seems like a strong defense. When everything is falling apart, people like being able to say, "We followed the plan," which really means, "It's not our fault." But, getting defensive bodes ill for everyone. Defensiveness means that communication has broken down and that people are failing to be honest, responsive, and cooperative. When things go wrong, planners want to dodge blame, so they lie. The plan diverges from reality. (Beck and Fowler, page 5)

From the developer's point of view, when you don't know how to solve a problem, planning feels like being set up. Whenever managers force developers to make plans, they suspect that managers will complain when anything deviates from those plans, which will assuredly happen. So, developers often react defensively to all planning.

The Good News and the Bad News

In spite of what we have written so far, we believe that planning is good for all software projects, within reasonable limits. The problem is that people cannot keep their expectations about planning modest and real. Planning is a tool to be less wrong, but nobody wants to hear that. People just want to be right.

Planning is Inevitable and Helpful

In *Planning Extreme Programming*, Kent Beck and Martin Fowler write about the benefits of planning for Agile projects. In *Managing the Software Process*, Watts Humphrey writes about the benefits of planning for CMM projects. Here, we describe more benefits from psychology and sociology.

Setting Goals is Human Nature: David DiSalvo writes that the brain is a prediction machine. (DiSalvo, page 16) People spend about 12% of their time (about 2 hours every day) thinking about the future. (Partnoy, page 123) (Gilbert, page 17) George Loewenstein wrote, "The drive toward goal establishment and goal completion is 'hard wired.'" (Ariely, page 81). People make plans because they do so anyways and they are comfortable doing so.

Countering Procrastination: Planning counters the bad habit of procrastination by giving people concrete and useful tasks to do now, as well as some sense that they are making effective progress toward goals. (Partnoy, pages 147 to 196)

Fighting the Flinch: The flinch effect occurs because people can react much faster than they can understand, which is useful when responding to lions and tigers and bears, but is not so good for making software. "Even in the case of quite unfamiliar tasks, people seem to prefer to act than to reflect." (Hallinan, page 176) Planning encourages reflection and deliberation.

Stepping Back to See the Big Picture: Task saturation is the tendency for people to obsess over small tasks. (Hallinan, page 77) Ken Jacobson noted, "In many situations, the path of least resistance is to simply do another low-level task." Small tasks are more knowable and tractable, which makes them easier to understand and get excited about. Planning can return attention to the bigger, harder issues that matter.

Adding Delay before Deciding: Planning helps people to take time before making important decisions, like what they want and what matters most. People who never take time to address these questions should never expect to answer them well. Delay provides an opportunity to make a better gestalt assessment of a situation.

Adding Delay before Acting: Planning both adds delay before real work starts and provides a rationale for waiting. When REs and SEs need feedback on prototypes, they should wait as long as they can before proceeding, to get as much feedback as possible. Additionally, Partnoy writes that you want to put off what doesn't need to be done. (Partnoy, pages 147 to 196) Partnoy argues that in many situations, if you cannot assess a situation correctly, you will fail anyways, so you shouldn't even start. (Partnoy, pages 63 to 80) When you are unsure what should be done, planning helps to increase delay.

Exploring More Options: Ancillary issues may matter more than the resulting plans. For example, planning may help people explore and appreciate a broader range of options, so that when things do go wrong, they have a broader palette of responses at hand. Planning allows (or forces) developers to spend time to consider their implementation options before jumping to coding conclusions. This may be the essence of Carl von Clausewitz's maxim, "Plans are of little importance, but planning is essential."

Control: Control is good for everyone's mental and physical health. In one study, nursing home residents were given a house plant for six months; twice as many residents died when the plant was cared for by the staff (30%) as when the plant was cared for by the resident (15%). (Gilbert, pages 22 and 23) Planners make more choices and probably feel more in control of their destiny, which helps their mental and physical health.

Illusion of Control and Agency: The illusion of control provides the same psychological benefits as actual control. People will even make themselves the agent of control when none exists, for example gamblers may believe that their system will eventually win them big money. (DiSalvo, page 65) Similarly, managers and architects may come to believe that they personally cause their projects to succeed, going beyond overconfidence or ego.

Big Bets are Fun: People are fascinated by bold efforts, like putting a man on the moon. Small, incremental work can feel tedious, boring, and slow. Planning can enable bigger, more interesting, more daring bets, even though they entail greater risks.

Note that none of these advantages concern being right or perfect. They all concern doing better or doing something anyways regardless of the outcome. Also note that some are rationalizations for delay and others merely provide artificial peace of mind.

Less Wrong

More and more software engineers seem aware that planning has limits and that planning should occur only within those limits. Both Barry Boehm in "Architecture: How Much and When" and George Fairbanks in *Just Enough Architecture* recommend that before normal development starts, regardless of their circumstances, everyone should "plan as best they can, but no more." REs and SEs naturally want to start projects with the best priors that they can get because starting with better approximations to the real requirements, architectures, and source codes helps to minimize the learning and revision (i.e. the hard work) that they will have to do later. A wide spectrum of initial plans and priors can be useful, depending on what is and isn't known.

50-50: When you really don't know what will happen, Agile processes can start right away, with empty projects and no significant planning. The empty app is like Bayes starting with 50-50 because it could evolve into anything, though it may take a lot of work to get there. 50-50 is appropriate for projects with new hires, new technologies, or volatile or unknown requirements. When projects have experienced developers, well-understood technologies, and stable, known requirements, odds are that somebody can find a better prior. Any fixed project could be used as the default starting point, but the empty project is the obvious one.

Yesterday: In weather, one fairly accurate model is that today will resemble yesterday. Likewise in software, one project often effectively approximates the next. Many square-root functions use the previous result as the seed for the next because within apps, inputs to sqrt() are usually similar. Before maintenance, an app often closely resembles what the app will be after maintenance, which makes the existing app an excellent prior. Companies often specialize in specific markets or "product lines," so that one project will resemble another. When Microsoft decided to market their SQL server, they purchased the source code from Sybase to get a head start. Large companies often purchase smaller companies with established products to enter new markets. Google bought Android to compete with other smart-phone OSs. Of course, when a weather front moves in, then all bets may be off about tomorrow's weather. Likewise, when your next project uses a new technology or has a new client, then all bets may be off.

BDUF: When you have a good idea of what your project will become and you believe that you can plan better than copying an existing project, then "big design up-front" may help. BDUF covers a wide spectrum of degrees of effort in its own right. Some Agile processes devote the first iteration to planning and architecture. In the *Mythical Man-Month*, Fred Brooks suggests devoting 17% (1/6) of the project to initial planning. In "Architecture: How Much and When?," Barry Boehm suggests that initial planning should take from 5% to 37% of the total project effort, depending on the size of the project. (Oram and Wilson, page 179) How much BDUF helps is a function of how well you can predict the future, how stable your requirements and technologies are, how experienced your developers are in the tasks at hand, and so on.

BDUF is not about getting the architecture right, but about getting it less wrong than copying another architecture. Likewise, copying another architecture may be less wrong than starting with no architecture. The precondition for choosing BDUF as the prior is that you must subjectively expect that you can plan better than you can copy an existing project. The key word is "expect," as opposed to "hope" or "guess" or "demand." Likewise, the precondition for choosing a specific existing project (yesterday) as the prior is that you must subjectively expect that it is more representative than the empty project.

The Right Amount of Planning: Fairbanks encourages "sufficiently precise" planning. (Fairbanks, page 298) When developers plan a lot up front and changes or errors occur, then planning effort will be wasted (and probably a lot of developer effort, too). Conversely, when developers fail to plan where they can, they will waste development effort, later. The optimal solution is the less wrong one in between. The greater the unknowns, the looser the planning must be.

But You Can't Handle the Truth

Nobody wants to be less wrong. Nobody wants to admit that they could be wrong. Nobody ever says in a project bid, "We are less wrong than our competitors." Nobody ever says, "Formal methods are less wrong than ad hoc development." Everybody just wants to be right.

And there is good reason. Duncan Watts noted that only one future will emerge, so people really do want to predict it. (Watts, page 161) "When we think about the future, we care about what will *actually happen*." (Watts, page 145)

Many people believe that planning is the essence of success. Benjamin Franklin, Winston Churchill, and the Sphinx have all stated something like, "If you fail to plan, your plan will fail." This attitude is so pervasive that many people believe that results cannot turn out any better than they can plan. Selection bias reinforces this conclusion whenever someone remembers the situations where their plans worked and forgets the situations where their plans failed.

Planning Causes Failure

But, caring about what will happen and planning to produce good results are not enough. Plans that go awry are legion.

Market-Garden (also known as "A Bridge Too Far") was a wartime disaster. The U.S. invasion of Iraq was much worse. Before being ejected into space, Ford said to Arthur, "My plan rather involved being on the other side of the airlock." Watts notes that in the 1990s, both Sony (with mini-discs) and Apple (with the iPod) had great strategies, but only one worked. (Watts, pages 178 to 180)

Hewlett-Packard planned cool software for Palm-based tablet computers, which failed. Microsoft planned cool software called Metro, which failed. Customers refused to buy either one. These companies have enormous resources and obsessive proclivities for planning. As a practical matter, if teams at Hewlett-Packard and Microsoft cannot make and carry out effective plans, then you don't stand a chance with your projects, either.

The Standish Chaos Reports claim that most software projects are late. The list of our own failures is too long and humiliating to recount, but for example this chapter is over two years late and many of our own programs never got finished. Based on the observed facts, we conclude that planning in RE and SE causes many more failures than successes.

Having a plan is not enough; you need a good plan. So, why not just get a good plan? That is the crux. Everyone would if they could. But for all the reasons listed in the first section (unknownness, preference for bad plans, and politics), people only make bad plans. It is much easier to state what you want to happen, than to infer what will happen. All plans are flawed and must evolve to remain useful.

There is No Alternative

We suspect that a few well-intended souls will take this chapter and say things like, "Now that we know about the limits of planning, we should make a plan to avoid those limits." or "We need to characterize what we don't know so that we can find out specifically what we need to learn." These intentions are admirable, but deluded. They might do a bit better, but probably not much.

Either way they will make a new plan and then for all the reasons listed in the second section (anchoring, attachment, fig leaf for rationalization and wishful thinking) they will come to believe that their plan predicts the future. And because change feels like loss and everyone clings to the past, they will not allow the plan to change. And because they tried so hard, they will become even more schizophrenic.

All planning leads people astray. Rational people should not naïvely hope that their plans are perfect and they should be skeptical of all plans. But, most REs and SEs are all too human and unfortunately they irrationally delude themselves.

Conclusion

Our analysis contradicts the classic approach that says, "just make a plan," which was epitomized by Fred Brooks in "Calling the Shot" (Brooks, pages 89 and 90) and continues today in processes like CMMI, IEEE 12207, and RUP. We note that the PMI has ditched goal-driven processes and adopted Agile and that others are replacing RUP with AUP and DAD. Planning is a tool, not a solution or an ideal or an end. Neither a hammer nor a blueprint can guarantee that a building will serve its occupants. Software plans cannot guarantee good results, either.

We were tempted to call this chapter "Planning Considered Harmful," but that would overstate the problem. Many benefits of planning do exist, but they are murky and indirect. Since plans can cause so much harm, they should all be used with much more care than ever seems to occur. As Robert Burns noted centuries ago, even the best laid plans gang aft agley.

Notes

Threats to Validity: Much of this chapter is based on contemporary research from behavioral economics, psychology, and sociology. We have applied numerous observations from psychological and sociological studies out of context. Further, software geeks probably differ from average people in many ways. However, we believe that the principles apply broadly and our uses are in the ballpark.

Risk versus Loss: In this chapter, we treat risk and loss as synonyms, even though there are differences. The term loss is often used in the context of making choices, while the term risk is often used in the context of achieving specific goals. Government and business workers seem to prefer the term risk. For example, in *Just Enough Architecture*, Fairbanks uses the term risk consistently. In this chapter, we use the term loss, which seems more common in decision theory.

Acknowledgements: Many friends and colleagues contributed ideas and reviews to this chapter. We especially want to thank Mina Yamashita and Anthony J. Giancola.

Bibliography

Douglas Adams, "The Hitchhiker's Guide to the Galaxy," TV-series, BBC, 1981.

Dan Ariely, *Predictably Irrational*, Harper, 2010.

Dan Ariely, *The Upside of Irrationality: The Unexpected Benefits of Defying Logic*, Harper, 2011.

Kent Beck and Martin Fowler, *Planning Extreme Programming*, Addison Wesley, 2000.

Barry Boehm, "Architecture: How Much and When?" in Andy Oram and Greg Wilson (editors), *Making Software*, O'Reilly, 2010.

Frederick P. Brooks, *The Design of Design*, Addison Wesley, 2010.

Frederick P. Brooks, *The Mythical Man-Month*, Addison Wesley, 1975.

Robert Burns, "To a Mouse," wikipedia.com, 1785.

John Cacioppo and William Patrick, *Loneliness: Human Nature and the Need for Social Connection*, Norton, 2009.

David DiSalvo, *What Makes Your Brain Happy and Why You Should Do the Opposite*, Prometheus, 2011.

George H. Fairbanks, *Just Enough Architecture: A Risk-Driven Approach*, Marshall and Brainerd, 2010.

Daniel Gilbert, *Stumbling on Happiness*, Vintage, 2006.

Watts S. Humphrey, *Managing the Software Process*, Addison Wesley, 1989.

Michael Lewis, *Moneyball*, Norton, 2004.

Andy Oram and Greg Wilson (editors), *Making Software*, O'Reilly, 2010.

Frank Partnoy, *Wait: the Art and Science of Delay*, Public Affairs, 2012.

Kathryn Schulz, *Being Wrong: Adventures in the Margin of Error*, Harper Collins, 2010.

Nate Silver, *The Signal and the Noise*, Penguin, 2012.

Peter Sims, *Little Bets*, Free Press, 2011.

Diomidis Spinellis, "Quality Wars: Open Source versus Proprietary Software," in Andy Oram and Greg Wilson (editors), *Making Software*, O'Reilly, 2010.

Duncan J. Watts, *Everything is Obvious Once You Know the Answer*, Crown, 2011.

13
Postscript

In most of this book, we strive to understand the limits of what can be known, the ebbs and flows of quality, and how people get carried away with their hopes and ideals. But, we don't want to seem pessimistic. While we believe that "you cannot predict the future," we also believe that "you can play the game."

Five chapters in this book describe techniques for playing the software-engineering game. In "Sponsoring-Organization Obligations," we discuss Bride-of-Agile practices. In "Determinism versus Emergence," we argue that everyone should combine deterministic or Waterfall practices for planning out what they want with emergent or Agile practices for coping with whatever actually happens. In "A Sunrise Primer," we argue that everyone must continually satisfice, repeatedly and arbitrarily choosing that *this* is *good enough for now*. In "Polish versus Rot," we discuss the sources and tradeoffs of technical debt. And in "A Subjective Search Primer," we discuss Bayesian foundations for Agile and Bride-of-Agile practices.

However, we are only beginning to understand what it means to play the game. While Agile is a good start, much remains to be learned. Our Bride-of-Agile practices are only a first sketch of sponsoring-organization obligations. We don't yet know how to best combine deterministic and emergent practices. And, we don't yet know how to define *good enough for now* beyond using the existing rules of two, three, six, and twelve. We are now working to understand these and other issues and, as noted throughout this book, many other software engineers are doing so as well.